D0998985

Being

Jewish

in the New

Germany

JEFFREY M. PECK

Being

Jewish

in the New

Germany

RUTGERS UNIVERSITY PRESS
NEW BRUNSWICK, NEW JERSEY, AND LONDON

Publication of this book was supported, in part, by a grant from the German Historical Institute, Washington, D.C.

Library of Congress Cataloging-in-Publication Data

Peck, Jeffrey M., 1950–
    Being Jewish in the new Germany / Jeffrey M. Peck.
        p. cm.
    Includes bibliographical references and index.
    ISBN-13: 978-0-8135-3723-8 (hardcover : alk. paper)
    ISBN-13: 978-0-8135-4206-5 (pbk. : alk. paper)
    1. Jews—Germany—History—1945–   2. Jews—Germany—Identity.   3. Germany—
Emigration and immigration—History—20th century.   4. Germany—Ethnic relations.
I. Title.
    DS135.G332P43 2006
    305.892'4043'09049—dc22   2005004831

A British Cataloging-in-Publication record for this book is available from the British Library.

Manufactured in the United States of America

To HCS—mentor, colleague, friend

Contents

Preface

As a Jewish American scholar who focuses on Germany, I have been repeatedly asked, or even reproached, by Americans, especially Jewish Americans, about my intellectual interests and academic career that has now lasted for over twenty years. Questions such as Why are you interested in Germany? or How can you live in that country? have pursued me as I studied the language, literature, and culture of the country that perpetrated crimes against the Jewish people. Once, after giving a public lecture on Jewish life in contemporary Germany, a particularly angry and aggressive audience member chastised me and later sent a postcard suggesting I leave the United States for Germany permanently. Such reactions, most of them less hostile and merely inquisitive, force a scholar and teacher to think about the relationship between what he studies and who he is: in short, about identity. I became keenly aware how identity and personal histories shape the stories scholars tell, even those who try to be as objective as possible. This attention to my personal investment in my work forced me to think more deeply about what I studied and what it meant. Thus, studying Jewish life in Germany became both a personal and professional project, a combination I welcomed for the satisfaction and knowledge it provided. It also encouraged me to share these perspectives in this book.

However, it was only into the second half of my career that I focused on this German-Jewish subject. This happened when anthropologist John Borneman and I researched and published an ethnography, *Sojourners: The Return of German Jews and the Question of Identity* (1995) and completed a video documentary about the Jews of East Germany who had returned from exile after the war. The book I present here continues, at least chronologically, where this one left off, while still addressing fundamental questions about Jewish identity in Germany from new social, cultural, political, and religious perspectives. These have, of course, emerged and intensified since 1989, when the Berlin Wall fell, Germany was reunified, the Soviet Union disintegrated, and Europe was fundamentally transformed.

Why and how do Jews live in Germany today? Sixty years after the end of the Second World War and the liberation of the concentration camps, many Americans, especially Jews, are still preoccupied with what has come to be called "the Holocaust" and Germany's responsibility for this crime. Some cynical critics call this victimology; more generous observers merely note the strong identification of American Jews with this single, historical overarching event. Such a reaction is in part understandable, especially for those who have been personally touched. Clearly, it should not cloud our memory nor allow us to forget those who died. But it should also not blind us from recognizing the complexity of postwar German and Jewish society nor that Jewish life in Germany is more than the sum of these twelve terrible years.

The Federal Republic of Germany has taken responsibility for the horrible deeds of the Nazis. The fall of the Berlin Wall in 1989 and the peaceful revolution that brought reunification in 1990 confirmed Germany's commitment to liberal democracy that has flourished in the West since the end of the war. West Germany's "special relationship" to Israel since its founding, of which Americans know little, has also grown stronger. West Germany did more to remember and rebuild relationships with its Jewish population than any other European country, and continues to do so now after reunification. Still, there remains a gap between external judgments and internal experience, between those outside of Germany who cannot understand or accept Jewish life there and those Jews who actually live in Germany today and have made it their home. Consequently, my goal in this book is to educate an unfamiliar American public to the real-life experience of Jews in Germany and to acquaint them with the differentiated picture that makes up Jewish life since 1989, without glossing over the many problems and uncertainties that remain. I believe that understanding the new Germany, precisely because of its complex history with the Jewish people, will enhance tolerance and understanding in the transatlantic sphere.

In 1988, when my research on Jewish life in Germany began and just one year before political events would dramatically change the German and European political landscape, no one could have imagined that in the future the two politically and ideologically divided Germanys, the legacy of World War II, would become one. The dissolution of the Soviet Union and its empire would create an opportunity for the disparate countries of Eastern Europe to enlarge their union with Western Europe. And a little over ten years later, the United States would become the victim of a terrorist attack that led to war in Afghanistan and Iraq that would create inter-European tensions and fissures in the transatlantic alliance. The longstanding postwar relationship of Europeans and Americans, which the events of 1989–1990 had strengthened further, became strained when other geopolitical flashpoints like war in the Middle East and what is called the Second Intifada of the Palestinian Arabs against Israel took their toll on prospects for peace. It strained European-American relations as well.

In this new, globally interdependent environment, Germany, as a geopolitical and economic force at the crossroads of the new Europe, may still seem a small player. However, in the transnational context of Jewish Diaspora life, the status of its Jewish population, swelled by rapid and massive immigration from the former Soviet Union, draws international attention as the country that was known for so long as "the land of the murderers." In addition, Germany's postwar legitimacy and any future "normality" are intimately linked to the status of its Jews and often to other minorities in an increasingly multicultural country where the definition of a "German" is no longer as clear as it historically once was. The presence of a large Turkish population in Germany has forced a rethinking of immigration and naturalization policies. Until the year 1993, Germany's policy on asylum was one of the most liberal in Europe, but it still did not officially consider itself a "land of immigration," when it de facto already was. As of 2000, it has become easier to get citizenship; as of 2005 an immigration law is in force, although "becoming German" is another story.

Today, there are more than 100,000 registered members in the official Jewish community and many more Jews who are not affiliated. Berlin, the new capital and focus of this study, has the largest Jewish population with approximately 12,000 Jews registered. Frankfurt and Munich follow. While the Jewish population is still relatively small in relation to the total German population of approximately 83 million and its capital with 3.8 million, its moral and political significance outweighs its size. In 1933, it was estimated that Germany had about 500,000 Jews of which about

160,000 resided in Berlin. At war's end, as is well known, Germany's and Europe's Jewish population was decimated to a mere remnant of survivors.

Now in the new millennium, there is all the more reason to celebrate the triumph, as many see it, over Hitler's Final Solution. Germany's Jewish population has gained prominence as the fastest growing Jewish community in Europe and the third largest overall. Jewish Berlin has become a popular tourist site and home of major international and Jewish organizations. The leaders of Jewish institutions, like the American Jewish Committee (AJC), understand the importance of a sustained Jewish life in Germany. Far ahead of the Jewish public, they have established positive relations with Germany for decades. Yet, American Jews are often unable to overcome old stereotypes and prejudices. Many American Jews still feel uncomfortable traveling to Germany or even buying German products. In their minds all Germans, even those born after the war, are tainted by the genocide. Such issues about guilt, responsibility, and identity, however, concern Jews living in Germany, as well as other Germans and other Jews of all kinds, making Jewish life in Germany a focal point for Jewish concerns. There are no simple answers for Jews or for Germans; the names in themselves betray the limitations of categorizing individuals in fixed terms that do not capture the constant transformation of identities, especially in multicultural and global societies such as Germany, the United States, or Israel. And such transformations also include Jewish-Muslim relations since the Second Intifada which began in 2000 and the outbreak of waves of anti-Jewish violence in Europe, perpetrated primarily by disaffected Muslim youths but bolstered by a general revival of anti-Semitism.

I hope that this book, the culmination of more than ten years of close observation and study of Germany's and Berlin's transformation as the home of a "new Jewry," will contribute an illuminating chapter to German and Jewish history and culture. I also hope it will stimulate a new way of thinking about Jewish and Diaspora identities worldwide. There is no question that Jewish identity and Diaspora relations to Israel are changing. On the one hand, there is heightened insecurity and fear for the survival of the Jewish state reemergent in the Diaspora. On the other hand, many Jews who support Israel question its policies toward the Palestinians and its stance on religious diversity. Whatever the positions, Jewish identity in general is fraught with the push-and-pull of national, religious, ethnic, and cultural affiliations. This is particularly true in Germany where it complicates simple definitions of who is a Jew or who is a German. Once identity is not based solely on presumed blood descent, but on civic allegiances, precise definitions become all the more difficult.

And while I had hoped to complete this book before 2001, ironically, the tragic events of September of that year and their aftermath have altered my perspective on the relative significance of any single historical event like that of 1989 or even 9/11. The particular European watershed made many feel that the end of the cold war would reduce threat, increase security, and even, for some idealists, ensure peace and harmony in the world. A look at the earlier moment of 1989 from the distance of the second, and again from today, reminds us not only that such an ahistorical point of view ignores the impact new hegemonies, shifting priorities, and unexpected actors have on history and our understanding of it, especially as it affects contemporary political policies in the United States, Germany, Europe, and Israel. Of particular importance in this context are the changed bilateral perspectives on transatlantic relations where Jewish and other issues are concerned. While these events can never be fully dealt with in a study such as this, if there is anything we can learn from the confluence of events that unsettled our world so profoundly, it is that we are all vulnerable to historical, political, and cultural transformations, some of which can be explained and others cannot. The study of Jewish life in Germany I present here is only one piece of a larger historical puzzle that continues to defy completion and full explanation.

Two short comments about the methodology and organization of this book: My approach too has benefited from transatlantic movement of theoretical thinking. This interdisciplinary and international orientation moves beyond, or at least complements, more quantitative or empirical studies of many political scientists or sociologists. It brings the perspective of a literary critic/anthropologist to bear on topics that require a different kind of analysis. As a reader and interpreter of "texts," central to the intellectual project of both these fields, I analyze imaginative literature, critical journalistic writings, political speeches, interviews, and other forms of discourse that symbolically represent how individuals and sometimes groups understand themselves or want to be understood. Sometimes I am, in the tradition of anthropology, a participant observer, who textualizes moments in time and space replete with interpretive possibility. President Bill Clinton's visit to the Brandenburg Gate in Berlin, which I discuss in chapter 7, was one such ethnographic moment. In the tradition of a literary critic, I interpret written discourses, in particular essays and novels, to see how they are critical and often emotional interventions into public renderings of German-Jewish identity. My attention to the German-Jewish writers Barbara Honigmann and Rafael Seligmann, as well as the publicists Henryk Broder and Micha Brumlik are such analyses. Particularly interesting is the contrast provided by the Russian-Jewish immigrant author Wladimir Kaminer, who now lives in Berlin. This book is descriptive to provide information generally not known to the North American reader, but fundamentally it is interpretive, exposing and giving meaning to statements and events that the players themselves are not always aware of. As a scholar on Germany, I see it as my task to uncover and explain these rich offerings for what they may mean, in this case, for Jewish life in Germany fifteen years after reunification and for Americans who continue to be fascinated by Nazism, its persecution of the Jews, and the Jewish-German relationship.

My attention to American perspectives does not mean that what I present here would not be of interest to German or European audiences. It is clear to me, as I point out above, that my identity as an American Jew shapes my approach. Similarly, the American Jewish community and Israel are powerful frames in which to position the questions of identity that arise within Germany, both of these countries' best friend in Europe. The establishment of the American Jewish Committee's Berlin office is one of the most obvious symbols of this power. Similarly, albeit less politically influential, is the high status of Jewish American academics who study Germany and its Jews, or the Holocaust. Without statistics, an anecdotal look at German literature, history, or political science departments in the United States will show a high percentage of American Jews, besides myself, focusing on German questions. Names such as Sander Gilman, Charles Maier, or Andrei Markovits, all of whom are cited in this book, respectively represent these three major disciplines—literature, history, and political science—contributing to German Studies. They also differ from their predecessor generations in not being refugees from Nazi Germany. In short, academic interest in Germany must be explained by means other than national affiliation. I suspect that at least in part the Jewish heritage of these scholars—whether they admit it themselves or not—influences their political and intellectual subjects of study if they often write themselves or their interests into their research.

To the book's organization: the eight chapters encompass a narrative covering approximately the decade and a half since German reunification

Weiler, Klaus Milich, Irene Kacandes, Karen Remmler, Leslie Adelson, Zafer Şenocak, Anetta Kahane, Jürgen Lemke, and many others.

Finally, I am indebted to my editor at Rutgers University Press, Kristi Long, whose faith, enthusiasm, and above all, advice and hard work have made this book what it has become. I am so very grateful to her.

While German-Jewish identity has dominated my research agenda for many years and influences my thinking in almost all my work, I must acknowledge those publications from which some of the chapters in this book have emerged more directly than it would be appropriate to cite only in endnotes.

Chapter 2: "Die Konfrontation mit dem Holocaust: Deutsche und amerikanische Perspektiven." In *Die USA und Deutschland im Zeitalter des Kalten Krieges, 1945–1990: Ein Handbuch*, vol. II, *1968–1990*, edited by Detlef Junker. Stuttgart and Munich: Deutsche Verlags-Anstalt, 2001, 602–610. Also published as "German and American Confrontations with the Holocaust, 1968–1990." In *Germany and the United States in the Era of the Cold War, 1945–1990*, vol. 2. Washington, D.C.: German Historical Institute and New York: Cambridge University Press, 2004, 402–407.

Forum: "Being a Jewish American Germanist after Goldhagen: A Response to Herbert Lehnert, 'Was wir von Goldhagen lernen können.' " *The German Quarterly* 70, 2 (spring 1997): 168–174.

Chapter 5: "Turks and Jews: Comparing Minorities in Germany after the Holocaust." In *German Cultures Foreign Cultures: The Politics of Belonging*, edited by Jeffrey Peck, *AICGS Humanities Series*, vol. 3 (1998): 1–16.

Chapter 7: "Cultural Studies and Foreign Policy in a Strategic Alliance, or Why Presidents of the United States Should Learn German." In *A User's Guide to German Cultural Studies*, edited by Scott Denham, Irene Kacandes, and Jonathan Petropoulos. Ann Arbor: University of Michigan Press, 1997, 79–90.

Chapter 8: New Perspectives in German-Jewish Studies: Towards a Diasporic and Global Perspective." *Bulletin of the German Historical Institute* 35 (fall 2004): 33–42.

and eating a croissant, I sit in an Italian café a few blocks from the synagogue on Oranienburgerstrasse and around the corner from another bagel
shop. Sitting on one of the four stools, I watch the people of various races,
ethnicities, and religions go by the large picture window that allows the patrons to enjoy the variety that is now Berlin. It is not unusual to see a man
with a *kippah* or a woman in a headscarf. Inside the warm and cozy café,
no larger than a spacious closet, the owner speaks with his wife in Italian,
chats in Turkish with one of the regular customers, while other patrons
communicate in French or English and a woman sits next to me noncha-
lantly reading an Israeli newspaper. Jews, as well as others who publicly
demonstrate their difference in language, clothes, or symbols on the street,
are no longer a strange appearance. Bagel shops, not necessarily Jewish
ones, abound, as do other restaurants offering foreign cuisines in major
cities like Berlin. What might have seemed "virtual" in the mid-1990s, be
it Jewish or other, now represents, as in North America, a more common
experience for Jews and non-Jews alike in a changing Germany.

While this café, a bagel store, or other Jewish establishments in this
popular Hackesche Markt neighborhood bordering on traditionally Jewish
areas might represent to a purist like Gruber the absence of or merely an
imagined Jewry, I would rather see this new Jewish presence as a positive
part of renewal and real experience for Jews and non-Jews alike. Almost a
decade after the first scenario I recounted, Jewish life makes its presence
known more broadly and more diversely as part of cosmopolitan Berlin
where difference, while not always readily accepted, is contained in everyday life. For better, and sometimes recently for worse, Jewish life is lived in
Germany and Berlin, and the differences in my own experience that I re-
count here mark significant changes in the Jewish and German landscape
that make it possible to talk about a new Jewish life in Germany.

The question of definition and authenticity of a Jewish life in Germany
covering almost fifteen years after reunification is complicated by many
contrasts and contradictions that I have introduced above and also by the
terms that describe the people who are the subject of this book. Being
"German" and being "Jewish," separated identities that have a long history, especially since the Holocaust, are no longer mutually exclusive. Before the Second World War, most German Jews thought of themselves as
Germans. They felt uncomfortable with their Eastern European brethren
who congregated in the Scheunenviertel (barn quarter), an area near the
famous Alexanderplatz, whose name became associated with the disdained

Ostjuden. For many of the secular co-religionists, in their own words, Hitler turned them from Germans into Jews. After the war, the terminology separating Germans and Jews connoted the alienation and separation for those Jews remaining, most of whom were not "Germans" but displaced persons from Eastern Europe who came to be known by those ignominious initials as DPs. Then, it was simple: the Germans were the perpetrators and the Jews were the victims. As a postwar Jewish community took shape, albeit until recently very small, the term "Jews in Germany" became the dominant description of a people who were not fully comfortable or integrated into the society around them. My own prognosis looks toward a potentially new categorization, a "new" German Jewry that will represent a different status in both historical and contemporary terms.

Yet, all of the variations used to describe the population—"German Jewish," "Jew in Germany," "German of the Jewish faith," or even the favorite of well-meaning German politicians, "Jewish co-citizen"—connote the multiple ways of defining the relationships of Jews to Germans and of Jews who live in Germany to themselves and Jews living elsewhere. In other words, it is important to recognize that these varying terms show that Jewish identity is not static, but rather historical and dynamic. It is constantly being transformed by ever new positioning of one group to another, especially today in Germany's more heterogeneous society. However, the word "Jude" (Jew), which became so derogatory in the Third Reich, is still difficult for even liberal Germans to let cross their lips. To be a Jew in Germany today is still not "normal." As a prominent Berlin German Jew stated in 2003 as if to sum up succinctly the state of Jewish life in Germany today, "Abnormality is normality."[2]

The conference on Jewish American–German relations that had first brought me to Berlin was an encounter (and there are many of these meetings) that became more meaningful through these everyday, yet weighty, events in German culture. To be sure, anything that has to do with Jews in Germany is given special attention. In fact, it has even become trendy to be Jewish or to associate with anything Jewish. This attitude is certainly part of what has been called the "Jewish Renaissance," describing Berlin-Mitte (the center of the former East Berlin, the location of the most important sites), Oranienburgerstrasse with its "Jewish" restaurants, cafés, and renovated synagogue as museum and exhibition space. Jewish Americans trace the steps of old and new Jewish life with the popular *Goldapple Guide to Jewish Berlin* or a map called "Jewish Berlin." And now in the new millennium, as I already indicated, one can choose from a plethora of bagel shops that no longer seem so exotic, so specifically Jewish or American, nor quite the appropriate object of the ethnographic gaze. In Berlin, the controversial Holocaust Memorial designed by American architect Peter Eisenman and purposefully called "The Memorial to the Murdered Jews of Europe" is finally finished and opened in May 2005. Daniel Libeskind's Jewish Museum stands as an architectural masterpiece with its popular exhibition of "Two Millennia of Jewish Life in Germany." Cultural festivals and street fairs, television programs and exhibits fill in the picture of a growing Jewish life in Berlin in particular and in the rest of Germany generally. The Centrum Judaicum-Stiftung Neue Synagoge (Foundation for the New Synagogue) in the Oranienburgerstrasse (initiated in the late eighties immediately before the collapse of East Germany), the Ronald Lauder Foundation's Lehrhaus (learning center) for training Jewish teachers, Chabad Lubavitch, and the establishment of an office by the American Jewish Committee add an important institutional basis, one that is not coincidentally, at least in the latter examples, decidedly American. These institutions and the people they serve are indeed quite "real," concerned as they are with actual life experiences of Jews in Germany.

Now, more than fifteen years after the interviews and research for our book and video documentary on German Jewish identities, *Sojourners*, the Jewish terrain has changed considerably. Even back then our research convinced us that "German-Jewish identity" was constantly being redefined. In 1989–1990 the Jewish population was only half of what it is now. Although we addressed Jewish identity in Germany up until 1989 and immediately after reunification, questions about Jewish identity in Germany still persist. They are, however, colored by particular transformations based in large part on the expanded size and composition of the community made up to a large extent of Jews from the former Soviet Union. More recently, the proliferation of anti-Semitic statements and aggressive acts in Germany and other parts of Europe, especially France, has made the situation for Jews in Europe more complicated.

Nevertheless, since 1989–1990, the changes in the country have largely been positive and have essentially shifted the major question from why do Jews live in Germany to how should Jews live in Germany? Continuing to be taken aback by the presence of Jews living in Germany, American Jews are surprised to discover that the Jewish community in Germany is the fastest growing and the third largest in Europe after France and Britain. But beyond just the facts, the Jewish community in Germany is important for what it means for a new Jewish life in the Diaspora. This book is about these changes, the resulting complications, and ways to interpret them and their context.

The political, social, and economic reconfiguration after 1990 of two Germanys into one and the demise of the Soviet Union and its empire changed Jewish life in Germany. The major reason was, of course, the large influx of Jews from the former Soviet Union. To repeat a surprising fact for many North Americans: the numbers of Jews in Germany registers about 100,000 (12,000 in Berlin), more than two-thirds come from the Soviet Union, four times the size of twenty years ago. Ironically and erroneously, Germans when polled often overestimate the number of Jews in Germany at about 3 million. The latter case testifies to the misperceptions about Jewish status, influence, and power on the part of the Germans and the former case reflects an unfortunate ignorance and even prejudice by American Jews toward the Jewish community in Germany. Consequently, let us look at some of the facts and historical development of the Jewish community in Germany, primarily in Berlin.

The Jewish community in Germany is structurally quite different from communities in North America. Aside from the fact that there is no separation of church and state as in the United States and all official religious communities pay taxes and receive subsidies from the government, first and foremost, the Jewish Community in Germany is called "Einheitsgemeinde" (unified community). It has been defined this way since its reestablishment after World War II as a rump Community that needed to stand together since its near complete destruction in the Nazi genocide. The capital "C" signifies the distinguishing status of the German Community as a legal unit. More importantly, it has a hierarchical and all-encompassing umbrella-like structure directed from the top. It is also understood as a "Glaubensgemeinschaft" (religious community), primarily Orthodox, with some Liberal congregations, which would be called Conservative in North America. The Jewish community in Germany and Berlin answers to a single centralized entity, the Zentralrat der Juden in Deutschland (Central Council of Jews in Germany) in the former case and the Jüdische Gemeinde zu Berlin (Jewish Community of Berlin) in the latter. And as if to affirm its secure and public status, in January 2003, the Jewish Community and the German government signed what is called a "Staatsvertrag" (state treaty) officially establishing their relationship and substantially raising the amount of money the Community would receive as a religious institution. The Community's role is described in the *Goldapple Guide*: "The Jewish Community is the central organ of Jewish life in Berlin. It oversees all aspects of the synagogues, from cantor to cleaner. The Community administers welfare and social services; runs schools, adult education classes, and outreach programs; and maintains two cemeteries, and old-age home, two libraries, and three administration centers. It publishes a monthly magazine, sponsors religious and social clubs, and organizes cultural events. The organization represents local Jewish interests and 'the Jewish opinion' to the government and the media."[3]

There is no question that the Community dominates Jewish life in Berlin. But since Jewish prayer can take place anywhere a minyan (ten persons, traditionally men, needed for prayer) is gathered, in a home as well as a synagogue, it is sometimes difficult to establish a firm and stable profile of Jewish life, especially in Berlin, where the demography and religious orientations are changing so rapidly. In Germany, there are currently eighty-nine synagogues under the Central Council, twelve outside the Council, as part of the Reformed World Union of Progressive Judaism (WUPJ), and thirty rabbis. In Berlin, there are seven synagogues and an additional Orthodox synagogue, Adass Yisroel, which achieved independent legal and financial status after a long struggle. Included are also two houses of worship designated as "egalitarian," meaning men and women participate equally in the services. While such mixing is not acceptable in Orthodox shuls, it does not always coincide with a more liberal religious orientation. Adding to the transformation, another synagogue has moved from its prewar Orthodoxy to Liberal and two others are at a standoff if they should be Orthodox or Liberal. Other groups such as Sephardim and Jews from the Caucasus have their own minyans and talk about establishing a synagogue.[4] When one adds the strong presence of Chabad Lubavitch and the WUPJ, it is clear that diversity is in the making.

Politically, Community affairs are run by a representative governing board of twenty-one, elected by the membership, which is both vocal and complicated. For example, the board dissolved itself early in 2003 because of deep and persistent financial problems, called early elections for September, and then with great embarrassment had to annul the election and call for another vote in November. Such incompetence and confusion does not make a good impression either to internal or to external constituencies. Conflict often revolves around power and resources among various religious, political, and now ethnic factions within the official Community. Or it has to do with the Community's relations with those outside, such as with the Adass Yisroel or with the WUPJ. The latter recently launched a public and aggressive challenge to the Community. Chabad Lubavitch exists for more devout Orthodox Jews and is attracting many unaffiliated Russians. On the other end of the spectrum are feminist groups such as Bet Deborah and even a gay and lesbian group called Yachad. The Jewish Cultural Club, started in East Berlin by Irene Runge before the reunification, draws secular Jews and others to lectures and discussions and provides an important "Jewish" outlet for many who cannot, or would not, define themselves as religious. Populated by cultural and religious groups with such a variety of orientations, Berlin's Jewish landscape is the most interesting in Germany, and the one that still, amid all the turmoil and conflict, functions as a unified Community. However, the domination of the Einheitsgemeinde, defined as it currently is according to strict rules of Halakhah (Jewish law), means that the proliferation of such differences may well lead, in the opinion of some members, to a future dismemberment of the traditional community structure. Whether internal divisions in the Berlin Community will lead to a complete break remains to be seen.

The central issue in the Community concerns, in fact, the religious definition of membership, based on either the Halakhic law of maternal lineage or conversion by an Orthodox rabbi. This rule particularly affects Russian Jewish immigrants, whose Jewishness was recognized in the former Soviet Union patrilinearly and stamped into their passports as "national" affiliations were for other groups. Non-Halakhic Jews, for example, those with Jewish fathers and gentile mothers, therefore cannot become members, but may participate in the Community's activities. It is important to note here as well that only these Jews are counted in Community membership figures and thus reduces the total number of "Jews" in Germany, which some estimate to be thousands more. As anywhere, the reasons why some Jews who are religiously eligible to become members do not join are manifold. For example, it may be for lack of interest, identification, or money. This may be true for the Russian Jewish immigrants specifically, as well as their resentment toward the stringent religious rules

In a dramatic realignment, Europe's center moved eastward toward Berlin, the new capital of the united Germany, while the global balance of power moved in the opposite direction toward the United States.

This global shift has no doubt entailed a heightened presence of Jewish topics in German public discourse. Among the most prominent have been the acrimonious debates, even involving former Chancellor Helmut Kohl, about the Berlin Holocaust Memorial as to its design, its location, and its focus; the heated disagreements over a Jewish Museum in Berlin regarding its subject, its responsibility, and narrative; the visit of President Ezer Weizman, the first by a high-ranking Israeli official to Germany, which coincided with a debate about German Jewish reparation claims; the publication of Daniel Jonah Goldhagen's book *Hitler's Willing Executioners*, reviewed and debated in Germany as soon as it was published in the United States and months before its German publication date; the very public confrontation about interpreting the past between the writer Martin Walser and Ignatz Bubis. A short time later Walser's new novel, *Der Tod eines Kritikers* (Death of a Critic), whose main character, a Jew resembling the well-known literary critic Marcel Reich Ranicki, is murdered by a revengeful, angry author; the debate about "deutsche Leitkultur" (a dominant German culture); the Wehrmacht exhibition that accused the German army of war crimes during World War II; and the reappearance in 2002 of blatant, openly expressed anti-Semitism. This was prompted externally by the Middle East conflict and internally by FDP MP Jürgen Möllemann's attack on the television talk show host Michel Friedman, a vice-president of the Central Council of Jews in Germany, and president of the European Jewish Congress. Möllemann was publicly discredited by this cheap trick to win votes and by a financial scandal ending in his suicide in June 2003. Shortly afterward Friedman ironically was accused of cocaine use and involvement in a female prostitution ring from Eastern Europe. Friedman was fined and resigned all his posts amid a flurry of journalistic and public comments about whether his being Jewish affected the investigation either for or against him. And then, when it seemed that German politicians had learned a lesson from Möllemann, in October 2003, on the occasion of the German reunification celebration, MP Martin Hohmann embarrassed himself and his Christian Democratic Union/Christian Social Union (CDU/CSU) faction by calling Jews who participated in the Bolshevik Revolution "Tätervolk" (people of perpetrators) in an obvious attempt to relativize German guilt. He was dismissed from the party and a prominent general who defended him had to leave the army. Still, the debate and repercussions continued in his party and in German public discourse about how far a public figure could go in criticizing Israel or Jews in general. Although Hohmann's speech demonstrated his deficient historical knowledge and spurious references to famous anti-Semites such as the American Henry Ford, the general tone and substance of his speech was taken seriously enough to raise the long-standing question of Jewish "exceptionalism" to German criticism.

These events stand out as dramatic and decisive moments in the turbulent history of Jewish life in Germany in the last decade. I will show later how they affect Jewish outsiders to Germany through the comments of Israeli President Weizman during his visit and of an American second-generation survivor in the Goldhagen case. In particular, the presence of American Jewish organizations, discussed later on, shows how dominant American Jewish interests play out in Jewish German relations. They remind us how intensely the world, in particular Israel and the United States, concerns itself with Jewish life in Germany after the Shoah and how symbolic this relationship has become for Germany's "normal" place in the world. Ten years ago, Jewish life in Germany was viewed as exotic or quaint, on the one hand, or more seriously, aberrant or even despicable, on the other hand, proving that philo-Semitism and anti-Semitism are not so far apart. Little room is left for Jews to be regarded as "normal" people, subject to the ups and downs of mortal men and women. Their relationships with the "Germans" are always a subject of major national and often international concern. The specter of anti-Semitism or xenophobia resonates more deeply in Germany than in other European countries, although the rise of attacks on Jews in France is quickly achieving an equally negative status and, in fact, has come to overshadow concerns about Germany.

Of course, there are the many less dramatic presentations of Jewish lives in Germany that remain unknown to American audiences but are present in the German media. These illustrate an important internal debate that never reaches the other side of the Atlantic. For example, *Der Spiegel*, the most prominent weekly newsmagazine, published a lengthy and important interview with Ignatz Bubis in April 1996. In July of that year the Jewish newspaper of Germany, *Jüdische Allgemeine Wochenzeitung* (Jewish weekly newspaper), ran a cover article entitled, "The Bubis Factor. For many German citizens, the Head of the Central Council shapes their image of Jews."[11] There was also a provocative piece in December 1995 in the popular Berlin magazine *Tip*, called "The Young Jews of Berlin,"[12] highlighting the attitudes of the younger generation of Jews. These are just a few examples from a short period that typify attention to Jewish German matters. Some three years later, Bubis died. After what seemed a successful and honorable career, regrets about his failed accomplishments were published in a prominent interview with Rafael Seligmann in the popular magazine *Der Stern*. This sharp change in Bubis's attitude disturbed and even shocked readers. To add further irony, his requested burial in Israel was surrounded by ignominious circumstances when his grave was attacked by a mentally disturbed German-Jewish Israeli. The election of Paul Spiegel to Bubis's position followed. Right-wing agitation continued and there was even an attack on a Düsseldorf synagogue in the year 2000. Last, but definitely not least, the acrimonious debate about "Leitkultur" (dominant or leading culture) coalesced the discomfort and frustration of Jewish Germans and the next three years were marked by numerous anti-Semitic incidents.

Unfortunately, not much is heard in the United States about the German debate. This may be due to language problems or, more likely, that the American media, aside from being provincial, focuses on German or Jewish-German topics only in those instances when there is a taint of (neo) Nazism or anti-Semitism. In the 1990s Roger Cohen of the *New York Times* and Marc Fisher of the *Washington Post* were two exceptions. Scholars, mostly Jewish and female, publish widely on this subject. However, their writings, published in academic journals, remain largely confined to narrow university circles and receive little public coverage. Works such as Sander Gilman's *Jew's in Today's German Culture*, Gilman and Karen Remmler's collection, appropriately entitled *Reemerging Jewish Culture in Germany: Life and Literature Since 1989*, Michal Bodemann's *Gedächtnistheater: Die jüdische Gemeinschaft und ihre deutsche Erfindung* (Theater of Memory: The Jewish Community and Their German Invention), Bodemann's edited volume *Germans, Memory, Reconstructions of Jewish Life in Germany*, his recent book *In den Wogen der Erinnerung: Jüdische Existenz in Deutschland* (In the Surge of Memory: Jewish Existence in Germany), John Borneman's and my own study, Michael Brenner's *After the Holocaust*, and an edited collection by Leslie Morris and Jack Zipes, *Unlikely History: The Changing German-Jewish Symbiosis, 1945–2000*, as well as Elena Lappin's *Jewish Voices, German Words: Growing Up Jewish in Postwar Germany and Austria* and Susan Stern's *Speaking*

Out: Jewish Voices in a United Germany, all attempt to study or just present, to put it somewhat crassly, contemporary Jewish life rather than death. Rafael Seligmann, in his novel *Rubensteins Versteigerung* (Rubenstein's Auction) and in his essays, reminds us, as the title of an article in *Der Spiegel* claims, "The Jews are alive."[13]

Focusing on Jewish death, rather than celebrating Jewish life, as Seligmann continually repeats, obviously points to the preoccupation with the Holocaust, sometimes to the exclusion of the growing and vibrant new Jewish community. Concentrating on the genocide committed by Germany against the Jews reinforces opposing categories of "Jews" and "Germans." This rigid dichotomy created both by Germans and Jews makes it difficult to constitute a different kind of Jew as exists in Germany today who defies absolute identities of "us" and "them." In Germany, this attitude can give the impression that murdered Jews can be invoked and commemorated at the appropriate moment, but overshadow the real lived experience of non-Jewish Germans with their Jewish neighbors. In the United States, this position reinforces a preoccupation with the Holocaust as the only way American Jews identify these groups: namely, Germans as perpetrators, Jews as victims, and the new Jews in Germany as merely pariahs. Ironically, for both American Jews and non-Jewish Germans, being Jewish in Germany seems to be more about death than life. For the Jews in Germany, depending on whether they are indigenous or newly arrived, being Jewish falls somewhere in between and offers the possibility of creating an entirely new identity.

Of course, struggles in identity politics between Germans and Jews remain tightly linked to a dominant idea of what it means to be German. Although the racial policies of the Third Reich that extolled an Aryan race were discredited, a more benign notion of at least a homogeneous white and Christian German population remains a pervasive strand in the German postwar narrative. Many of the issues that I will discuss here return to particular assumptions about the definition of a German identity, as it constitutes "others" who may belong to or be excluded from the German nation. Reunification replayed these concerns when East Germans were welcomed as brothers and sisters and then suddenly were unmasked as different versions of their Western German counterparts. Their difference was ideological, rather than religious and ethnic, as it was with the now infamous Turkish "guest workers," who came to Germany in the 1960s to power the German economic miracle, stayed and brought their families.

Now, asylum seekers from the third world, skilled foreign workers from India, ethnic Germans and the Jews from the former Soviet Union have contributed to the multicultural mix that undermines a uniform German identity.

These identity questions surface repeatedly in different guises and varied locations. In the post-reunification period, one of the most typical was the very public debate about "Leitkultur," the notion of a dominant (read: German) culture that erupted between Paul Spiegel and the leaders of the conservative CDU/CSU. This conflict typifies the constant sparring that goes on in Germany when any hint of exclusionary nationalist politics emerges that might mark any group as "other." Initiated by CDU politician Friedrich Merz and reinforced by party chair Angela Merkel as part of a platform on the problem of integration of "foreigners" in Germany, the notion goes to the heart of what defines German identity. Spiegel spoke out publicly at the commemoration on November 9 in the year 2000, "What is all this talk about a German defining culture? Put an end to incendiary speeches." He continued, "Does a defining German culture include hunting down foreigners, setting synagogues on fire, killing homeless people?"[14] For the conservative politicians of the CDU/CSU who stood in silence at Spiegel's provocative remarks, Leitkultur "is [clearly] a chance," from their point of view, to support a benign and optimistic, yet prescriptive concept of "Germanness" that will contribute to a more coherent and solid notion of nationhood for the Germans. Particularly, in Germany with almost 8 million foreigners, among them 2.6 million Turks, it was not surprising that the Muslim community also spoke out against the notion of Leitkultur, as well as Möllemann's anti-Semitism.[15] In fact, Martin Hohmann's speech could be interpreted as rekindling the discourse on Leitkultur since he was encouraging a version of national pride that was promoted by setting off Germans against Jews. Ultimately for people like Hohmann, race, ethnicity, and religion, the markers of an identity that is different, may exclude groups such as Turks and Jews, as well as reinforce the fact that in multicultural societies, such as the United States, Canada, and now Germany, identities are constantly changing and are inclusive rather than exclusive.

Whatever German Jews like Seligmann or other Germans may feel about the Holocaust or anti-Semitism, the triumph of life over death in the shadow of the Shoah in Germany is obviously not easy, nor meant in any way to detract from remembering, commemorating, or honoring those

and career in Germany." He continues, however, "Whether Germany will become the beloved homeland (Heimat) again remains rather doubtful for the coming twenty years."[20] Although a Jewish community is being established in Germany, it remains to be seen if it will be normalized, whether it will be a society where Jews do not constantly need "to question their identity" in a democratic and sovereign country like Germany.[21]

Tolerance of difference sets the standard for such changes and Germany will continue to bear more scrutiny than other European countries when the issue of anti-Semitism, xenophobia, or right-wing extremism rears its ugly head. Perhaps the "unification of Europe" is one new avenue for repositioning what defines the new "German Jew," different than its prewar predecessor, but more representative of Jewish life in Germany fifty years after the war's end and ten years after reunification. Perhaps the transnationalism and globalization, which shift and eliminate borders in Europe (as well as the rest of the globe), will reconstitute Jewish life as well, as a "European Jew" or in a new form of cosmopolitanism whose effects and name we cannot yet articulate. Whatever this category might be, what happens in Germany to the Jews living there will be a significant marker for the future of Jewish identity. This book will trace the details of that lively and complicated process since the years 1989/1990.

2

Shadows of the Holocaust in Germany and the United States

There is no question that the Holocaust continues to cast its shadow over Jewish life in Germany, the United States, and of course, Israel. The resonance of the organized genocide of Europe's Jews is pervasive in its immense scope, emotional depth, and discursive power. Often the invocation of the Holocaust in debates is quite literally about memory, monuments, or memorialization of the event itself. Sometimes it plays out in ongoing identity questions about Jewish self-definition. And other times, as more recently since the Iraq war, it underpins conflicts about anti-Semitism, anti-Zionism, or even anti-Americanism. Consequently, the Holocaust continues to affect Jewish, American, German, and transatlantic relations even if not explicitly expressed but translated into questions about a Jewish voice, Jewish power, or Jewish influence. Understandably, both the victims and the perpetrators, as well as their descendants, are still sensitive about guilt and responsibility for the crimes of the past. How they are acknowledged affects policies in the present, and who will preserve its memory in the future.

Any potential normalization of relations between Jews, in Germany or the United States, and non-Jewish Germans must find a way to remember and memorialize the Holocaust, while at the same time recognizing changing historical contexts and the intervention of other events that may alter its meaning and status. Today, for example, the controversial discussions about German suffering in the fire bombings of Hamburg and Dresden or about a center for ethnic Germans who were driven out of Poland and other areas in the wake of the war precipitate emotional debates. In January 2005, for example, state parliamentarians from the right-wing NPD party walked out of the Saxon legislature during a moment of silence for Holocaust victims. One of them called the Allied bombings of Dresden "mass murder" and a "Holocaust of bombs." Leading German politicians and newspapers condemned these statements. These controversies are not only about the events and victims themselves, but also about their meaning in relation to the crime itself and its uniqueness in the minds of most Jews. In short, the underlying concern here is about who "owns" the past and whose memories and suffering will prevail when histories are written and stories are told about these times. Even words like "victim" are contentious, since they signify different attitudes about history and its interpretation, in this case, about who suffered, how much, and why. While the memory of the murder of the European Jews persists, it is yet to be determined how it will affect the future of Jewish life in Germany that will increasingly have to contend with alternative claims on the German past.

In 2004, as I tell this story, almost sixty years after the war, the particular history of Jewish identity in Germany is inextricably connected with the genocide of the Jews by Nazi Germany and its collaborators. Of course, other significant political events configure this contemporary consciousness as well. These include Germany's defeat, its division, the establishment of two German states, each aligned with different political systems and ideologies, and the restructuring of Europe after the fall of the Wall, and German reunification. Nevertheless, the Holocaust remains a central and unique component of how Jews understand themselves as Jews, especially in Germany. For example, the debate and finally the building of the "Memorial to the Murdered Jews of Europe" that stands next to the Brandenburg Gate at the hub of Berlin testify to this event's centrality in German and Jewish consciousness. While all such problems about claiming and representing the past were not immediately solved with the merging of two Germanys into one, reunification did tidy up, so to speak, at least officially, conflicting and competing versions of German history and the Holocaust. Let us look briefly at this story.

Until 1990, both Germanys had their own interpretation of this past, what historian Jeffrey Herf aptly calls "divided memory."[1] The Federal Republic constructed out of the American, British, and French occupation zones instituted de-Nazification procedures that were meant to cleanse the Germans of fascist ideologies and make them good democrats. These grand efforts of purification were not very successful. Konrad Adenauer, the first chancellor of German Federal Republic, instituted the controversial policy of "Wiedergutmachung" (reparations) to Jewish survivors and the State of Israel not only as a good will gesture of literally "making good again," but also to endear Germany to the Western Allies. In the German Democratic Republic, converted from the Soviet-occupied zone, an ideology Herf calls "German Communism's master narrative of anti-fascism" became the mantra of guiltless East Germans whose socialist "new Germany" absolved them of any responsibility for German crimes of the past.[2] Although the GDR pictured itself as idealistic and utopian, its projected "workers' paradise" turned out to be an unrealized dream. As more and more of the regime's abuses were revealed, a mass exodus of East Germans in 1989 for the West bluntly demonstrated its failures. The GDR collapsed more quickly (and more peacefully) than even its strongest critics would have imagined.

Until the 1960s, the goal in both Germanys was to establish their individual states as separate entities and to build diverse futures apart. According to historian Alan Steinweis, there was little interest in the Holocaust in either West or East Germany, or in the United States, for that matter, even among Jews. He notes, however, several important events that finally changed German attitudes toward the Holocaust, at least in the West. There was, for example, the televised Eichmann trial in Jerusalem in 1961, a proliferation of swastika smearing, the Auschwitz trials between 1963 and 1968, as well as the debate from 1965 over extension of the statute of limitations for the prosecution of Nazi war criminals. After four parliamentary sessions, the last in 1979, the statute of limitations was lifted.[3]

However, the new generation of West Germans, born during and directly after the Second World War, was coming of age in a country that could not shed its responsibility for the Nazi crimes as easily as had been done in the East. Even such grand symbolic gestures as President Ludwig Erhard's recognition of Israel in 1965 that preceded the overwhelming German support of Israel in the 1967 Six-Day War did not take away the burden of guilt. As they tried to come to terms with an inexplicable past and a contentious present, these "second-generation" Germans questioned the authority and legitimacy of their elders. The student movement, Vietnam protests, and anti-establishment fervor in West Germany in the 1960s, which also distinguished the West from the East, expressed their disillusionment with the older generation and a sharp critique of social and moral assumptions that ultimately contributed to opening up discussion of what had been done to the Jews. Ironically, the questions that often led these young people to reproach their elders also contributed, at least in the case of the demonstrative New Left, to a reversal of sympathies for Israel after the 1967 war. According to political scientist Andrei Markovits, the New Left "used anti-fascism to displace the Jewish question from its prominence among paradigms of historical analysis. . . . Ironically the intensity of the New Left's anti-fascist convictions furthered the marginalization of the Holocaust in German discourse. Whereas the student movement had sympathized with Israel in reaction to the students' fathers' generation, the New Left's sympathies drifted increasingly toward the Arab viewpoint after the Israeli victory in 1967."[4]

In other words, the New Left's strong anti-fascist rhetoric against Germany's Nazi past was transformed into harsh critiques of American and Israeli "imperialism," a semantic slippage that ignored significant historical dimensions. In the GDR, anti-fascism became the state-supported narrative that in East Germany contributed to the interpretation of the Holocaust in crass Marxist terms. The communist resistance was privileged above the Jews and the Holocaust was interpreted primarily in class terms. For the East Germans, it was simple, too simple: the Federal Republic, the ally of the United States and Israel, inherited and continued the tradition of "fascist" Germany. Although between 1945 and 1949, according to Herf, "the Soviet occupation authorities convicted 12,500 persons of war crimes in the Nazi era . . . after 1950, East German authorities claimed that justice had been done and that most of the Nazis were among the hundreds of thousands annually fleeing to the West."[5] In official GDR policy, the Nazis had left the GDR and socialist Germany held no responsibility for the Nazi past. From the GDR perspective, the division of Germany was now even more apparent because of their own version of "de-Nazification."

In America, cold war consciousness was even more blinding, according to Edward Linenthal, the author of *Preserving Memory: The Struggle to Create America's Holocaust Museum* (1995). "Indeed, if the Holocaust 'lived' in postwar American life," he writes, "it often did so in the subterranean anxieties surrounding meaningless mass death, with the Bomb replacing the gas chamber as the agent of extermination."[6] He even goes so far as to say "active memory of the Nazi past was considered a needless complication in the struggle to win the Cold War."[7] However, Linenthal also recognizes how Israel's precarious position affected a change in the

American Jewish public. He states dramatically, "After Israel's military victory, complacency did not return. 'Never Again' was heard not only from the Jewish Defense League, but also from the mouths and pocketbooks of many American Jews. This time they could celebrate a different ending to a potential holocaust."[8]

In fact, Linenthal links the emergence of Holocaust commemoration in the United States to the cold war by way of Vietnam and draws attention to the Holocaust imagery used by the anti-war movement. He goes so far as to see the protesters' interest in persecution of Native Americans and American involvement in Southeast Asia as establishing a moral yardstick derived from their reading of the Nazi persecution of the Jews. Quoting the renowned Holocaust historian Raul Hilberg, he tries to answer the question of why American college students became so interested in the subject in the 1970s. Hilberg states, "After the disorientation of Vietnam . . . they wanted to know the difference between good and evil. The Holocaust is a benchmark, the defining moment in the drama of good and evil. . . . Against this single occurrence, one would assess all other deeds. And so, memorialization began in earnest, that is to say, it became organized."[9] In the United States, no better example of this institutionalization of memory was President Jimmy Carter's decision to form a Holocaust commission. It would "make recommendations with respect to the establishment and maintenance of an appropriate memorial to those who perished in the Holocaust."[10] The United States Holocaust Memorial Museum opened in 1993.

The year 1978, however, became a major turning point in Holocaust awareness due to the mini-series "Holocaust" shown on American television on April 16–19, and a year later in Germany. These television programs became significant for educating a broad public about the events in Germany and Europe that produced the genocide of European Jewry. In both countries critics argued about similar issues. On the one hand, they complained about the aesthetic merits of a commercial television (NBC) docudrama that was, aside from its simplistic portrayals of Germans and Jews, crudely interrupted in the United States by advertisements for deodorants and cleaning products. On the other hand, they recognized the pedagogical and informational value of such a nationally televised program. In Germany at least, this program, still relegated to the less popular German Channel 3, was, in fact, a watershed in educating the public to the deeds of their leaders and compatriots. Sitting together in front of the television set, parents and children were confronted with a German past that had never surfaced so widely and publicly. These intimate familial moments often turned into angry confrontations of a younger generation accusing their parents of being perpetrators. More organized public discussions were also held after each installment to a broad popular response.

The year 1978, the fortieth anniversary of the November pogrom the Nazis called "Kristallnacht" (night of broken glass), marked, as such commemorations often do for Holocaust awareness, a significant moment not only in West Germany but also in East Germany, even though the GDR would not air the television program. It is important to remember that not only did a Jewish community, albeit quite small, exist in the GDR, but reaction to the revelations was also a measure of the communist regime's allegiance to cold war ideologies promoted by the Soviet Union. Although the thirtieth anniversary of the GDR in 1979 gave GDR Jews a chance to affirm their dual identities, as Jews and as (East) Germans, they continued to struggle with their regime's hostile policies toward Israel as an "imperialist Zionist state" aligned with the United States. Nevertheless, they tried whenever they could to affirm their commitment to the communist state as Jewish citizens.[11] It was in 1982, however, even after many other commemorations offering public recognition as well as confirmation of how secure they felt in the GDR as Jews, that the Israeli invasion of Lebanon intensified their quandary of being Jews and loyal citizens of the state.

In 1985, the United States and Germany were also intertwined in the next major milestone which unfortunately displayed a lack of sensitivity on the part of both nations' leaders. President Ronald Reagan was to visit a military cemetery in the town of Bitburg where some SS officers were buried among others. Reagan refused to cancel the visit despite widespread protest. Although it turned out that those buried there were members of the Waffen SS (combat units) not the Totenkopf Division that carried out the Final Solution, the damage had been done. Accompanied by Chancellor Helmut Kohl, Reagan's visit created a furor in America and became a turning point in German-American and German-Jewish relations. This visit, a symbolic gesture of cold war reconciliation, was meant to assuage Kohl's disappointment and even anger for Germany's exclusion from D–Day ceremonies in Normandy. For Kohl, this was a measure of Germany's acceptance into the Atlantic Alliance and the power of Germany's postwar transformation to counterbalance memories of Nazi Germany's horrible deeds. In short, it seemed to be time to look to the future and not the past. In President Reagan's words, when he decided on this trip to cancel a proposed visit to a concentration camp, "I don't think we ought to focus on the past. I want to focus on the future. I want to put that history behind me."[12] Weren't solid German-American relations forty years after the end of the war just cause to celebrate symbolically even at the graves of Waffen SS officers who in Reagan's mind were also "victims of Nazism . . . just as surely as the victims in the concentration camps"?[13] Such comparisons were sharply condemned not only by Jewish groups, but also by other religious and ethnic organizations.

Bitburg, however, did not, as either Reagan or Kohl might have hoped, succeed in removing the Nazi stain from postwar West Germany ready to celebrate its allegiance to the West, in particular to the United States. Rather, Bitburg became a reminder that historical understanding was still needed, especially by Americans and the president himself. What Jürgen Habermas called the "forced reconciliation" orchestrated in the name of state powers was not to be trusted. It was German President Richard von Weizsäcker, who, three days later on May 8, spoke out forcefully against what Bitburg had come to symbolize in a speech to the Bundestag (parliament) as it commemorated the fortieth anniversary of the end of the war.[14] Delicately, albeit decisively, he reminded his fellow Germans that May 8 was "an aberration of German history,"[15] and "a day of liberation."[16] Yet he differentiated between guilt and responsibility when he addressed the generation of Germans born after the war who "cannot profess a guilt for crimes they did not commit,"[17] yet still "must accept the past."[18] Bitburg symbolized not only the complexity of German-American relations regarding the Holocaust, but also the ways that cold war imperatives continued to be colored by the historical past. Bitburg proved that the past would simply not disappear and that Americans, not only American Jews, would not allow Reagan to forget the Holocaust.

In 1985, another public event occurred that required Jews in Germany to speak up, this time not against politicians, but against the artistic community, which showed that it too had power to set agendas. What came to be known as the "Fassbinder Affair" was to affect the political culture of the Federal Republic for years to come. The play *Der Müll, die Stadt, und der Tod* (Garbage, the City, and Death), by avant-garde filmmaker, sometimes playwright, and general enfant terrible of the German cultural scene Rainer Werner Fassbinder, was to be produced in Frankfurt. In particular, the character of the "rich Jew" drew accusations of anti-Semitism.

Consequently, on opening night members of the Frankfurt Jewish community, leading among them Ignatz Bubis, who not only resembled the main character in the play, but also was the future popular president of the Central Council of Jews in Germany, protested on stage and stopped the performance. They engaged in a heated discussion with the audience not only about anti-Semitism, but also about artistic freedom. The play was canceled and, according to Andrei Markovits, "for the first time in the Federal Republic, Jews had participated in a protest qua Jews."[19] The response was likened to the results of the production of Rolf Hochhuth's controversial play *Der Stellvertreter* (The Deputy), twenty years earlier. At that time this play created a furor because it presented Pope Pius XII's unwillingness to intercede with the Nazis to save the Jews of Europe, a sore point between Jews and Catholics. Pickets also protested the performance.

A less fortunate "reinterpretation" of the historical past occurred a year later, in 1986, during what is known as the "Historikerstreit" (Historians' Debate). This controversy over the uniqueness or comparability of the Holocaust set the tone for heated debates about "normalization" and "relativization" of the Nazi genocide of the Jews in German history and historiography. It also dealt with how memory mediates the past in the present, as that past becomes increasingly distant and filtered through second-hand accounts. Spawned by the writings of two respected German historians, Andreas Hillgruber and Ernst Nolte, and the response by social philosopher and critic Jürgen Habermas, the debate quickly moved beyond historical methodology to even more profound questions of defining a German nation after Auschwitz. Nolte compared the Nazi death camps to Stalinist gulags and underplayed the specific historical differences between fascism and communism. Habermas rejected these simplistic comparisons. Referring to the Historians' Debate, American historian Charles Maier advanced an intriguing thesis stating, "It may just be fortuitous that a bitter controversy over the legacy of the national past has erupted at the very moment when a Soviet-American agreement to eliminate intermediate missiles and the advent of a Reformist leader are changing the variables of the East-West balance."[20] Questioning the centrality of the Holocaust for German self-understanding, according to Maier, means that "the debate over the national past will have served to have licensed a debate over the German future."[21]

The fiftieth anniversary of Kristallnacht, November 9, 1988, would be the last under the cold war order. One year later, on that exact date, the fall of the Berlin Wall would decisively point the way to a new German nation that could not have been imagined one year earlier. It is ironic that these dates coincide. While November 9 would preoccupy historians since it marked many important moments in German history, many Jews feared that the joyous event of 1989 might overshadow the tragic memories associated with 1938. Still, the commemorations of 1988 marked a move forward for the Jewish community with the East German government. The president of the World Jewish Congress, Edgar Bronfman, visited the GDR at the request of the government, special sessions of the GDR Volkskammer (People's Congress) where Erich Honecker, leader of the communist party, spoke about Jewish suffering under Nazism, and other meetings were convened with foreign Jewish dignitaries, including Heinz Galinski. Honecker bestowed gifts on the Jewish community and announced the reconstruction of the synagogue in the Oranienburgerstrasse, as well as the founding of the Centrum Judaicum, which would become a center for commemoration as well as research. In fact, reflecting more openness toward the West whose financial support was needed, many commemorations were held in Berlin and throughout the country recognizing not only persecution of Jews but also their accomplishments and contributions to German life. Publications about the Holocaust by GDR historians also multiplied, as well as a Jewish Community publication in many languages, a small booklet called in English "Beware Lest the Nightmare Recur."[22]

The fall of the Wall and the reunification in 1990 that followed were momentous in ending the cold war order. But Jews in both the United States and the two Germanys were most fearful about what this political transformation would mean for them. For many, the calls in East Germany of "We are the people," which quickly melted into "We are one people," smacked of a resurgent German nationalism, which for Jews meant renewed anti-Semitism. Neo-Nazi demonstrations and skinhead attacks on innocent people were to multiply in the years directly following reunification making such cities like Hoyerswerda and Rostock in the East and Mölln and Solingen in the West synonymous with xenophobia, racism, and anti-Semitism. The comparison between Jews and Turks, anti-Semitism and xenophobia is the subject of chapters 5 and 6. Jews around the world feared what reunification might mean for the future of security for Jews in the new Germany. However, the events which first seemed to portend dark trends in Germany's ability to deal with "others" as part of resurgent uncontrolled nationalism were seen to be unfounded. Questions about German reunification became more about economic than security matters.

Since 1990 the differences between the way Americans and Germans confront the Holocaust have become ever more distinct. In the former case, the opening of the Holocaust Memorial Museum on the National Mall in Washington, D.C., and many other museums and monuments around the country focus attention on representations of Holocaust memory. The popularity of these public institutions has exceeded all expectations. Controversies surrounding the return of property in Europe to Jews, the payment of pensions to survivors living in Eastern Europe, and more dramatically, the revelations about Switzerland's collaboration by receiving "Nazi gold," all draw the attention of Americans to the Holocaust and the ways that its legacy still affects the lives of Jews today. Articles appear with great frequency in the *New York Times* about such issues, as well as personal stories of survivors, all reinforcing the Holocaust's place in contemporary American consciousness. Whether or not such focus is an antidote to forgetting, media attention in the United States leaves little doubt that there are significant individuals and institutions seeking to keep memory alive, although there are those who present a strong argument that such attention will do precisely the opposite. Those critics would say that while universalization of the Jewish experience makes the Holocaust more accessible and more relevant to early twenty-first century America, it also adds both a grand moral dimension and the potential for decoupling the Shoah from identity-affirming Jewish victimhood and suffering.

Increasingly, popular culture plays a persuasive role in educating the public to the Holocaust, particularly films with works like the French filmmaker Claude Lanzmann's nine-and-a-half-hour documentary *Shoah* (1985), the better-known *Schindler's List* by Steven Spielberg (1993), the controversial Italian comedy *Life Is Beautiful* (1998), or Roman Polanski's *The Pianist* (2000), as well as many television documentaries. Making the case for the influence of popular movies on German-Jewish reconciliation, historian Frank Stern cites the proliferation of films in the 1990s that show the difficulty of German/Jewish relations, such as in the romantic feature *Meschugge* (1998) in which an American Jew and the granddaughter of a Nazi who thought she was Jewish declare their love. For Stern, film has the power to transform how Jews and Germans understand and even, as in this case, love each other. "Jewish Weeks of Film and

Culture as in Berlin and Vienna could be more important than the politically important statements of [Jewish] Community leaders."[23] In fact, many critics, such as Alvin Rosenfeld, have claimed that most people (read Americans) get their information about the Holocaust not from historians but "rather from novelists, filmmakers, playwrights, TV program writers and producers, popular newspapers and magazines, political figures and other public personalities."[24]

The popularization and even what Michael Berenbaum, former director of the Research Institute at the Holocaust Memorial Museum, calls the "Americanization of the Holocaust"[25] emphasizes some fundamental questions about the status of the Holocaust in contemporary American and German life. Popular books like Daniel Jonah Goldhagen's very successful *Hitler's Willing Executioners: Ordinary Germans and the Holocaust* (1996) are at the top of the list. This so-called Americanization continues with the publication of studies such as Peter Novick's *The Holocaust in American Life* (1999) and the controversial book by Norman Finkelstein, crassly entitled, *The Holocaust Industry: Reflections on the Exploitation of Jewish Suffering* (2000), both of which stirred public debate. In the same vein Rosenfeld warns that "images of mass suffering may awaken conscience, but they also have the power to perversely excite the imagination. A pornography of the Holocaust, in other words, may undercut a didactics of the Holocaust."[26] Whereas the 1960s initiated discussion of the Holocaust in both countries, these last forty years reflected, understandably so, increasingly divergent preoccupations and concerns. The success of the Holocaust Museum and other such institutions has fixed Holocaust memory in the American consciousness, in fact, it has fixed it to such an extent that Jewish educators worry it may too strongly define American Jewish identity with what some call "victimology." In Germany, it remains to be seen how the Berlin "Memorial to the Murdered Jews of Europe" will be received since the history of the monument in its planning stages has been so controversial and troubled. The Jewish Museum showcasing "2000 Years of German Jewish History" (discussed in chapter 4) definitively does not see itself as a museum dedicated to the tragedy. Continuing to grapple with how the past is to be remembered in Germany and the political vicissitudes of who will control that memory in a still newly reunified nation continues to make the task profoundly more difficult for Germans than for Americans.

However, for both Germans and Americans in the new century, such comparisons raise questions whether the Holocaust will continue to be understood as what Fred Kempe, the former Bonn correspondent for the *Wall Street Journal*, calls "the old rituals" of "guilty Germans" and "Jewish victims."[27] Or will it go beyond a pseudo-acceptance of Jews (or foreigners as well) in the growth industry of philo-Semitism, what Michael Daxner, former president of the University of Oldenburg, calls "the new love of Jews," a kind of "backward salvation"?[28] Such questions have become increasingly ubiquitous as not only the most cynical critics talk about the "commodification" of Auschwitz as the "Shoah business" and a fixation of Jewish-American identity on the Holocaust as more and more survivors pass on. In Germany, some complain about the overwhelming attention to the topic in public and media culture, while many Jews remind them that such awareness must be maintained. Still confronted with anti-Semitism and those who would like to draw a line in German history between the past and present—the infamous *Schlußtrich* (line of closure)—Jews in Germany have new and complex issues to deal with that do not, however, escape the shadow of the past.

In the late 1990s two events and their repercussions stand out in Holocaust discourse and German-Jewish relations. One comes from the United States that spawned unexpected reverberations in Germany—the publication of Goldhagen's *Hitler's Willing Executioners* in 1996 and its German translation in 1997. The second is the so-called Walser-Bubis debate of 1998. One should not forget that these events, which called on historical memory of the Holocaust and its relevance today, took place in close proximity to the election in 1998 that brought about the SPD/Green coalition of Chancellor Gerhard Schröder and Foreign Minister Joschka Fischer. These politicians, and many in their administration, not only created an entirely new political coalition and culture at the top of Germany's federal government. They were also representatives of the 1968 generation of student activists who had questioned their elders so harshly about their role in the persecution and extermination of the Jews. As part of the generation whose relationship to Israel and the Jews had been shaped by events of the 1960s and 1970s such as the Vietnam conflict, the Six-Day War, and the other Israeli policies toward their Arab neighbors, their election was both a political and emotional break with the past and the policies of the previous government of Helmut Kohl.

To be sure, academic scholarship on Jewish life in Germany and especially on the Holocaust is prolific. Some would even crudely call it an "industry." However, rarely does a book promoted as a scholarly study on German anti-Semitism have as massive an effect on popular and public discussion as did Daniel Jonah Goldhagen's *Hitler's Willing Executioners*. Goldhagen's book was an anomaly when it became a major bestseller in the United States and Germany, even before its German publication, and made Goldhagen a media star overnight. What was it that attracted American and German audiences to Goldhagen's thesis of "eliminationist anti-Semitism"? Perhaps one answer is to be found on the book jacket that dramatically claims that many beliefs about the killers are fallacies: "They were not primarily SS men or Nazi Party members, but perfectly ordinary Germans from all walks of life, men (and women) who brutalized and murdered Jews both willingly and zealously. . . . They acted as they did because of a widespread, profound, unquestioned, and virulent antisemitism that led them to regard the Jews as a demonic enemy whose extermination was not only necessary but also just."[29]

This thesis that "radically transforms our understanding of the Holocaust and of Germany during the Nazi period" was undeniably provocative. Goldhagen was, at least, implying that the Germans inherently hated the Jews, which made all Germans collaborators, if not outright perpetrators.[30] He offered a rather simplistic explanation of what many wanted to hear on both sides, but for very different reasons. But the success of the book was based not only on its subject. The incredible proliferation of discourses surrounding the book, such as the reviews, the interviews, the criticisms, in fact, all of the statements made about the person and the book, created a reputation and "hype" unfamiliar to observers of German history and politics. The Holocaust became a popular topic of debate in a way that had not occurred so publicly since 1979 when the television series premiered. Unfortunately, aside from serious flaws in historical analysis and use of sources, the book's graphic descriptions threatened to become sensationalist and gruesome accounts that titillated the senses more than the mind.

Hitler's Willing Executioners is not literally about postwar Germany or Jewish life today and it is more than a scholarly study of the roots of the Holocaust. However, it is a book that was marketed brilliantly to the general public, reached bestseller lists in America and Germany, and whose following demanded police barricades to protect crowding viewers at public forums at which the author was present. Goldhagen's supporters and critics have dealt with the thematic aspect ad nauseam. However, I am far more interested in its resonance for us today. Although Goldhagen may have written the book from a "detached" perspective, its emotional import engaged scholars and general readers, Germans and Americans, Jews and non-Jews.[31] Goldhagen made a point that it is irrelevant that he is Jewish and his father is a Holocaust survivor. As he says, "People's backgrounds are not relevant to the story."[32] But the book is precisely interesting to me because of who Goldhagen is and the personal investment he has in this history. By the same token, the book compels each reader to take a position toward the incisive question of German guilt, that is, eliminationist anti-Semitism and the German and Jewish relationship, and to come to grips with what it means for us today, especially as Germans, Jews, or Americans. It is an intense, personal lesson on how to relate to history and the complexity of historical understanding. Goldhagen inadvertently challenges his readers to take a stand on history, as did another popular success, *Holocaust*, fifteen years before.

After reunification, Goldhagen's book brought us back to a topic that struck a new chord in Americans and Germans. I was concerned, however, not only about what Goldhagen actually said, but also what the book did as a "cultural event" that constructed meaning about the Holocaust in the minds and imaginations of Germans and Americans in the postwar period. Surely its success tapped into an emotional vein. Although Goldhagen denied that a "*timeless* [his italics] German character exists," this point is easily inferred from his analysis.[33] The situation after 1945 is discussed in only two footnotes, but has been more extensively elaborated upon in the many public and private discussions as part of what I call above the book's "cultural event" character.[34] Many commentators have pointed out that Goldhagen's evaluation of postwar Germany is naive and limited, aside from the fact that he discusses only West Germany. His point is too simple: the Germans learned to be democratic from the conquering Americans. Yet, if the Germans are inherently anti-Semitic, how could they change into liberal democrats? If this is not the case, then the analysis of postwar Germany is simply unnecessary and insufficient. This gap in logic is one, if not the strongest, of the targets of criticism. Because the claim about Germany pre-1945 is so extreme, it exaggerates a post-1945 temper in its uncritical and rosy picture of Germany today. On the one hand, his book is fodder for those Jews, especially American Jews, who can unequivocally hate Germany and all Germans since they have not kept abreast of Germany's efforts toward "Bewältigung der Vergangenheit" (coming to grips with the past). On the other hand, the book may posit a far too positive image of Germany, democratized by the Americans, toward liberal democracy. In short, Goldhagen over-stigmatizes Germany before the war and underplays racism and anti-Semitism since the war's end. Thus, Goldhagen reinforces a notion of "Stunde Null (Zero Hour)–1945" that has all but been discarded by most critics since anti-Semitism did not suddenly disappear at the end of the war.

Although no other event surrounding questions of the Holocaust has had an equally great impact in Germany and the United States, there have been "local" German debates that have turned into significant German media events. In 1998, the year of the election, an acrimonious and public debate erupted between Martin Walser, a respected writer, and Ignatz Bubis, FDP politician and president of the Central Council of Jews in Germany. It was additionally fueled by the support Walser received from the prominent SPD politician Klaus von Dohnanyi whose own father had been executed for resistance in the Third Reich. This event represented many of the tensions between Jews and Germans, about normality and uniqueness, about historical understanding and responsibility, about the past and the present, about generations, and as always, about identity.

Walser's remarks came on the occasion of his receiving the Frankfurt Book Fair's Peace Prize. Bubis's quick and sharp response filled the newspapers. The controversy concerned the status of the Holocaust in everyday German society, how it is interpreted and then used by Germans and by Jews to define who they are today. This self-identification necessarily implies questions about the definition of Germanness and is part of, as was the debate about Leitkultur, in short, who belongs to the new Germany. Walser's radical questioning of Germany's responsibility to remember fifty years after Auschwitz smacked of anti-Semitism to Bubis and many in the Jewish community. But to many non-Jewish Germans, Walser's words finally expressed what they had feared to say: they wanted to be liberated from constant reminders of German guilt.

The story was brief, but sharp and painful. Walser suggested that Auschwitz was being used as what he called a "moral cudgel" against the Germans to keep them forever guilty about the horrible deeds perpetrated by the Nazis.[35] To Walser and many of his generation, the Holocaust had become an "instrumentalized crime."[36] Bubis responded by criticizing the author's "provocative incendiary sentiments" that were minimizing these past events that were so defining for Germany's present and future.[37] The contentious debate drew attention to the ethics of public political and cultural figures' statements about Jews and what could be construed as anti-Semitic discourse. It was a part of the ongoing German project of coming-to-terms with the past that was proving "tiresome" and "empty" for many people of Walser's generation and younger. It was also the beginning of what many saw as a breaking of a taboo about how Jews were to be discussed in public discourse and became a reference point for years to come.

This debate resurfaced again in June 2002 when Walser's novel *Death of a Critic* released a storm of accusations of anti-Semitism hearkening back not only to his earlier speech, but also to the Fassbinder controversy in 1985. In the new Walser novel, the main character appears to be another public Jewish figure, this time Marcel Reich-Ranicki, a well-known Jewish literary critic and television personality, who had not always been kind to Walser's work. While this controversy cast Walser's status as a public spokesman for Germany into doubt, it reaffirmed Bubis's role as an outspoken and respected representative of the Jewish Community. Until shortly before his death, when he radically questioned the impact of his commitment, he remained an important Jewish leader and role model who saw himself as both a German patriot and an observant Jew. He actively reminded his fellow Germans of their responsibility to remember the Holocaust, to stand up against prejudice of any kind, and to recognize Jews as full members of German society.

Emboldened by Bubis's work, the Jewish Community will indeed become stronger. But a new German Jewry will also face the disappearance of generations who experienced on German soil or under German occupation the destruction that defined them for so many years. For a largely Russian Jewry whose relationship to Nazi Germany is either absent or overshadowed by Stalin's crimes, the Holocaust wanes in significance for their identity compared to other Jews in Germany or in the United States. While the new massive "Memorial to the Murdered Jews of Europe" stands in the center of Berlin next to the rebuilt Potsdamer Platz, the Brandenburg Gate, and the erstwhile location of the Berlin Wall, sites so filled with various stages of past German history, new German and German-Jewish identities may consider other German spaces more meaningful for evolving self-definition. How will the memorial and the Holocaust survive time and historical change?

This particular Holocaust memorial has a contentious and acrimonious history. Some might say that what came to be known as the "Mahnmal Debatte" (Memorial Debate) created a serious public discussion among many important factions as to how the Holocaust should be remembered in Germany, not unlike the effects of the Historians' Debate in the mid-1980s. Especially after ten years passed from the initial idea to the beginning of construction, many feel that too much talk, too many personalities, and too much politics complicated the process. In other words, the path to the memorial was not paved with gold. Initiated in 1989 by journalist Lea Rosh, the construction of such a memorial produced persistent questions about location, size, and design, as well as whether only Jewish victims should be included in this remembrance. Many sympathetic professionals, mainly directors of established historical Holocaust remembrance sites such as concentration camps, questioned whether Germany needed a central memorial since so many of the actual Holocaust sites still existed. One such site is the well-known "Topography of Terror" exhibition directed by rabbi and former president of the Berlin Community Andreas Nachama, which is housed in the exposed basement of the Gestapo headquarters only a short distance from the Berlin Memorial. These directors, many of whom are historians, were concerned that such a large central edifice that was only symbolic would diminish interest and support for their historical sites which have existed over many years and offer visitors education and experience of the locations themselves.

In 1995, the first competition for the design was announced and drew worldwide attention and many submissions. A plan was accepted by the distinguished selection committee: an enormous so-called gravestone with the engraved names of millions of murdered Jews. Chancellor Kohl rejected this plan. In 1997, another competition was announced and finally Peter Eisenman and Richard Serra's stark field of 4,200 concrete blocks was chosen. But the discussion continued, changes were made, Serra withdrew. New suggestions, including a "Haus des Erinnerns" (House of Memory), were then made in 1998 by the recently appointed State Secretary for Culture Michael Naumann. In 1999, after much debate again, the Bundestag accepted a revised Eisenman proposal that included an information center. On January 27, 2000, the symbolic construction began marking the day that Auschwitz was liberated, a date that since 1996 has become an official day of remembrance for the victims of the Holocaust in Germany.[38]

With such a controversial, divisive, and politicized history, it is not surprising that the discussion surrounding the memorial has itself become a subject of study. It represents how seriously, and unfortunately, to what ends such issues are taken up in the German public sphere, where sensibilities are raw and egos are large. Clashes are often instigated by the rather notorious German television personality and member of the Memorial's Board, Lea Rosh, a non-Jew, who fashions herself literally and figuratively as a Jewish spokesperson. In 2004, for example, she led a protest against the Degussa Company which was providing chemicals to protect the memorial's stones from graffiti. Since a Degussa subsidiary had manufactured poison gas used to exterminate Jews in the camps, she wanted the company to withdraw from its work on the memorial. Eisenman disagreed with this position. Then, some months later, she walked out of a meeting in support of Alexander Brenner, former president of the Berlin Jewish Community, who attacked Eisenman for a joke he made during a visit to his New York dentist. Apparently, Eisenman related the Degussa controversy and the dentist asked Eisenman if he should remove his teeth since he had just used Degussa products on the architect. Eisenman was asked to apologize for insulting the victims of the Holocaust. Again, in comments about the controversy by other prominent Berlin Jews like Nachama and Schoeps, it became clear that resentments were still strong, since many Jews felt that the memorial was a decision of the German Parliament and not of the Jewish Community. Consequently, according to Schoeps, "There will continue to be disputes . . . because the basic question of who is building the memorial for whom and for what purpose is and remains unanswered." It was left to Wolfgang Benz, speaker for the foundation's advisory board and respected professor and director of the Center for Anti-Semitism Research at the Technical University in Berlin, to mediate the tension. He noted, "Eisenman was certainly not clear how Brenner would react to his story . . . [Eisenman] has introduced us Germans to American humor. In the States, they are much more easy-going about themselves and their history, even Jewish history."[39]

Benz wisely recognizes that Americans and American Jews have different sensibilities and broader thresholds of humor, based on the way that local histories shape Jewish identities. Such differences should be a reminder about the different experience Russian Jews bring to and have in Germany. In Germany, jokes about Jews, even those made by Jews, as is common in the United States, are still rare. In July 2004, the monument had an official opening, although the laying of the slabs is not even complete. Crudely, some people claim the monument will mainly benefit dogs who want to relieve themselves on the stone blocks rather than be the intended reminder of Nazi atrocities against the Jews of Europe. Others still feel the money would have been better spent on other sites or that other groups should have been included, such as the Roma and Sinti or homosexuals. The discussion continues. It remains to be seen what role Holocaust remembrance will play when illusive memory, on the one hand, and concrete stone slabs, on the other hand, are the only traces remaining from an event that has defined Jewish life in Germany so profoundly.

3

Russian Immigration and the Revitalization of German Jewry

Since 1990 a mass migration of Russian Jews has been under way, primarily to the United States and Israel. However, literally tens of thousands have also settled in Germany. The Jewish immigrants have since transformed the life of a community that had an uncertain future at best. Ironically, this massive population movement has certain parallels with a similar movement of Jews from East to West at the end of the Second World War when the concentration camps were liberated and thousands of displaced persons (DPs) moved across the Continent. Homeless, lost, and mostly destitute, many then resided—primarily in DP camps—on the soil of the nation that had almost succeeded in wiping out their people. In contrast to that earlier migration, however, Jews are now coming to Germany willingly, this time as seekers of a permanent stable home. This time they did not migrate in the aftermath of war, but nevertheless in a period of intensive change and insecurity. The East has moved west and the West has moved east, altering European spaces of identity that, typical of diasporas, no longer coincide with territorial boundaries.

In 1989, before the Berlin Wall came down, the point at which my main narrative begins, the story of Jewish life in Germany had improved, but it was not particularly optimistic. There were 20,000 to 30,000 Jews in the Federal Republic (West Germany), 6,000 in Berlin, and about 500 Jews in the German Democratic Republic (East Germany), 200 in East Berlin.[1] Most were elderly and their numbers were diminishing. Then came the opening of the borders, followed by the disintegration of the Soviet empire. Those decisive years, 1989–1990, marked the beginning of a flood of immigration. Few Americans seem to be aware how this population shift has, in fact, saved the Jewish community in Germany from certain extinction and made it the third largest in Europe, the ninth largest and fastest growing in the world. And few people, as the thesis of my book contends, understand how this migration and the reconstitution of the Jewish community in Germany may change our thinking about diaspora.

Today the German Jewish Community proudly announces a membership of more than 100,000 (estimated most recently at 108,000), with 12,000 in Berlin. Eighty-nine synagogues are under its aegis, ranging from the largest in Berlin to smaller ones, such as in Rostock in the East or Kassel in the West. In some, Russian Jews make up virtually the entire community. In fact, 85 percent of the Jewish population in Germany is from the former Soviet Union and since 1989, over 190,000 Jews have emigrated from that dissolved empire and its successor states, primarily from Russia, Ukraine, and the Baltic states. While the numbers indicate a sizable immigration, more importantly a closer analysis shows that not all Jews from the former Soviet Union, nor all Jews in Germany for that matter, are members of the official Jewish Community and therefore counted in these figures. An examination of the obvious question why all Jews are not official members reveals important idiosyncrasies about Jewish life in Germany, the relationships of German Jews to their immigrant brethren and of these "new Jews" among themselves.

Migration of Jews from Eastern Europe to Germany is not unprecedented. In the early decades of the twentieth century, before Hitler's accession to power in 1933, an uneasy peace existed between the so-called Ostjuden and their overwhelmingly secular German Jewish hosts. Eastern Jews were more religious, more Orthodox, and outwardly more clearly distinguishable. They were also generally poorer and more provincial. In Berlin many lived in the area called the "Scheunenviertel" (the barn quarter), a less than desirable part of town adjacent to the well-known Alexanderplatz, the scene of Alfred Döblin's famous novel of the same name. Coincidentally, I lived in this area when I did my research on Jews in the GDR in the early 1990s. At that time one could still see traces of Hebrew inscriptions on crumbling walls. The new "Ostjuden" who populate Germany today are also met with ambivalence, although the Community is officially committed to integrating them into German-Jewish life. Aware of how these large numbers of Jews would not only reinvigorate, but also repopulate a community that needed them, the social welfare arm of the Community helps them with housing, jobs, language courses, and navigating the complicated social system. Nevertheless, these Jews have a very different outlook on what it means to live in Germany than the Community that receives them. In common, both groups suffer from hope and frustration.

The Jews from the former Soviet Union were often the victims of blatant anti-Semitism in their homeland—graffiti or attacks on synagogues, desecration of cemeteries, and public invectives against Jews by political figures were common occurrences. However, their relationship to the Holocaust itself and German history is less familiar and sometimes less fraught than for Jews in Germany and elsewhere in Europe. While they know about the genocide and its horrors, very often their personal nemesis was Stalin who murdered millions of Soviet citizens, including Jews, and sent millions of others to gulag labor camps in Siberia. They seem more immune to German history and the Holocaust because of the country's postwar isolation from the West. Buttressed by Soviet propaganda, they identify strongly with Russia's suffering at the hands of Hitler's army as proud Russians as well as Jews. It is quite common for aging Jewish war veterans from the former Soviet Union to display their red stars proudly in the Berlin Jewish Community, as if to acknowledge their immutable link to their former homeland. Others, who may feel more at home, state, even amid the beginnings of the anti-Semitism discussions of June 2002, "They [American Jews] keep asking me why I want to live here, but Germany does not mean fascism for me and America is not so great. I have lots of German friends. Why should I hate the whole nation?"[2] Many choose to live in Germany, sometimes selecting it over Israel or the United States, because in Eastern Europe Germany is seen as a major economic powerhouse and a land of economic opportunity. Some like its proximity to Russia and its familiar European heritage and others prefer Germany because it is presumed safer and more secure than Israel. Stories of Russian Jews being blown up on Israeli buses or in cafes do not encourage migration to the Jewish state, while Germany can provide the personal and financial security Russia was lacking. Others wind up in Germany more by chance than purpose, simply because of complications or idiosyncrasies of their immigration process as they enter the West via Vienna or Rome. Attraction to Germany rather than Israel also results from "Germany's liberal policy in accepting ex-Soviet Jews and a desire by many to live in a country that is both a solid democracy and a firm member of the European Union." Yet ultimately, Germans encourage Soviet Jews: "It is connected with its responsibility for the Holocaust. After the fall of the Soviet Union in 1991,

Germany established a liberal immigration policy for Jews."[3] Although not all German officials or even all Jewish functionaries are happy with these immigrants' choices, no one could imagine barring Jews who willingly want to settle in Germany. Still, the demographic shift creates an opportunity for a new domestic German Jewish future and for positive international publicity for Germany.

Yet the story is even more complex and ambivalent when viewed from several sides—the German, the German Jewish, and the immigrants themselves—on issues of identity, belonging, and Jewishness. Before changes in the German citizenship law in 2000, which has made it easier for foreigners living permanently in Germany to become citizens after an initial waiting period, but more difficult to gain a quick haven, Germany had one of the most liberal asylum laws in Europe. But there was no "immigration law" per se. A liberal immigration policy toward Jews from the Soviet Union developed in 1990, when in the last days of the former GDR, according to sociologist Robin Ostow, "the de Maziere government, hoping to survive in some form, was looking for ways to lend itself legitimacy."[4] In the words of this first elected minister president of the soon to be defunct GDR, "For humanitarian reasons, the GDR government is for the first time offering domicile in limited numbers to foreign Jewish citizens who are threatened by persecution or discrimination."[5] Referring to these new openings for Jews, expert Jeroen Doomernik calls this moment "between the fall of the East German socialist regime in the autumn of 1989 and the incorporation into the German Federal Republic a year later . . . a time of remarkable politics."[6] The uncertainties of transition created opportunities for citizens to take initiatives, in this case toward encouraging state regimes, specifically the GDR, to admit Jews from the Soviet Union.[7] After reunification, as Ostow continues in her 1992 report in the *American Jewish Yearbook*:

> In the fall of 1990, the West Berlin Jewish community began to take over. In mid-September, with unification approaching, the West German government ordered its consulates in the USSR to stop processing immigration application forms from Jews and advised the GDR to do the same. On October 2, West Germany closed its border to Soviet Jews. From then until the end of the year, Soviet Jews continued to arrive illegally or semi-legally, i.e., with "invitations to visit relatives." . . . In the final months of 1990, Heinz Galinski, the president of the Central

Council of Jews in Germany and of the Berlin Jewish community, organized a staff of administrators and social workers for the Soviet Jews and publicly insisted that they be admitted to Germany on a non-quota basis and granted residence rights. He maintained this position against pressure from the German government, the Israeli government, and a large part of the membership of his own community.[8]

In January 1991, after German reunification, Soviet Jews were now admitted under the "Kontigentflüchtlingsgesetz" (quota refugee law) granting them rights ironically only accorded to the so-called ethnic Germans, whose relationship to contemporary Germany after many generations of living in remote areas of the Soviet Union is more imagined than real. This legislation was a turning point for Soviet Jewish immigration since it allowed masses of Jews to enter Germany as immigrants rather than on tourist visas as had previously often been the informal practice.

The special refugee status of these Jews was not the only reason that they were not always welcomed with open arms by the German Jewish community, many of whom had emigrated themselves in the 1970s during an earlier flight from the Soviet Union. Most of the newcomers—an estimated 80 percent—are halakhically not Jewish, meaning they do not have Jewish mothers or do not fulfill other requirements, such as an Orthodox conversion. Many claim they are Jewish because in the Soviet Union, Jews were considered a nationality that was marked plainly on the infamous fifth line of their passports, a category that did not distinguish how that Jewishness was determined. Even most of those who fulfilled the requirements of Jewish law had little or no formal Jewish education and knew little about Jewish traditions or rituals. In the words of Paul Spiegel, they "know they are Jews but they don't know what Judaism is." [9] Further, their arrival put a financial, psychological, and emotional burden on the existing communities who simply did not have the infrastructure to handle such a large number of newcomers. They were often regarded as merely "using" their real or supposed Jewishness to get out of the Soviet Union for a better life in the West, or using the Jewish Community to make the best of a difficult situation, for example, to get social welfare or language instruction. In the unfriendly words of one German Jew, "They exploit anything that they can get for free."[10] In this new situation, however, in the words of one former GDR Jew, "a minyan could now be arranged," which had frequently not been the case in East Germany. Still, the sheer need for jobs, housing, education, and emotional support overwhelmed the Community structure. Many of these immigrants were also older and would never learn German;[11] many were well-educated and could not find equivalent work in Germany and simply had to settle for a lower professional status. Engineers, the largest professional group, as well as teachers, doctors, and intellectuals found their personal social worth as devalued as their credentials when they could not find acceptable work. The resulting anger, frustration, and jealousy on both sides were mitigated by the satisfaction of finally having a substantial Jewish Community in Germany whose future was no longer so bleak. While the newcomers are welcomed by the Community and by the German government, who are pleased that Jews want to live in Germany, it still adds a burden to Jewish and German institutions.

Whatever the attitudes, the Jewish community in Germany and especially in Berlin has been permanently marked by the presence of this new group, its culture, and its expectations. The Russian language dominates not only in the small congregations which are not infrequently almost completely Russian, but also in the larger communities like Berlin where it is common to hear only Russian in the Joachimstalerstrasse synagogue or in the Fasanenstrasse library. In fact, it can be said, as Michael May, a high-level Community administrator, claims, that the Community in Berlin operates literally "in Russian." This means that the employees, from secretarial to financial and service administration—from those who do accounts, taxes, and wages to those who perform kitchen help—speak Russian among themselves. The Community's monthly magazine *Jüdisches Berlin* (Jewish Berlin) is published bilingually in German and Russian and postings on the bulletin boards advertising goods and services are almost all in Russian. Jewish-Russian newspapers are popular as well. Russian children predominate in the Jewish elementary schools, however, not because of religious fervor, but as was patently made clear by one member of the Community, because the length of the school day and the provision of a warm meal. As Judith Kessler, a social activist and journalist who studies the immigrants and emigrated herself from Poland to Berlin in 1972, remarks, "The Germans, the Israelis, and the Poles complain that only Russian is spoken anymore. . . . They say, 'This is not my community anymore. It is no longer that which I remember from earlier. I am getting out.'"[12]

For the future of the Community, some of these cultural strains can be overcome by increased political involvement on the part of the immigrants, for example, in the representative governing body of the Community. It is said that one cannot govern the Community anymore without either speaking Russian, as in the case of the former leader Alexander Brenner, who is Polish born and speaks Russian, or being a leader who speaks directly to the problems of the Russians. Such a case was Andreas Nachama, whose Greek-born father, Estrongo Nachama, was the esteemed cantor of the Community. Nachama was singled out at his election as a member of the first post-Shoah German-identified generation to lead the Berlin Community and made a special effort of accommodation toward the Russians.

The Jewish Community in Berlin is the largest, the most diverse, and the most contentious, if communal elections signify the attitudes of its members. In 2003, after one canceled election because of a scandal about questionable voting practices, the most recent community election in Berlin (November 2003) took place. This time it was also marred by acrimony and bitterness. Repeating the previous results, again over half of the fifty-five candidates and notably the executive council members are of Russian origin from the voting bloc optimistically named "Kadima" (Forward).[13] Albert Meyer, a German Jew, was elected president. As a Pole, Brenner who came in second was the only candidate who was not a member of this bloc. This election was markedly different from previous ones when more "German" Jews of Polish origin were prominent. Also of note is the fact that Meyer, who is not Orthodox but Liberal, admits he only goes to synagogue once a month, and even wants to hire another Liberal rabbi for the Community. The last one, Rabbi Walter Rothschild, was unceremoniously fired when he displayed condoms as well as gave radical advice to his congregants. Meyer's greatest challenges are integrating Jews from the former Soviet Union, primarily through language courses, and improving the abysmal state of the finances and administration in the Community. He came on board without even a budget in place. Since only 35 percent of the Community's members even voted in the election, most likely reflecting the frustration and cynicism in the wider community, Meyer must enlist the support of over two-thirds of those who voted otherwise or not at all.

The public meeting for the Constitutive Assembly on January 6, 2004, that followed the elections captures some of the vicissitudes of the current Berlin Jewish Community. Allow me to share with you my experience of that evening. After entering the Fasanenstrasse community center, past the guards and the security check, many of whom were Russian-speaking, I climbed the stairs to the large second floor 500-seat meeting room across from the kosher restaurant Arche Noah (Noah's Ark). Filled with what I presumed were members of the Community, but also, as I later noticed, with journalists, television cameras, and the stray visitor like myself, the atmosphere was upbeat, if not a bit unruly and chaotic. Many people stood on the sidelines chatting, others were greeting friends, and then some were taking their seats in preparation for the evening's festivities. Before the official presentation of the winning slate and the election of the Executive Council (EC) that apparently was already public knowledge, there would be the required speeches. These proved to be particularly interesting for what they showed about the past and future of the Community. The audience had some trouble settling down; the Community leaders and the twenty-one successful candidates who sat in parallel rows in the front of the hall, however, contributed to the unsettled atmosphere as many continued their private conversations and greetings. The entire environment seemed a little like an Orthodox shul (synagogue) where people move in and out and talk among themselves, seemingly unconcerned with any conventional propriety or protocol. With some help from a friend, I identified the new president of the Berlin Community: tanned, good-looking, and healthy, extremely youthful for his fifty-six years, and stylishly dressed. He obviously was going to distinguish himself from his predecessors in other ways than just his administrative abilities. Before the official activities began, Meyer walked over to the widow of the deceased and highly respected first president of the Berlin Community Heinz Galinski, as if to pay his respects to the "dowager queen," who sat in the front row. Then, the oldest member of the Community introduced the evening by first respectfully invoking the name of Galinski who, as he stated, proved Hitler wrong by forcefully leading the reborn Jewish community after the Shoah. The audience solemnly rose to honor Galinski's memory. His speech began with a reminder of current dangers "in a time when the security of every Jew is threatened."[14] He continued to the obvious issue of integrating the immigrants and finally, he moved on, hoping to heal the more corrosive topic of the divisive election process, "We are all in the same boat."[15] A series of long-winded speeches by local rabbis, one in German tinged with a Yiddish accent, followed.

The audience was, however, growing increasingly restless. Because of the comings and goings and the shuffling back and forth, it was quite difficult to hear the speakers. A woman next to me, well-dressed, heavily made up, and decked out in fine jewelry, spoke, not surprisingly, in her Russian mother tongue to another similarly coiffed matron. It seemed to me that I had discovered a new international Jewish stereotype that I resisted acknowledging even with the smile it produced on my face. Although we had not been introduced or spoken, she looked at me knowingly during the speeches—as if to say "let's get on with this, I have better things to do"—which seemed endless, verbose, and clichéd about the importance of Jewish identity and the need for a strong community in Berlin. Finally, the elections began with pro forma nominations and secret ballots that tried everyone's patience. More people got up, circulated, and chattered on. It seemed as if everyone suddenly had to go to the restroom.

Having accomplished my goal, I left before the end to read the results in the morning papers. As demonstrated that evening, this slice of a complicated community coming to terms in their new elections with misused finances, bad blood, and voter inconsistencies did not present the decorum of a world that one might, even prejudicially, have associated with sophisticated German Jewry rather than less well-heeled Ostjuden. In the new representative assembly (EC) work obviously remains to be done. With the "Poles" absent from the leadership, it remains to be seen if the alliance of German Jews and Russians can bring the Community together, even though a few months later, one of the prominent German Jewish EC members resigned.

Aside from depicting the controversies, the scene also reminds us how ethnic divisions continue to plague the Jewish community. "Poles," "Germans," and "Russians" are all national and ethnic categories that one would hope would disappear in a Jewish community that is supposed to be based on religious rather than national or ethnic affiliations. Moreover, it is a community whose very existence depends on migration, integration, and consensus among diverse groups of Jews. Yet, as I have repeatedly pointed out, religion, which defines the Jewish Community, allows little diversity; Orthodoxy dominates, some Liberal (Conservative) synagogues fill out the picture, and no official Reform offerings are available, except for the controversial World Union of Progressive Jewry (WUPJ) still fighting for recognition. While well-integrated, the "Poles" who have become "Germans," most of whom were DPs, are still not "German Jews," who have centuries-wrought identity and tradition in Germany, and of course, the Russians are another story.

The Russians' attitudes toward the Germans can indeed often be aggressive, either in words, deeds, or just attitudes. Many educated Russian Jews disdain "high" German culture and regard the classical Russian tradition on a par or even better.[16] For many, this culture replaces the religious participation from which they are excluded or which they themselves reject. Nevertheless, it is reported that "the Community Center in Berlin now organizes chess tournaments and ballet evenings instead of rounds of Skat, Germany's favorite card game."[17] One observer of the Düsseldorf community, whose comments are applicable to Berlin as well, humorously captures the Russians' cultural appetite by entitling her report "Vitamin 'K' für Kultur."[18] And while I am on culinary and more profane matters, the popular supermarket Real in East Berlin now sells kosher solanka, a favorite soup from the Soviet Union (Ukrainian/Russian) that was a popular item on the menus of their most western satellite, the GDR. But to return to more sacred themes, at least to German Jews, it appears that the powerful German *Bildungstradition* (tradition of [moral] education), which also shaped German Jewish identity up to the Nazi period, no longer has the universal status it once had. This was neither the case for the Russians' self-image nor for their regard of prominent German Jewish figures in the Community. As was flatly claimed by one observer, "You can't win elections today in the Community by using flowery German and quoting from Goethe and Schiller."[19]

Although Albert Meyer, a lawyer who studied business and administration, is strongly identified with this German-Jewish tradition, he is using a pragmatic, no-nonsense plan for solving the financial and administrative problems in the Community as well as pursuing Russian integration that will attract the new majority. However, as if to remind the public of Meyer's origins, German-Jewish journalist/author Rafael Seligmann calls Meyer in an article about his election: "*Jude, Preusse, deutscher Patriot*" (Jew, Prussian, German patriot).[20] For Seligmann, who uses his own writing to prompt the Jewish Community to more action, Meyer's "ethnic" as well as professional background fosters his unquestionable sympathies for the Russian Jews who are, in Meyer's own words, "Menschen in Not" (people in need).[21] Meyer's background and the entire complex of relations also illustrate the increasing "ethnicization" of Jews in Germany.

Indeed, the immigrants are in need of all kinds of support. Although most of the Russian immigrants had little Jewish education or knowledge of tradition and rituals, some have tried to educate themselves and to create links to the Community. This attempt at attachment has been done primarily through participation in what was called "life cycle events."[22] Bar mitzvahs, bat mitzvahs, circumcision (bris), weddings, and most of all Jewish burials have become significant links to the Community and to their sense of Jewish identity. These events, such as burials, as many as 150 a year, bring the entire family together; they can occasion even the building of tombs at great expense, as was reported to me, in odd shapes in the manner of an extravagant marble computer for a deceased technology entrepreneur. In a recent survey of the Jewish Community (2002) conducted by Judith Kessler, a Jewish burial was rated most important for Russian immigrants. To cite the study, "It is important for almost 80 percent of all Jews to be buried in a Jewish cemetery—above all this is the case for the immigrants even when among them one-third are atheists and the others haven't described themselves as anything. The relationship [to their Judaism] remains even without religious connections."[23] This "relationship" to a tradition that is often asserted, claimed, and felt rather than substantiated through the blood of maternal lineage or Jewish knowledge can bring these immigrants into the Community.

Still, the resentment goes both ways and the German Jews remain skeptical of the Russians' legitimacy as Jews according to halakhic principles. It is difficult to say if these attitudes are really only religious or pretense for other social or cultural problems with Eastern European Jews. It may be a mixture of Western snobbery (since it seems that Jews from the former East Germany have a better relationship to the Russians) or frustration with the deceit and corruption in the Community. Nevertheless, I know of one story of an esteemed young Jew who was dismissed from a religious Jewish institution in Berlin when it was discovered that his mother's conversion was not properly Orthodox. Whatever the reasons that halakhic regulation remains so powerful in a community that some might say can ill afford to be so conservative, many in the Community see the Russian Jews as exploiting them for their own benefit without giving much back. They even see the Russians as destroying the very foundations of the Community with different traditions or nonexistent practices. Many feel that they are siphoning off precious financial resources and even take away burial sites and seats in the synagogue. While these traditional milestones are important symbolic events that bind these immigrants to their families, to the local Jewish Community, and to established Jewish traditions, they are obviously also being interpreted more instrumentally. Many immigrants are criticized for not reading Hebrew nor having any interest in a Jewish education. They are accused of playing a game that is expected of them to take advantage of the Community. As I will show later, it is a "game" that one scholar accuses the Community of playing as well.

But first, let us take a close up of one Russian Jewish immigrant who is angry and cynical about her experience in the Community. She has even compiled a book of interviews with other Russian Jewish immigrants who confirm her experiences. LD is a woman in her fifties, now a teacher, whose journey to Berlin took many twists and turns, beginning with her application for emigration from the Soviet Union in 1978 to her final arrival in Berlin in 1987. She and her husband, who is not Jewish, live with their son in a comfortable yet modestly furnished apartment in a pleasant middle-class section of Berlin. Approaching the apartment building and entering her apartment one might expect someone who is content with all the amenities she needs. She is an attractive middle-aged woman and very proud, clearly less well-off and showy than her Russian compatriot I saw at the Community meeting. She speaks forcefully, yet calmly about topics that have obviously caused her some anguish.

The fact that she and her husband originally wanted to go to Canada may explain some of her ambivalence about Germany. Apparently, a friend of her husband convinced them to come. She told me bluntly that Israel was out of the question because her husband was a "Russian"; in other words, he was not Jewish. This ethnic category, like the traditionally exclusive terms dividing "Germans" and "Jews," distinguishes her husband's situation, which has little to do with religion (since being Russian or German does not preclude being Jewish), but rather with accepted categories of belonging. They had suffered considerably in the Soviet Union since they filed for exit and were anxious to get out as soon as possible to wherever they could find refuge. They did not come as *Kontingenten-flüchtlinge* (quota refugees). Their life was very difficult after their arrival since as is typical, their diplomas were not recognized and she and her husband had to go back to school. Immigration meant a reduction in self-esteem as well as income. In the beginning, LD notes, she had contact with the Jewish Community, but has since dropped out. She says bluntly, "The Jews in the Community think they are better [than we are]."[24]

Her problem, as it is for many in her cohort, is not about "being Jewish," but rather about being a member of the Jewish Community overloaded with bureaucracy, rules, and financial obligations that she was

expected to fulfill. In her own sharp terms, LD found the community simply chaotic, "a circus."[25] Although she was the breadwinner for her family
for a long time, she was still expected to pay her taxes to the Community.
They would not take her poor economic situation into consideration. She
feels herself to be Jewish, although she is not religious, her son who did not
have a bar mitzvah even less, and her husband who is not Jewish remains
completely excluded. She reminded me again that to be Jewish was not
dependent on being a member of the official Community, but how one
felt inside. However, she admitted that she felt equally marginalized in
Russia and says that in the Soviet Union, "We were something different."[26]
Although she does not feel "Russian," she admits that all of her friends are
Russian Jews and that she has little to do with German Jews who have a
different position in society and are separated from her by "money" and
"class."[27] However, like the majority of immigrant Jews, she remains a convinced supporter of Israel at any cost and has contacts with non-Jewish
Russians. LD's predicament is typical of many Jews from Russia: she
stands in between, never fully accepted in either country, neither by the
non-Jewish Russians nor by the German Jews.

Many other immigrants, even those who came directly to Germany as
Kontigentenflüchtlinge, have had a difficult time, but for reasons unexpected. An outstanding and controversial ethnographic study of the Russian Jewish immigration by the German anthropologist Franziska Becker,
*Ankommen in Deutschland: Einwanderungspolitik als biographische Er-
fahrung im Migrationsprozess russischer Juden* (Arrival in Germany: Immigration Politics as Biographical Experience in the Migration of Russian
Jews), presents the sharpest analysis and the most stinging critique of their
situation.[28] Using discourse analysis of interviews, case studies, and surveys
of media coverage collected during her field work at refugee sites, she
shows how the immigrants were often questioned about their "Jewish authenticity" even if they had the proper papers. She illustrates that the situation of these people in the Soviet Union was neither black nor white; they
were always confronted neither with anti-Semitism nor with positive acceptance. Both experiences existed simultaneously in a more complex
everyday life than the authorities in Germany expected. Consequently,
she uncovers how many of them assumed Jewish identities as "victims"
that the Community expected. She reveals shocking details from her case
studies of immigrants being questioned about racial categories and
whether "they looked Jewish" or asked whether they were lying because

their Jewish identity was based on ethnic rather than religious affiliations. In other words, their identity, according to Becker, was politicized: they had to take on the "victim" role expected of them, particularly toward the Holocaust, even if their Soviet experience was different, albeit also tragically shaped by Stalin's brutal anti-Semitic policies. For many, it became a constant necessity to prove that they were victims in order to be recognized as Jewish, by Jews as well as other Germans. Unlike in Israel or the United States, these Jewish immigrants had to assume a German-Jewish narrative of Holocaust victimhood and Soviet anti-Semitism that didn't necessarily belong to them in order to be accepted as Jews and be integrated into their new lives.[29]

Such religious and social conflicts that may seem strange to Americans represent some of the major problems and contradictions these Jews have to confront. In the Soviet Union, under succeeding regimes in the twentieth century until Gorbachev loosened state authority in the now infamous perestroika and glasnost, Jews were a tolerated and sometimes less than tolerated minority. On the one hand, they often bore the brunt of anti-Semitism, sanctioned even by political parties such as the well-known Pamyat. On the other hand, many Jews did not practice their religion nor pass it on to following generations, either by choice or by circumstance. Thus, many of the Jews who immigrated to Germany were Jews only by dint of the famous "fifth point" on their internal passports that identified them "ethnically" as Jews. It was a mark that some have compared to the Nazis' "J" stamp in Jewish passports. While some had tried literally to erase their "Jewishness" from their passport to improve their domestic situation, when the opportunity came to go to Germany as Jews, they did everything they could to reverse this situation by trying literally to have their Jewishness reinscribed in their passports. However, merely acknowledging or even creating a Jewishness that wasn't there was enough to gain them special status for emigration to Germany, but not enough to allow them to become members of the Jewish Community. In short, they were Jews in name only.

The issue of authenticity—a central issue in the Jewish world—became a major sticking point not only within the German-Jewish community, but also between the Community and the German Foreign Ministry responsible for granting immigration permits. Standards vary as to who is defined as a Jew; stricter for the Community than for the ministry since the former only recognizes the halakhically required maternal lineage and the latter recognizes both paternal and maternal heredity. In short, the Community recognizes only religion while the German government recognizes, in addition, nationality or ethnicity. However, German government authorities were certainly not about to decide who was, or was not, a Jew! Nevertheless, Jews continued to come—in fact, more Jews settled in Germany than Israel in 2002—19,000 compared to 18,000 (this includes non-Jewish family members). Rather than simply bemoaning this troublesome and even embarrassing situation, in the summer of 2003, for the first time a task force from the Jewish Agency in Israel came to Germany to assess the situation. They hoped to encourage young German Jews to look again toward Israel as their home. By the end of 2004, the Federal states sought to limit the immigration of former Soviet Jews to those who could work and did not need social welfare assistance. Unusually pessimistic about Jewish life in Germany, Paul Spiegel criticized this "selection" that puts Jews into categories and elicits bad memories, some would even say of Auschwitz.[30]

The continued attraction of Jews to Germany raises many questions for the Jewish authorities in Germany and Israel, not only about demography but also about identity. However, the migration also sharpens tensions toward alternative Jewish affiliations, both religious and cultural, which either question or fall outside the rigid system of the Einheitsgemeinde (Unified Community) that controls the religious life of Jews in Germany and maintains Orthodoxy and halakhic standards. The growth in Germany of the World Union of Progressive Judaism (WUPJ) is one such example. Since many of the Jews who come from the Soviet Union do not meet halakhic criteria or have non-Jewish partners who consequently produce offspring who are not "Jewish," they cannot become official members of the Community. They cannot participate in services nor send their children to religious school. Nevertheless, many participate in the cultural activities that the Community offers and benefit from that non-religious association. In Berlin, where the egalitarian service (men and women pray together) is part of the official Community and not part of the WUPJ, these Jews can benefit from both affiliations. However, in the rest of Germany, the two organizations—the Central Council of Jews in Germany and the WUPJ—vie, so to speak, for the souls of these immigrant Jews, as well as for money from the German government. For example, in 2003, after many years of negotiations, the Jewish Community signed an official "state treaty" with the German government, as the latter had with the Catholic and Protestant churches, which tripled its annual budget to nearly 3 million euros. Paul Spiegel called it a "historical event," and it proves that the German government is not only aware of the new Jewish community but also supports it and welcomes it.[31] The WUPJ wanted some of these resources, as well as other monies destined for NGOs from the "Remembrance and Future Fund of the Foundation 'Remembrance, Responsibility and the Future.'" In 2004, the WUPJ filed a lawsuit against the Community, although it was later retracted.

Founded in Germany in 1997, the Union has fifteen congregations in Germany (plus one in Vienna) from large cities like Munich to small towns like Hamlin. Its membership ranges from as few as twenty to more than one hundred, totaling three thousand, and may indeed offer an opportunity to "be Jewish" to these Russian Jews who halakhically do not qualify. Ironically today, the tradition of Reform Jewry that started in Germany in the early nineteenth century and became so identified with German Jewry had more success in the postwar era in the United States than in Germany. Two hundred years later, Reform Judaism is trying to reestablish itself in the country of its founding. With only lay leaders, no trained rabbis, cantors, or Jewish educators, the WUPJ has a rabbinical school at the University of Potsdam named for Abraham Geiger, an influential nineteenth-century Reform theologian, and founded a Jewish publishing house in 1999 in Berlin.

As part of the World Union of Progressive Judaism in Germany, Austria, and Switzerland, the case of this organization speaks, in fact, to conflicts within the German Jewish Community with regard to the distribution of financial resources, personalities, and of course, religious practice when it comes to the Russian immigrants who represent the future of the Community. The WUPJ states quite openly in its material that it has "not been enthusiastically welcomed by the traditional-oriented [sic] German Jewish organizations which have controlled the distribution of the government-collected religious tax since the end of World War II."[32] This situation represents the issue of who speaks for the Jews in Germany. It has been created precisely by the opportunity to win over converts to progressive Judaism from the Orthodox establishment in postwar Germany. The German government tries to remain neutral by leaving these "internal" battles to the Community itself. However, as if to signal its honoring of the long-standing German Reform Jewish tradition, which the WUPJ follows, in July 2003, the minister of the interior attended the seventy-fifth anniversary of the founding of the WUPJ in Berlin.

The battles between the WUPJ and the Community continue. One newspaper report claimed that the WUPJ wants to connect to their rich past and compete with the official representation of the Central Council of Jews in Germany. It reports that the Council under Paul Spiegel "avoids direct contact with the 'Union.' Letters of the (WUPJ) liberal Jews remain still unanswered."[33] However, in conversations with Spiegel in April 2004, he told me that he has been open to contact with the WUPJ and relations are improving.[34] Some Jewish leaders find their tactics too aggressive in that they enlist American Reform Jewish congregations to petition against the official Community. In August 2004 an apparent agreement was reached.

The battle among various factions as to how the German Jewish Community will be constituted and defined will have to address the many young Russian Jews who have come to Germany or are born there. The meeting in January 2003 of the Winter University of the Union of Jewish Students in Germany coalesced some of these central conflicts around identity and belonging that also plague the fifteen thousand Jews in Germany between the ages of eighteen and twenty-five. Most of them, as in the larger community, come from the former Soviet Union. Thus, this meeting on the topic What is Judaism? went to the heart of the identity issue even more directly in their eyes than those of the Jewish community organizations. As Uriel Kashi, the current president of the organization, has said, "Our goal is to listen and discuss in a Jewish atmosphere, to learn about our Jewish identity."[35] For Julian Voloj, the former president of the German student group and now leader of the 200,000-strong European Union of Jewish Students, the work they do on the Europe-wide level for those Jews from west to east is even more important than the grand plans of the expanding European Union (EU). This group also has a regularly sponsored the pan-European Summer University where five hundred young Jews gather to discuss issues that concern them as Jews and as Europeans. Voloj sees his organization as the future of a new European Jewish identity, even though he admits that the fact that he and Michel Friedman, the former director of the European Jewish Congress, are "German" has traditionally been regarded with some skepticism by other European Jews.

Consequently, Jews in Germany who lead important European organizations must also fight the same kind of prejudices that American Jews still feel for Germany. As part of a European organization of Jews and especially of Jewish young people, Jews in Germany can gain status and support for their fast-growing community that has brought Eastern and Western Jewry together again in an unexpected way.

Even more recently, a sociologist colleague and I met with two small groups of university-age Jews (August 2003 and December 2003); most were from the former Soviet Union and belonged to the Jewish Student Organization, which is decidedly more conservative in its communal nature. Two groups of about fifteen attended these informal sessions in the modest clubhouse located in the basement behind the Joachimstaler-strasse synagogue, next to the bagel shop and bookstore I introduced in chapter 1. In both cases the participants formed a mixed group as to gender, nationality, and political orientation. Given that the choice to belong to this group already implies commitment to some form of Jewish identity, it cannot be said that these students are typical of all young college-age Jews in Germany, especially those of Russian origin. Some wanted to emigrate from Germany to Israel or to the United States; many were increasingly fearful of the rise of anti-Semitism; all of them supported Israel. At the first meeting, their reactions focused on their feelings about living in Germany, their definitions of Jewishness, and their personal and professional futures. Two students from the WUPJ-sponsored Geiger Rabbinical School were the only ones who were adamant about staying in Germany in order to contribute to a future Jewish life. The hopeful and upbeat ideology of the WUPJ certainly seems to have rubbed off on them.

The students in the second session were generally more skeptical about their future in Germany as anti-Semitic incidents had increased since the summer when the Iraq war had ended. They were more outspoken about leaving Germany, although one young actor who had gone to the United States, Canada, and Israel admitted that he returned after his many travels because "he missed Germany and he learned to appreciate it in many ways."[36] They also had to admit, including the actor, that the unstable economic situation in Germany influenced them as much as political factors. Interestingly, these young "German Jews" leave Germany for North America because of financial insecurity and Russian Jews come to Germany to find a better economic life. It was a young woman from France, however, who provided a comparative and alternative perspective when she defiantly proclaimed, "I would rather live in Germany than in France."[37] She proved, as many other observers have noted, that attacks on synagogues, schools, and individuals in France raise more serious questions about an anti-Semitism that is clearly more dangerous there than in

Germany. Obviously, Germany's special past creates associations and fears that are less grounded in reality than in the continuing resonance of history. Contrary opinions also emerged from other young people from the former Soviet Union I interviewed who live and work in Germany with plans to stay. The diversity of opinions found among young people from the 1990s to 2004 reminds us that Jews, even in Germany, do not speak with a unified voice and that immediate political events can shift attitudes precipitously.

No matter what course their individual lives take, the future of a German and European Jewry will certainly depend on the enthusiasm, energy, and literally the staying power of these young people. Clearly, it will also depend on the political, social, and economic environment in which they find themselves in as to whether they will make Germany their permanent home. The shifts in attitudes since 1989 demonstrated in this study remind us that Jews in Germany, especially the majority Russian Jews, no matter how connected they are to the Community, define themselves as "Jews" and this affiliation affects their feelings about the country. Attention to being Jewish, no matter what their religiosity, affiliation, or membership, still makes a decisive difference to them.

Whether a new German Jewish space will evolve seems at this point dependent on how the former Russian Jews in Germany choose to become Jewish. They may choose the more religious path, as part of the Community, or the more liberal as part of a more progressive Jewish religious movement that could more easily recognize them even if only their fathers are Jewish, or as only ethnic or cultural Jews. It will also be important that the Community consider expanding its options for recognizing Jewish identity in its many forms, recognizing that it may not be possible to define the official Jewish Community exclusively in halakhic religious terms. Albert Meyer seemed at least to be hinting at greater inclusion in many of his remarks after the election. The choice of spouses, the birth and raising of children, and the potential "intermarriage" of Jews from different European countries who create a new European Jewry bred of mixed national Jewish parentage will certainly be criteria for establishing Jewish lives.

It continues to be of utmost importance, at least, to welcome the interest and enthusiasm for "things Jewish" in Europe even if they are created and promoted by sympathetic non-Jews. These "discursive communities," both real and virtual, in which Jewish topics are discussed and represented publicly, such as in cultural festivals, exhibitions, or museums, contribute to a significant Jewish presence in Europe. This presence is not vanishing, nor is it just virtual; it is a small yet importantly symbolic group of communities who have a voice in their individual countries that supersedes the power of their numbers. There is no question that the freer movement of these peoples and their ideas around Europe, as well as their connection to other world Jewish communities, will enhance the creation of Jewish spaces. The continued exposure and education of young people in succeeding generations to the wide spectrum of "Jewishness" will also contribute to supporting a new European Jewish identity.

Berlin and Germany are the most interesting stage for identity-building since they intertwine different kinds of Jews from East and West and different ways of being Jewish, from Reform to Orthodoxy. In the future, Jewish life, if it is to continue, will have to negotiate this rocky terrain that for most is paved more with cautious optimism than gold. Perhaps in the face of negative demographic figures and narrow definitions of Jewishness, one has to extend the position of Boris Feldman, editor of the Russian-language weekly *Russkii Berlin*, who emigrated from Latvia in 1990. He states, "The revival of Jewish life in Berlin is the revival of Russian-speaking Jews. . . . I think that today we shouldn't compare with the past. I don't look back, I look ahead . . . I think that Jewish life in Germany is still ahead of us."[38] What this future means for Russian Jews depends on how they shape a new German-Jewish community in this very unique context.

4

Representing Jews in Germany Today

Representing Jews or Germans is not only about "real Jews" or "real Germans," but also about how these and other groups conceive of and understand each other as depicted in various forms, such as television, film, literature, art, advertising and of course, the Internet. Even before the notion of the "virtual" became commonplace, knowing what is "real" and what is not was difficult. We live in a world inundated with images and words that project so many conflicting representations. This confusion is especially acute when representation concerns people who are different, unfamiliar, and even strange. Filtered through our imagination, representations compete with the urge to know objectively who people really are. It is easier to present what we may not know or understand in stereotypes and clichés, for example, seeing all Jews as victims and all Germans as Nazi perpetrators. The Holocaust's effect on the relationship of Jews and Germans has made these two groups particularly susceptible to such limited representations. When tolerance and integration into a democratic civil society are at stake, representations—which are about all most Germans have in a country with so few Jews—do matter. In short, "representations" are, as anthropologist Paul Rabinow once claimed, "social facts."[1]

For a study that is decidedly about Jewish life rather than Jewish death in Germany, conventional and flat representations proliferate, even overly positive ones. Who can forget the American love affair with the musical and film *Fiddler on the Roof* (known in Germany as the popular musical *Anatevka*), a romanticized and sanitized version of Eastern European shtetl Jewish life? The optimistic musical refrain "To life, to life, l'chaim" that echoes my own concern with Jewish life in this book, does not, however, really capture the harsh circumstances of Jewish lives under the

Russian czar that drove many Jews to leave for more secure havens. But then again, all the singing and dancing, the pathos and the tears made us American Jews feel good, since so many of our ancestors escaped this world and made it to a richer and safer America. While neither real nor objective, this vision of happy shtetl life, even with its poverty and prejudice, still colors the understanding of many Jews and non-Jews about life in these Eastern European villages. And while the musical and film are not about the Holocaust, one could not help but think that those Jews who stayed and survived the relentless pogroms were to perish some decades later under far worse circumstances. I remember seeing the musical on Broadway in the 1960s and thinking how lucky my family was to have left Eastern Europe, and how unlucky were those who stayed. As an American Jew, in fact, an Ostjude myself, I grew up seeing us as victims, a representation that was gruesomely depicted in the many documentaries on the genocide. These contrasted with the popular American World War II movies that portrayed Germans as one-dimensional evil Nazis, cardboard figures screaming or grunting in an ugly language my parents thought suited their brutality. The advent of the television comedy series "Hogan's Heroes" (shown in Germany years later) did little to mitigate the image of Germans running a prisoner-of-war camp for Americans as ludicrous, stupid buffoons. It wasn't until the 1980s that the German war film *Das Boot*, preserving its German title, showed American audiences German sailors not as brutal Nazis, but as humane victims with complicated psychologies and sensitive emotions.

Representations are, of course, always part reality or fact, part myth or fiction, and largely interpretive. We have seen how difficult it is to define who is a Jew. Yet, while legal definitions must be made for pragmatic reasons in civil societies, identities are built on experience. Having a Jewish father and a gentile mother, I may feel I am a Jew, but in Germany I am not Jewish enough to join the Jewish Community there. In the United States, I am Jewish, not only according to institutional Reform Judaism, but also as to how I see myself, feel, and am regarded as a Jew. Indeed, German citizenship is now granted more easily, but as a Turkish German, African German, or Jewish German, I may never feel that I am German, even with the proper passport, because belonging is more than an official piece of paper. Under conditions in which blacks or whites turn into shades of gray, it might be more useful to look at Jewish life experience through the lenses of various interpretations than trying to establish who or what is a real Jew. In fact, it might be more interesting if we juxtaposed the depictions or representations of Jews to see what they mean when compared with one another and with what we know, or at least suspect, to be objective historical truth. A search for a definitive answer to what defines Jewish identity seems, at least in this case, to be rather futile.

Linked to the question of identity then, representation has everything to do in a double sense with who we are as Jews. First, the invisible hyphen in "re-presentation" masks the mediating person who talks about, depicts, or displays Jews again and again in all kinds of settings and as a people always in the Diaspora, removed from the homeland Israel. When anthropologist Virginia Dominguez calls Diaspora Jews "twice strangers," she could, in fact, be addressing the unique situation of Jews in Germany.[2] They provide an even sharper focus on the distance between the real and its representation since they are not only Diaspora Jews, but also Jews who live in "the land of the murderers." Living in Germany, they are presumed to be alienated both from "the homeland" that links all Jews halakhically through their Jewish mothers and from their fellow Jews around the world who often see them lost in the German "fatherland" that had sought to destroy all of European Jewry. In fact, the representation of Jews in Germany offers a special window on how depiction of a group in public life and the media can be burdened with history and politics. In the case of the Jews in Germany especially careful attention is required to sort out what is "real" and what is not. As one critic rightly points out:

> The German public's perception of Jews is problematic . . . . : Besides an aggressive and latent anti-Semitism, less malicious clichés and even well-meaning efforts to relate to Jewish topics often fail to grasp the reality of Jewish life. Jews are predominantly associated with the Shoah, and thus with National Socialism. They appear in research projects, documentary films, political debates, and historical museums. If Judaism is portrayed in contemporary culture at all, it is exoticized through visual topoi such as synagogues and kippot, Torah scrolls and payees [side locks] and transformed into a mysterious and obscure religion. Germans' imaginations of their Jewish fellow-citizens have little in common with the reality of Jewish life in Germany today.[3]

I would not claim here to present the reality of Jewish life in Germany today. All I can offer are some educated reflections on a particular angle of a complicated story that requires multiple points of view and multiple kinds of representations that try to come to terms with reality. To illustrate the importance of representing Jewish life in Germany, I use three different forms of representation: imaginative prose (novels), journalistic essays, and public exhibitions. An analysis of literature, journalism, and museum exhibitions has the potential of highlighting the ambiguity and ambivalence inherent in all of these representations that reflect the status of Jews in Germany today. I, therefore, discuss Jewish authors writing in German and analyze characters and problems presented in their novels; I interrogate Jewish publicists who speak out on contentious issues within an enlarging Jewish public sphere; I look at the story that is being told about Jewish life in Germany in the first permanent exhibition of this kind in a new Jewish museum. What will become clear, I hope, is the way Jewish and non-Jewish German lives intertwine in all of these areas and are constantly changing based on the historical contexts and individual perspectives of those telling these stories. Identity itself is discontinuous and dynamic, always in flux, and ready to be redefined at any moment. Understanding German Jewish life, in fact, becomes exemplary for identity politics in general, especially after 1989.

It is worth noting that at the same time as Jewish identity in Germany was being questioned, similar issues emerged in the United States in the early 1990s according to curator Norman Kleeblatt of the Jewish Museum in New York. In the catalogue to the exhibition *Too Jewish? Challenging Traditional Identities*, he notes: "A number of Jewish artists . . . were using strident, provocative Jewish subject matter to assert a personal ethnicity and culture . . . who have rediscovered their identities by circuitous routes . . . to examine aspects of their subjectivity through personal struggles in certain areas . . . only to realize that their identities were more intricate, and that religious and cultural issues still remained unresolved for them."[4] Here is another proof that defining Jewish identity, be it in New York or Berlin, remains problematic. While Jewish life in New York or in the United States is more familiar to the broader non-Jewish public than it is in Germany, Jewish life in Berlin and in Germany is also becoming better known. The sociologist of Jewish life in Germany, Y. Michal Bodemann, calls this situation in Germany the increasing "Judaizing milieu" spurred by the philosemitism of the churches and student movements that seek out Jewish themes, Jewish topics, and Jewish interlocutors.[5] This expansion is also taking place, as mentioned above, due to the proliferation of things Jewish in public life, the media, and in the arts, as well as its negative counterpart in anti-Semitism.

Before I begin, however, to take on the three versions of representation—literature, journalism, and museums—a brief word must be addressed to one of the most popular, and in part, the most problematic form of Jewish representation in Germany today. The explosion of Klezmer music, not restricted to Germany, its most preferred site, but a Europe-wide phenomenon, has exposed, albeit not always faithfully or accurately, non-Jewish and Jewish Germans to a particular strand of Jewish life that had been wiped out by the Nazis. This is the Russian/Eastern European heritage based in Yiddish language and culture, but definitively not the indigenous German-Jewish tradition. In fact, as a young German Jew pointed out to me, "most Jews, especially the young, really do not care for Klezmer." The irony of the popularity it has gained in Germany does not elude the performers, public, or critics, especially since this musical genre displays as much American as broadly European influences, rather than German. Most popular in the mid-1980s and "explod[ing] a few years later after the Fall of the Berlin Wall,"[6] in the words of Ruth Ellen Gruber, the "Klezmer craze"[7] offered, especially in Berlin, "Germany's Klezmer capital,"[8] a chance not only to enjoy an unfamiliar brand of lively music that brought feelings of joy, hope, and affirmation. It also dealt profoundly with guilt, responsibility, and loss. For the minority Jews and majority non-Jews who performed as well as listened, the music also awakened specific ambivalences, always accompanied by an awareness of the feelings evoked by the clash between the past tragedy and present renewal. While the music's origins were in the East and never indigenous or even popular in secular Jewish pre-war Germany, for the new Russian immigrants in particular, some of whom do perform, it is a chance to connect personally to their individual pasts and illustrate the cultural contribution of the Ostjuden. It is not without irony that their musical tradition is now experiencing its popular moment in Germany, more successfully through German or American musicians seeking to revive a lost art form, than through Eastern Jews. This "virtual" state of Jewishness, in Gruber's terms, may also have a positive effect on a German public that still has little contact with Jews in their daily life:

> For a German public yearning to come to terms with the past but unable or afraid to interact with living Jews in their own cities, the new groups proffered a new image of Jews and Jewish music. It was a vision,

even if an onstage vision, of vigorous Jewish contemporary life, not a picture of Jews as antique shtetl dwellers or as prison-stripped victims in a history book or on grainy black-and-white-film. Nor did it fit the other common philosemitic stereotypes: noble souls to be put on a pedestal, or baleful reproachful witnesses constantly reminding German audiences of the sins of their fathers. Living Jewish musicians onstage created the illusion of real interaction with Jews.[9]

And an illusion it is, since most Germans never meet Jews. Yet, Gruber seems largely critical of the "virtual" Jewish experience, such as the one she describes here. In this regard she is like many Jews in Germany who cynically call the "Inszenierung" (staging) of Jewish life near the Oranienburgerstrasse synagogue "Jewish Disneyland" or "Jewrassic Park."[10] Yet, it remains to be seen how these kinds of representations of Jewish life primarily by non-Jews will affect actual German-Jewish relations, especially for the Russian immigrants and their transformation into a new German Jewry. To my mind, the writings of the Russian-Jewish author Wladimir Kaminer, whom I discuss below, or Klezmer music will have a profound effect on educating non-Jews, and even Jews, to the life experience of Jews whom they may or may not know. It will present alternatives to dealing with the weighty past of the Shoah, which is not as profound for the Russians, and the evolving present, which is very much about their present contributions to Jewish identity.

At stake in this entire chapter on representation is the question of "authenticity," what defines "Jewish," and whether "being Jewish" legitimizes the meaning of these Jewish representations and the judgments they inspire. Is Klezmer played by a Jew better than if performed by a Christian? How many Jews does it take to make an "authentic" Klezmer band? How many mothers must be Jewish? I do not mean this last question as a glib joke, but rather as an essential issue for Jewish identity, especially Russian Jewish identity in Germany today. While Gruber is right about Klezmer, both in a positive and negative sense, the entire question of "virtuality," as she frames it, still posits some notion of "real" that is becoming increasingly questionable and more difficult to support. Jewish identity, a prescient paradigm for all questions of self, plays out forcefully in Germany today.

As Klezmer gained popularity in the 1980s and 1990s, Jewish life was being documented and interpreted in literature primarily by the so-called second generation of German Jews. These writers confronted head-on the question of identity. Names such as Maxim Biller (b. 1960 in Prague; moved 1970 to Germany), Irene Dische (b. 1952 in New York; 1980 Berlin), Esther Dischereit (b. 1952 Heppenheim, Germany), Barbara Honigmann (b. 1949 East Berlin; 1984 France), Rafael Seligmann (b. 1948 Tel-Aviv; 1957 Germany), and in Austria, Ruth Beckermann (b. 1952 Vienna), Doron Rabinovici (b. 1961 Tel-Aviv; 1964 Austria), Robert Menasse (b. 1954 Vienna), and Robert Schindel (b. 1944 Vienna) have gained some notoriety in Germany, although their writings never reach best-seller lists nor do they find their way to the bookshelves of the most literary non-Jewish Germans. Marked by the special term "second generation," these writers' biographies—birthdates, birthplaces, and their immigration—reveal their stories as children of the Holocaust, offspring of the survivors of occupation, exile, or even the camps. It also shows them as Diaspora Jews, who have gone from one country to another, some from Israel to Germany, and who understand how such movement affects their search for a secure home. Aside from having changed spaces, they are also acutely aware of temporal movement: the relationship of the past to the present and how this historical perspective frames the specificity of individual experience and even connects them to a time before they were born. As writers operating in an imaginative medium, they also confront the problem of finding the appropriate vehicle to express and represent their difficult experiences. The forms they employ—novels, short stories, poetry, film, and radio-plays—offer a great variety in language, rhythm, character, setting, voice, tone, and perspective. Most of them do not write about the Holocaust directly. All of them were born after the war. However, the past resonates explicitly or implicitly in their writings as children of parents who experienced the genocidal cataclysm firsthand. These effects are apparent in their personal and professional lives, in their familial and romantic relationships, and are a dominating factor in their attitudes toward the Jewish and gentile worlds in which they live, be it Berlin in the case of Seligmann, Strasbourg, France, in the case of Honigmann, or Vienna in the case of Schindel.

The variety of locales associated with contemporary German-Jewish writing reminds us how a definition of what is German Jewish, in this case German-Jewish literature, draws on the multiple ways these categories of identity and place are defined. Must the writer be Jewish, if so, how Jewish? Must the writer be born or live in Germany? Must the book have a

Jewish topic? Are some topics more Jewish than others? For example, one of these popular second-generation writers, Irene Dische, who was born in the United States of Jewish refugee parents, came to Berlin to write her first collection of stories, *Fromme Lügen* (1989) that were actually translated from English (*Pious Secrets [Lies]*, 1979) into German. Assumed to be a German Jew because of the subject of her work and its publication in German, Dische addresses the ways Germans and Jews come to terms with the past through the various stories they tell, be they completely truthful or not.[11] The irony in the title acknowledges not only the importance of writing and representation as a way of creating meaning in life, but also that each story and each writer's perspective holds its own truth.

Like so many so-called minority writers in Germany, among them Turks, Spaniards, Italians, and Japanese who write in German, Jewish writers in Germany today often make a mark because a curious or sympathetic public sees them as revealing the unfamiliar lives of "foreigners" living among the Germans. From the time they started writing in the 1970s, and especially through the 1980s and early 1990s, these writers' works became a separate genre coined "Ausländerliteratur" (foreigner literature), taken from the negative term in German for foreigner (Ausländer). In American universities, where these writings were studied earlier than in Germany, the term "minority literature" has also been used. Few of these writers were pleased with either the pejorative term "Ausländer" or this special "minority" status since it undervalued their artistic qualifications or the aesthetic qualities of their work. Furthermore, as with German-Jewish writing, the category itself presumed a definition of "foreigner" that could only be rationalized against a notion of the German that was based on racial or ethnic purity. Rather than having their writing read naively as mere social documents about foreigners living in Germany, these writers wanted their works seen as complex interventions into hybrid worlds where simple answers do not suffice to explain the ambiguity and ambivalence they often feel as Jews or other non-Germans in Germany. In other words, they wanted to be accepted as German writers, rather than as Turks or Jews who are writing in German. A few of the Jewish writers, like Rafael Seligmann, are also publicists and are more familiar to the public through their newspaper columns and essays than their fiction. Nevertheless, those who do read their works published by major German houses, even in special Jewish series, and available in all bookstores, access the emotional and subjective experiences of what it is like to be living as a Jew in Germany after the Holocaust. Interested readers who want more on Jewish literature or Jewish topics in general can visit the Jewish bookstores in Berlin and Munich owned by Rachel Salamander, a prominent bookseller who was honored by the city of Munich, or the Judaica section of many smaller specialty stores. Interestingly, Salamander's two stores are named *Literaturhandlung* (literature shops) without any formal marking that shows their exclusive attention to Jewish material. However, the one in Berlin, which I introduced at the outset, might be more obvious since it is in the same building as a synagogue with the policeman standing guard.

In the United States, these Jewish writers are hardly known at all, although some portions of their work have been translated and collected, and even a few complete novels have been translated. Primarily, however, their writing is of interest to German professors like myself who see their work as an opportunity to teach American students about lives that exist in Germany that do not fit conventional molds. Such literary perspectives offer alternative ways of knowing Jewish life than those which can be gained from demographic statistics, sociological surveys, economic data, or political analysis. Some of the authors do appear at American academic literary conferences, for example, as guests of the Goethe Institute, the international German cultural center, or as writers-in-residence at major American universities like New York University or MIT. Still, they remain relatively unknown, even to American Jews who are particularly interested in Germany.

To remedy this situation in a small way, I would like to look more closely at just two of these second-generation writers. I will focus on Rafael Seligmann and Barbara Honigmann, who in my opinion address the issue of identity most interestingly in two respective novels, *Rubensteins Versteigerung* (Rubenstein's Auction, 1989) and *Soharas Reise* (Sohara's Journey, 1996). Both Seligmann and Honigmann have created characters who in many ways model their own lives. Although the relationship between authors and characters should not be overstated, it may indeed be that due to their marginal status as minority writers, they feel the need to assert their identities and draw more intimately on their own biographies.

Like Seligmann, Jonathan Rubenstein returns with his parents to Germany from Israel before the influx of Russian Jews that would change the face of the Community. He bemoans his life and chastises his parents for making him live in what he calls "Naziland." Hostile toward Germany and frustrated in life and love, Jonathan bears on his shoulders the weighty burden of the genocide and its impact on identity. Always angry, he seems to find an outlet only in his sexual exploits. When he finally finds a more fulfilling bond with a gentile woman, his mother, according to her frustrated son, destroys the relationship. His disrespect for his parents and the German world around him turns into resentment and the novel plays out his personal dilemma of defining who he is, a German or a Jew? The novel ends in an ambivalent acceptance of his dual identity, when he dramatically claims *"Ich bin ein deutscher Jude!"* [his italics] (I am a German Jew).[12]

Although Honigmann now lives in France, she was brought up in East Germany, whence her parents returned after their wartime safe haven in England. Not finding enough Jewishness in what was to be the "better Germany" in the East, as she once told me, she moved in 1984 to Strasbourg to be part of the large Jewish community and to live in a different environment. Her heroine, Sohara, is a North African Sephardic Jewish woman who, like Honigmann, leaves her country and comes to Strasbourg. Sohara goes into exile in France, marries a traveling confidence man who passes himself off as a pious rabbi and who ultimately kidnaps their three children. Sohara befriends a woman neighbor, a German Holocaust survivor, who helps her recover her children through an international network of rabbis. Through these experiences beyond the sequestered life she is forced to lead, Sohara learns to understand alternative ways of being Jewish and to be the head of a new kind of Jewish family.

Thematically, both Jonathan and Sohara question their Jewish identities as "foreigners" in the double diaspora sense, but both also learn to come to terms with the hybridity of their existence. Although both search for a home, they live on the border, Sohara literally in Strasbourg, a city both French and German, and Jonathan psychologically between German and Jew. Both come to terms with ambivalent identities that leave them, more in the case of Sohara than Jonathan, optimistic rather than merely resigned about the future. Neither have had direct contact with the Holocaust. Germany's Nazi past only casts a shadow on Jonathan's life and contributes to his neurotic and crass behavior. Although many experiences in her exile are reminiscent of those of Holocaust refugees, Sohara's relationship to the Holocaust comes vicariously from the experiences of her neighbor. Nevertheless, it is present, as both are embodied literally in her new friend who still hates Germany and metaphorically in reminiscent Holocaust language, metaphors, and symbols. These create parallels between her displacement from Algeria and that of the Jewish people throughout their history, culminating in their deportation by the Nazis. But for Sohara, this similar narrative ends optimistically with a new life rather than death.

Stylistically as well, Seligmann maintains a border between his story and his audience. Since it is not possible for him to tell this narrative in a straightforward, realistic manner, as a truthful rendering of Jewish experience in Germany in the 1980s, Seligmann must exaggerate Jonathan's spoiled and self-absorbed qualities to distance the reader who is expected to be critical of such an unpleasant character. Many Jewish readers in Germany, who probably read the novel too literally, criticized Seligmann for his portrayal of this Jewish Portnoy whose representation was, in their words, "dirtying the nest." Honigmann, by contrast, creates her Jewish world in simple, sympathetic, and almost lyrical language. Unlike Seligmann, she is gentle with her characters and touches them with a light rather than a heavy hand.

These literary representations of Jewish lives depict such situations critically, precisely because by creating fiction they show what might or could be possible, rather than what might be actual and real. Their worlds can be playful or serious, ironic or comic without need for real Jewish lives that might be limited by the requirements for realism or objectivity. They open a special entry into Jewish lives that are not easily defined and offer multiple meanings that are not unlike Jewish identity itself, whose fate it is to be reinterpreted again and again, generation after generation, in one historical context or another. These rich Jewish texts remind us of the importance of the "book" for the Jewish people. The fate of Jewish life in Germany is similarly written in many stories that remain open-ended and unfinished for generations to come.

In line with the seemingly limitless reinterpretations of Jewish identity through literature and reinterpretation of the past, the new voices of today must speak to the present and the future rather than the past. Already recognized by the media as a unique voice, Wladimir Kaminer, a Russian Jew who was born in 1967 in Moscow and emigrated to Berlin in 1990, represents the new kind of Jew who lives in Berlin today. A product of a different generation, a different tradition, and a different emigration, he is in tune with the beat of contemporary Berlin and the exciting multicultural world he finds there in the 1990s. He approaches identity without complaints or conflict. He represents a counterpoint to the other two Jewish authors in tone, attitude, and position. He is also different from many of his Russian compatriots. His humor and irony about life in the Soviet Union and in Germany counterbalance the frequently weighty perspectives of his fellow immigrants. As a best seller in Germany, Kaminer's novel *Russendisko* (2000; Russian Disco), one of many similar novels, illustrates an optimistic version of a multicultural Berlin, filled with Turks, Vietnamese, Greeks, and Africans, among others. Kaminer turns the often negative concept of "foreigner" connoting difference on its head and celebrates this difference and the benefits of diverse nationalities and ethnicities in Berlin. Like Kaminer, all of these new Germans make their home in Berlin without addressing the topic as explicitly or dramatically as the earlier generation.

Like Seligmann and Honigmann, Kaminer, the Jew from Eastern Europe, also writes as a "displaced person," but a quite different kind than the two authors or the DPs who formed the remnant of European Jewry after the war. Kaminer's narrator, seemingly identical with the author himself, represents an everyday world filled with trivialities that become adventures every time he turns a corner. The narrator, and apparently Kaminer himself, thrives in this new world they both embrace with naiveté and openness, even though it is sometimes confusing and uncertain. He talks about life in Moscow before the emigration as well as his experiences in cosmopolitan Berlin with a mixture of directness and subtlety. Kaminer's narrator lets the reader know the "facts," for example, of his spur-of-the-moment trip to what was then East Germany that became his immigration, but simultaneously gives his subjective view on what they mean for him in this new life. Kaminer's motto captures his attitudes toward Germany: "Don't think too much, but rather trust life."[13]

If Kaminer can represent anything to us in the West, it is a newer generation of Jewish writing in Germany that is not negative and complicated, nor overshadowed by the past. His work obviously reaches beyond a Jewish public. His readings are cult events packed primarily with young, hip Berliners who clamor to hear him read his work. He also hosts "Russian Disco" evenings of music and readings in an East Berlin café, as well as a radio show called "MultiKulti," a common abbreviation of the German word for multiculturalism. Kaminer's variety of artistic endeavors as well as his attitude, his flexibility, openness, and creativity, clearly mark him and his generation as a new breed. He is breaking ground and carving out a new direction that depends neither on the prewar German-Jewish tradition nor, as is the case with other Russian Jews, the trauma of the Holocaust. He exemplifies a new German-Jewish lineage, one that is more hybrid, more heterogeneous, and more deeply imbedded in a diaspora consciousness. Perhaps just as Kaminer experiences and defines his diverse world as one possibility among many, Jewishness and homeland will be defined in a radically different way.

More important perhaps than the second and even third generation of Jewish writers in Germany I have just presented are those who can be called publicists, journalists, and commentators who write for the public and are better known than any of the literary writers—names like Micha Brumlik, Henryk Broder, Michael Wolffsohn, Richard Chaim Schneider, and Rafael Seligmann himself. Their writings contribute to a public discourse that gives a fuller, more complex, and critical picture of German-Jewish life in prominent German newspapers and magazines such as *Die Zeit* (national), *Der Spiegel* (national newsmagazine), *Der Tagespiegel* (Berlin), *Die Süddeutsche Zeitung* (Munich and national), or *Die Jüdische Allgemeine Wochenzeitung* (national Jewish newspaper). They often appear on television in the ever-popular German roundtables where intellectuals slug it out over questions of political, social, or cultural interest. They are public Jewish figures, prominently all men. While they do not speak in any official capacity as the voice of the Jewish Community, with whom they often disagree, they are nevertheless listened to with interest and respect. These younger intellectuals are a welcome presence to differentiate and critique the generalities (and sound bites) of political policy makers who are beholden to a different public. They have the luxury of being public figures in an intellectual milieu whose judgments are based as much on discursive or rhetorical flourish as on substance or critique. Often they add a needed corrective or addition to official policies that may be too harmonized with government wishes. None of these men could be accused, as leaders of the Jewish Community are, of pandering to officialdom or becoming what is negatively termed a "Hofjude" (court Jew).

Like the three authors, these three men that I have selected, Brumlik, Broder, and Seligmann, have to be understood as to how time and place have shaped their individual biographies, especially as Jews in Germany. Therefore, not surprisingly, they too deal profoundly with questions of identity and home. These are children of survivors, the first generation to be born after the Shoah, the event that distinguishes the chronologies of all Jews in Germany, that is, those born in Nazi-occupied Europe from what Germans call "Nachgeborenen" (literally, those born afterward, i.e., of later generations). The second generation bears the mark of being living symbols of survival. Producing Jewish babies at that time was literally an act of victory! These children were the offspring of a generation that had emerged from complete hopelessness to give life to a new Jewish progeny. In the end, Hitler's *Endlösung* (Final Solution) to the so-called Jewish question did not accomplish its goal of wiping out all of European Jewry. However, the psychological burden for the second generation, borne of their parents' survival and their birth as a kind of "proof," became a weighty legacy of the genocide that has most likely driven many of them to write and speak in public forums.

Brumlik, Broder, and Seligmann (besides Wolffsohn born in 1947 in Tel-Aviv, who moved in 1954 to Berlin, and Schneider born in 1957 in Munich), all were born in the period of 1946 to 1947. All three arrived with their parents in Germany in the 1950s, the period when most of that first and second generation returned: Brumlik in 1952 and Seligmann in 1957 to Munich and Broder in 1958 to Cologne. The families of Seligmann and Brumlik returned to the country they had left behind, while Broder's family came from Poland, after surviving the camps. All of them have a relationship to Israel. Born in that country, Seligmann spent the first ten years of his childhood there; Brumlik lived there for almost two years (1967 and 1968) as a young man who was a fervent and then disappointed Zionist; and Broder, as an adult, commutes between Jerusalem and Berlin. Brumlik and Seligmann are German Jews and Broder is an Ostjude, a member of a group whose history in Germany and even in the Second World War and the camps illustrates a well-known internecine hostility.

Broder, Brumlik, and Seligmann are quite different in their attitudes toward Jewish life in Germany; each has a distinctive personality and way of expressing his own Jewish identity. Many observers would agree, I think, that Broder is the most cynical, Brumlik, the most accommodating, and Seligmann, while sarcastic and sharp, maintains through his longer imaginative works (he is the only novelist of the three) a sense of humor, an attitude that to my mind often fails the other two. Each then in his own way takes to task the vicissitudes of every aspect of Jewish life in Germany (and for Broder in the United States as well with his biting critique of what he so unceremoniously termed the "Shoah-Business").

Religion, identity, politics, sexuality, education, business, and culture all figure into the mathematics of commenting on a Jewish population that, as I have documented, has grown by leaps and bounds. It is also one that increasingly is on public view to critics such as these. But above all, one notices how one line of thought threads its way through all of these subjects, just as it does in the novels: namely the notion of home or *Heimat*. This German term carries with it a weighty tradition of patriotism, national identities and affinities, and even ideology. The German term is more akin to the somewhat out of fashion English word "homeland" that was revived by the Bush administration to name the Office of Homeland Security. Date and place of birth, immigration history, present domicile, as well as critical attitudes and perspectives are always about the existential questions of identity and belonging expressed in the question of home for Jews living in Germany. Even with the advances I discussed in chapter 1, the question is still being asked whether Germany can be a Heimat for the Jews.

I want to focus on this primary theme of home in selected works and articles, such as Brumlik's 1996 autobiography, *Kein Weg als Deutscher und Jude* (No Way as German and Jew), alluding to Jakob Wassermann's autobiography, *Mein Weg als Deutscher und Jude* (1921; My Way as German and Jew). Broder's 1993 collection of essays, *Erbarmen mit den Deutschen* (Take Pity on the Germans) and *Der ewige Antisemit: Über Sinn und Funktion eines beständigen Gefühls* (1986; The Eternal Anti-Semite: On the Meaning and Function of a Constant Feeling) as well as short journalistic pieces and his appendix to Lea Fleischmann's memoir, *Dies ist nicht mein Land, eine Jüdin verlässt die Bundesrepublik* (1980; This Is Not My Country: A Jewish Woman Leaves Germany). For Seligmann, I look at part of his article entitled "German Jewry: Squawking at the Approach of Danger" in an English collection entitled *Speaking Out: Jewish Voices in United Germany* (1995), edited by Susan Stern, which summarizes many of his points in other articles and in his own essay collection, *Mit beschränkter Hoffnung: Juden, Deutsche, Israelis* (1991; With Limited Hope: Jews, Germans, Israelis). All three have also written forcefully about the political situation after the Iraq war.

In an English collection, entitled *Jewish Voices, German Words: Growing Up Jewish in Postwar Germany and Austria, An Anthology* (1994), edited by Elena Lappin, Broder goes to the heart of the issue in an essay entitled, "Heimat, No Thanks," while at the same time uncharacteristically delving into his own biography. It is not surprising perhaps that addressing the notion of home calls up personal ruminations on the author's own relationship to place, which in Broder's case describes his early feelings about moving with his family to Germany from anti-Semitic Poland through Vienna in 1957, and possibly his peripatetic existence between Germany and Israel. His observations on Heimat are not particularly new. He does, however, try to define the Jewish notion of "Heimat" by historicizing the concept as regards the situation of German Jews. He says, "Thus, at the beginning of this century, Jews had three different concepts of Heimat to choose from: a spiritual one, in the sense of a portable fatherland [from Heine]; a national one, in the sense of Zionism; and a 'symbiotic' one, in the sense of assimilation. We know which course history chose." He concludes the article claiming, as any good poststructuralist critic would do today, that "the big problem with Heimat . . . is that a person is expected to choose one. It would be better simply not to have one. Or best of all: to have a whole lot of them."[14] Here Broder, without any self-awareness, targets a focal point of my argument. Jewish life, especially in the Diaspora, necessarily multiplies affiliations and undermines the possibility of a single identity or solitary home.

To Broder's credit, he has always been in the right place at the right time with his commentary. In fact, Broder is one of the most insightful and sharpest observers of German- Jewish life whose best work is precisely when he uses his sharp tongue to cut through the self-righteousness and inauthenticity of do-gooders, even if they are Jews. While his points of view are often controversial, he lets no one off the hook and no stone unturned until he exposes what he sees as hypocrisy and contradiction. However, such ambivalence and ambiguity are precisely the stuff of identity construction, even in Broder's own words. Perhaps it is his particular emphasis on ferreting out anti-Semitism, what he calls "a constant feeling," that makes him seem so uncompromising, especially toward what he has called "Antisemitismus lite" (Anti-Semitism Lite). Broder himself admits elsewhere, of course, that we in the United States "find a way to live with intractable problems. Nobody there denies that anti-Semites and anti-Semitism exist. And the Jews there take in stride the role of the scapegoat that is assigned to them."[15] Uncharacteristically, Broder here seems generous toward Jews in the United States, who in his opinion have found "a third alternative, somewhere between the impossibility of solving a problem and the wish to ignore it."[16]

Seligmann is close to Broder in style and stance: sarcastic, witty, and determined to lay bare the complexities of German-Jewish life. I mentioned briefly how in his novel *Rubensteins Versteigerung*, Seligmann created his German-Jewish antihero, Jonathan, to question in an ironic and even cynical way the problem of being Jewish and being German. Seligmann has his finger on the pulse of Jewish issues and the Jewish community in his journalistic pieces, which are published in a variety of newspapers and magazines. For example, he conducted a now well-known and insightful interview for the magazine *Der Stern* with Ignatz Bubis, shortly before the latter's death, in which the then-debilitated and frustrated leader of the Jewish Community questioned whether all of his work had advanced the cause of Jews at all.[17] Seligmann wrote about the scandal of Michel Friedman in 2003. In early 2004, directly after the new elections at the Berlin Community, Seligmann praised the election of Albert Meyer as a "break" with the past, since the new president was born after the Shoah, and the man himself as a "Jude, Preusse, deutscher Patriot (Jew, Prussian, German Patriot)."[18] Seligmann always returns, as he does in his novel, to the need for Jews, as ambivalent as they may be, to consider identifying themselves as Germans.

While Seligmann and Broder can be equally harsh in their opinions about Germans and Jews, Brumlik is calmer, more tempered, and reasoned. Less flashy and probably less well known outside of his home state of Hessen to a non-Jewish public, Brumlik is a pedagogue in spirit as well as in academic degree. He is the director of the Fritz Bauer Institute and professor at the university in Frankfurt. His writings appear primarily in Jewish publications and he is a former co-editor of the journal *Babylon*, a quasi academic-intellectual journal, published in Germany about German-Jewish issues. Brumlik has been more involved recently with religious issues such as the establishment of a Reformed service in Frankfurt. His autobiography, *Kein Weg als Deutscher und Jude: Eine bundesrepublikanische Erfahrung* (No Way as German and Jew: An Experience of a Citizen of the Federal Republic), is also a story about home, specifically in the Federal Republic, as each chapter represents a literal stage in his development as German and Jew, a kind of modern Jewish *Bildungsroman* (novel of education). The memoir is the personal story of a complex identity—Zionist commitment and disillusionment, leftist political engagement and critique—that parallels the trajectory of the young Federal Republic moving from infancy to adulthood. In Israel he himself realizes what Seligmann's Jonathan Rubenstein struggles with, "That a Jew in Germany [in 1972] can find not only Germans but also Jews as a kind of monster."[19] Just as Jonathan discovers his unique position though a relationship, Brumlik realizes in his relationship with an English girl that he "was a part of German society and that life in Germany was a part of him. Might I not have at least expected to have recognized this part of my self?"[20] The relationship fails, this time for the Jewish man with a Jewish woman for the same reasons—being a Jew in Germany—Jonathan Rubenstein was unable to succeed.

Like Seligmann's novel, Brumlik's autobiography is interesting also for his ability to stand back, unlike Broder, and to see himself as a man commenting on this very particular evolution in Germany. In retrospect these pages reflect a constant musing and critique of who he is and how he acts, both as a Jew and as a German. Of all three writers, he seems best able to accept the anomaly of his position, most willing to make a life for himself in Germany, most open to other causes, and less preoccupied with self-promotion and casuistry. While this might be explained through his involvement with a new religious identity in Germany, he has devoted himself to the cause of the Sinti and Roma as well. In the last words of his book, he doubts whether the new Jewish community has many future "ways of living, belief and piety" because "the status quo conquers all."[21]

Precisely because they are all so different, their writings have contributed substantively to creating a diverse Jewish identity in Germany beyond the narrowly defined political line. Their different styles and critical positions are needed to amplify the alternatives and opportunities for Jewish men and women alike. Micha Brumlik has published a collection of interviews with third-generation Jews in Germany. He seems to be more optimistic, as are these young people, than he was earlier. Seligmann moved to Berlin at the end of the 1990s, to be closer to a center of political and cultural activity, and Broder keeps up his nomadic existence. While there is no question that a Jewish life will have a place in Germany, all of these writers are as unsure as before exactly what kind of Heimat that might be.

The Jewish Museum in Berlin is probably the most important contribution to recent representations of Jewish life in Germany. Since the organization, presentation, and materials of a museum exhibition obviously tell a story, especially in historical museums, this new Jewish Museum in the capital city creates a narrative that must do justice to two thousand years of Jewish life in Germany it presents. What that story will be, however, depends on those telling it. The creation of such an institution in Berlin itself signals its significance in the developing story of the new Berlin and the new Germany.

Even before the exhibition opened, the striking building, designed by the American Jewish architect Daniel Libeskind, who has also been chosen to design the World Trade Center site, was an exhibition in its own right. Visitors viewed the empty building enthusiastically and could even walk through its interior. Some people felt it should remain empty, standing as a monument rather than as a museum. The creation of the historical exhibit of the museum, which opened officially in September 2001, was placed under the directorship of Michael Blumenthal, an American Jew who escaped Germany as a child via Shanghai. Initially, he was aided by several colleagues in complementary roles. Now the exhibit is in the capable hands of Cilly Kugelman, a sociologist and art historian, who has a long and notable history working on Jewish topics in Germany. Blumenthal and the many North Americans and other non-Germans involved in the project bring a broader perspective to the difficult task of representing two thousand years of Jewish life in German-speaking lands. In his "Welcome" printed in the book *Stories of an Exhibition: Two Millennia of German Jewish History*, the official documentation of the museum, Blumenthal states: "The Jewish Museum Berlin is no ordinary museum. As a major institution of memory, it occupies a unique place in Germany's capital city. As a national institution supported by the Federal Government, the State of Berlin, all political parties, and a broad cross-section of the public, its mission has sociopolitical meaning that far transcends the story it tells of the 2000-year history of German Jewry. It symbolizes, in fact, a widely shared determination to confront the past and to apply its lessons to societal problems of today and tomorrow."[22] Blumenthal's message and mission is optimistic, as it should be coming from the director of such an important institution. Jewish life in Germany "with its ups and downs"[23] will have multiple educative functions. It encompasses not just the past, but the future, not just for Jews, but for all those who might visit. By presenting a chronological history of the Jews from their earliest settlement in the areas that became the German-speaking lands through the present, it reminds the visitor, especially non-Jewish Germans, that the Jew is not an "other," an exoticized foreigner who does not belong, but an integral part of a historical German identity.[24] While the urge to harmonize German-Jewish identity is understandable, I would suggest that this exhibition is also a contentious site for definitions of what it means to be German as well as Jewish. Blumenthal acknowledges "what becomes possible when religious, cultural, or ethnic minorities are able to contribute their unique talents to national life—and how terrible the consequences for all can be when intolerance and prejudice prevail."[25] However, while the upbeat tone of the introduction may set a desired mood appropriate to the voice and genre of the essay, it may also conceal important controversial breaks that emerge when the exhibition is interpreted in a broader context.

Just as the exhibition itself ends with young Jews in Germany presenting personal objects of meaning—a child's Torah, records, and even a Jewish Barbie doll—so does the entrance to the museum begin with young Germans, mostly non-Jewish, welcoming the visitor with studied friendliness. Clearly, an institution shaped in the American museological mode does not begin and end with the exhibition itself, nor with just this impressive building. Rather its creators seek to provide a total experience. From the moment one enters the old Baroque building that leads to the Libeskind structure, one is greeted warmly and directed to the security check, and into the foyer where the coat can be checked, information can be had, or surprisingly, one can buy typically American sweets such as brownies, chocolate chip cookies, and Ben and Jerry's ice cream that until recently was unavailable in German cafés or restaurants. A little further on one can partake of a more substantial meal, this time prepared by Israeli chefs serving hummus and other Middle Eastern specialties. American and Israeli culinary specialties represent the two major influences on Jewish life in Germany, here in the museum and, as I will demonstrate in chapter 7, on politics and identity as well. These two strains of influence may also target the two nationalities constituting the majority of visitors to the museum, aside from reminding Germans that German-Jewish life is connected to these two largest Jewish communities in the world. On the occasion of my visit just before Chanukah, visitors were offered the traditional Eastern European latkes and Israeli sufganiot (potato pancakes and jelly doughnuts respectively). Jewish or American identified food becomes, like bagels, a step into another version of Jewish experience for the German or non-Jewish visitor.

Let us, however, walk through the exhibition after entering the bright foyer of the museum. One can choose to go downstairs to the multiple

Axes and to the Void or upstairs to the exhibition itself, in a sense choosing the optimistic path upward or the tragic way down the stairs. The building overlaid with meaning by Libeskind's stringent design, which some find burdensome since it leaves little room for interpretation, is hidden by the full exhibition except for what museum staffers ironically call "Libeskind moments," where the architect's design shines through or is used as part of the exhibition. The exhibition as well as the building have garnered both praise and criticism. "Two Millennia of German Jewish History" opened in September 2001 in a building that many have called an architectural masterpiece. To quote from one of the exhibition catalogues that cite Libeskind, "The building is structured around 'two lines of thinking. . . . One is a straight line, but broken into many fragments, the other is a tortuous line, but continuing indefinitely.' "[26] While a great deal has been written about the building, the exhibition is much less known to Americans, although the museum and the exhibition have become standard stops on Jewish American and Jewish tourist itineraries. Visiting a building and viewing an exhibition dedicated to the people that the Germans tried to wipe out holds an irony and fascination for many, aside from mere interest in this chapter of Jewish history. To the museum's credit it is not fixated on the Holocaust. It is definitively not a Holocaust museum, as every member of the staff, including Michael Blumenthal, will point out. And yet, the design of the building does point to this focus. The lower floor of the museum concentrates on what the catalogue calls "The fate of German Jews in the 20th century: emigration, extermination, and survival,"[27] with its Axis of Continuity leading in and out, the Axis of Exile leading to the outdoor Garden of Exile and the Axis of the Holocaust leading to the Holocaust Tower. Large window displays containing pictures and personal memorabilia present the history of German-Jewish families' experience in the Nazi era. At least on this floor, a veil of sadness shrouds what should be an upbeat and forward-moving chronological history of Jewish life in Germany that was cut short by the rise of Nazism. Separated from the chronological and thematic path of Jewish history from the Middle Ages to the Present, this lower level and its severe architectural space with dizzying slanted floors and the dramatic, eerie Voids can thematically and structurally overwhelm the history above. Unlike the chronological history above, this section does provide, as the catalogue duly notes, "biographical perspective of the exhibits in the Axes"[28] that apparently, according to the catalogue, was the wish of "surviving relations . . . that a parent, cousin or friend be remembered in the country where they lived and felt they belonged, before being driven into exile or murdered."[29] The powerful impression these two floors evoke tends to overwhelm the exhibitions on the two upper floors, where the thematic structure pales in comparison and the architecture often seems lost and becomes a mere backdrop to the objects and texts comprising the historical narrative. Nevertheless, this challenging interplay between space and story provides an interesting stage for the representation of Jewish life, the first such permanent exhibition in Germany, and more intellectual fodder for the continuous discussions of German and Jewish identity. Still, the question remains for some, at least rhetorically, if the museum would have been more powerful and dramatic had the space been left empty, thus creating a monument rather than a museum, a symbolic rather than literal representation of Jewish history.

On the lower level, glass cases display donated objects of memory and remembrance of those who went into exile or those who perished. Upstairs in the exhibition itself, objects, as is the stated objective of the curators, dominate the story, which is thematically focused and organized historically around interesting Jewish figures such as Glikl Bas Juda Leib, better known as Glickel of Hameln, and Moses Mendelssohn, as well as themes such as "Rural and Courtly Jews," "Family Life," "Tradition and Change," "Modernity and Urbanity," "East and West," "Persecution, Resistance, and Destruction," up through "The Present. 1945 and After." As one museum critic has noted, "The museum attempts to highlight the similarities and the differences between Jewish and German lifestyles, traditions and progression from the Middle Ages to modernity. Picking out individual characters for the visitor to concentrate on is a well-known method of achieving empathy and understanding in an audience, while also making it easier for visitors to take in information effectively."[30] These noble efforts are sometimes undone by the confusing zigzags of the structure. In fact, the museum was forced to post red arrows on the floor to help lost visitors find their way. The earlier sections feel confined and crammed with objects trying to show Jews as "people with artifacts as multi-faceted as their culture," and the latter section, especially after 1945, seems thin and dislocated among the rich earlier history.[31]

Throughout the exhibition, however, Jews in their many historical and religious incarnations are presented as an integral part of the German tradition, one that stretches back thousands of years even to the time, where the exhibition begins, when the "Children of Israel" were expelled into the

Diaspora and first came to the Germanic lands. One sees how Jews not only tried to participate in German society that would create the so-called German-Jewish symbiosis that was destroyed by the Nazis, but also that this interrelationship was longstanding: "From the beginning, the history of what is now Germany was a German-Jewish history" or "Jewish merchants were among the first inhabitants of medieval German cities. Often they were among their founders." German-Jewish life in all of its traditional forms is represented: rituals, religion, culture, society, and family. Interspersed among the specific significant moments of German-Jewish history are the more universal educational interludes of Jewish ritual and religion, presented in interactive videos, boxes, and drawers that open and close to reveal information and answers to the questions posed.

At the beginning of the exhibition, for example, in "The Medieval World of Ashkenaz," a Jewish man and woman in traditional dress are presented next to a series of drawers with anti-Jewish stereotypes of the time. Clearly, they are designed to educate a non-Jewish public about Jewish life in general, presenting information about religious ceremonies, defining "kosher," and even asking questions meant to challenge stereotypes and prejudice; for example, an interactive screen asks, "Is it appropriate today in Germany to tell Jewish jokes?" While some of these interventions seem important for raising social consciousness and others for religious education, they interrupt the narrative the exhibition sets out to relate due to their simplistic and naive structure that tries too hard to relate Jewish history to universal values about prejudice. In my opinion, one of the most disturbing moments is when visitors are asked to write their names in Hebrew letters. While the activity may be a simple way to arouse empathy for Germans among Jews and to make the former feel that they are Jewish, it seems a cheap convention for constructing a Jewish identity in the Hebrew or Yiddish alphabet, which aside from being in the former case primarily the language of prayer and of the Israeli people, or in the latter the language of Eastern Jewry, has little to do with German-Jewish life. In reaction to this entire exhibit and in the same vein, one non-Jewish German I spoke with felt that this tour through German-Jewish history was constructed to grant the feeling of absolution to the "guilty" Germans who had just walked literally through two thousand years of German-Jewish life. At least, in this more cynical view, a German who navigated the exhibit could feel good for having completed this tour.

Skepticism aside, the exhibition's success lies in the fact that it draws large non-Jewish audiences to its historical representation of the everyday life of Jews in Germany and elsewhere. The museum receives about two thousand visitors a day. In 2002, for example, 650,000 people visited the museum, primarily non-Jews. In July 2004, the museum received its two millionth visitor. The museum's narrative shows literally how German Jews lived, how they loved, how they died, and importantly, how these Jews tried to be Germans (the example of the assimilated ceremony of "Weinukkah" and Jewish Christmas trees is a favorite), how they were successful in that endeavor, and as we know, how they failed. This ambivalence is at the heart of the exhibition, yet there are other important contradictions that are omitted, such as the history of Jews on the political Left. For example, Karl Marx and Rosa Luxemburg are completely absent from the story. Planned changes, as members of the staff told me, will reflect more of the tension between Germans and Jews, such as in the period between 1800 and 1914, presenting the different attitudes about emancipation, identity, and later Zionism and patriotism. The exhibition has the difficult task of composing a narrative that illustrates an intertwined history; it must simultaneously reveal and question the breaks and challenges in this story, one that is typical for Jewish life all over the world.

Temporary exhibitions will also be added periodically to expand or fill in gaps in the German-Jewish story, often targeting contemporary issues. One of the most powerful was, not surprisingly, composed by Henryk Broder. Shortly after the first anniversary of September 11, 2001, the day of the World Trade Center bombing, Broder, always on the heels of a newsworthy story, published a book called *Kein Krieg, nirgends: Die Deutschen und der Terror* (No War, Nowhere: The Germans and Terror). Broder also created a special exhibition with the editor of the *Jüdische Allgemeine Wochenzeitung*.[32] Called "Ich bin kein Antisemit" (I am not an anti-Semite), the presentation presents the many letters and e-mails sent to Jewish personalities like Broder and others in Germany proclaiming, ironically, their tolerance toward Jews while spouting anti-Semitic invectives or thinly veiled slurs. It stands at the conclusion of the permanent exhibition and is revealing in light of the new anti-Semitism that broke out in Germany in 2002 and attracted so much attention. Letters and e-mails written to him after a controversial *Spiegel* article are displayed as if "dirty" or "clean" wash hanging out to dry and visitors can post their own comments on a large board that may be similar to those displayed. As a gloss, a book entitled *Was ich den Juden schon immer mal sagen wollte . . .* (What I always wanted to tell the Jews . . .) lies almost unnoticed on a table. This exhibition confronts the viewer with questions of self-definition precisely through the language they use to excuse, deceive, and protect themselves as they spout anti-Semitic invectives or even philo-Semitic hyperboles of how much they love Jews. This dissimulation and the bitter irony of the difficulty of even finding a space to talk about Jews in Germany is a reminder that the "'new' anti-Semitism" debate in Germany is not about Jews causing the problem for themselves, as Möllemann would have had it in his critique of Friedman. Rather it is about Germans coming to terms with their own national identity in a democratic postwar culture, an identity that is and will increasingly be marked by difference. It is clear that accepting the "other" is still a significant problem in Germany. At least, there have been calls for more solidarity and cooperation between Jewish and Turkish communities in fighting anti-Semitism, xenophobia, and racism issued by individuals in both groups.

Particularly in the new millennium, as the Shoah generation is dying out, the exhibition must demonstrate the centrality of the Holocaust and how to remember it. However, it must also accommodate a changing world and show how this affects the evolving Jewish community since the Second World War and the different Jewish stories that are a part of the history of Jewish identity in Germany: the German-Jewish, the Ostjüdisch, and the Russian-Jewish. Based on the entire experience of visiting the museum, I would add the American-Jewish influence as well, since it shaped the building, the focus on the visitor, and the presentation of the story. All four strands of Jewish tradition and ethnicity surface and recede at different moments, each with its contribution to this grand narrative. As Broder's contribution shows, more emphasis will be placed on the contemporary period with exhibitions and installations on topical issues as a reminder that Jewish life is present today in Germany and plays a role in German society, as well as among world Jewry.

The museum is a monument to both the continuity and discontinuity of Jewish life in Germany. Today Jews form an important, though not singular, segment of a society increasingly composed of immigrants. Since identity constructed by the representation of Jews will become increasingly hybrid, increasingly defined among different kinds of Jews and various "others" living in Germany, it will also continue to change in response to new influences and events from inside and outside of Germany. The Jewish status quo to which Brumlik refers may simply change because of generational shifts that will make his contemporaries more conservative or subject to the critiques of younger and different Jewish voices. While the "second generation" dominated the thinking about identity for much of the postwar period, in the millennium new voices like Wladimir Kaminer will continue to surface and shift the terrain of Jewish identity in a more diverse society. In coming years, writers, commentators, curators, and artists may well imagine and represent Jews in ways we cannot surmise.

Nevertheless, the theoretical problems of representation highlighted here will be at least structurally similar for other minority groups who are imagined in ways that do not coincide with who they are or how they understand themselves. The largest immigrant community in Germany, the Turks, find themselves portrayed as rampant criminals, juvenile delinquents, political radicals, religious reactionaries, or simply lazy immigrants who do not want to work. In broader political terms, the Turks in Germany also must contend with European and international attitudes toward Islam and terrorism that affect their status in Germany as much as that of their fellow Turks in Turkey, a country that sits between East and West. They will become, even more than before 1989, a major force in how one comes to define non-Germans in this century. The relationship between the Jews and Turks is the subject of the next chapter.

5

Jews and Turks

DISCOURSES OF THE "OTHER"

"I look at everyone in the face, she says, and wonder if he could also be a murderer."[1]

Ominous words from a German or Polish Jew in postwar Germany or from a Russian Jew in Germany after 1989? In fact, this reference is not a Jewish voice, but rather the outcry of a Turkish resident of Berlin after Solingen. This small town was one of the sites of deadly violence in 1991–1992 against foreigners (primarily Turks and asylum seekers). Places like Hoyerswerda and Rostock in the former East Germany and Mölln and Solingen in the West gain national notoriety. The names of these towns are now emblazoned in the minds of Turks and sympathetic Germans as icons of prejudice, intolerance, and even persecution. While they invite comparisons to places like Auschwitz, which objectively bare no resemblance, these events also seem to have become a bridge between Turks and Jews in Germany.

What do such comparisons mean in Germany for identity and for the ways in which people who are seen to be different from the Germans, such as Turks and Jews, are regarded? While both Turks and Jews are minorities in Germany, their histories and current status in a country known for its reluctance to accept foreigners and immigrants are very different, even though until 1993 Germany had one of the most liberal asylum laws in Europe. While 2.3 million Turks, 28 percent of the 7.3 million foreigners, live in Germany, there are only about 100,000 Jews registered with the Community. Even counting the hundreds or even thousands of unaffiliated residents, Jews constitute a much smaller group than the Turks and make up only a minuscule percentage of Germany's total population of

83 million. Clearly, the Jews have a long history in the area that is modern-day Germany, more than two thousand years as the Jewish Museum in Berlin reminds us. The Holocaust grants Jews a higher status (what some would call "symbolic capital") and governmental financial support that Turks simply do not enjoy. The Jews are also part of an extensive world Jewish community, largely in the United States and Israel, which has an interest in the German-Jewish Diaspora. The Turks have none of these global benefits.

In fact, German-Turkish relations only became a flashpoint in the early 1960s when in 1961, Germany concluded an agreement with Turkey to invite what was termed "Gastarbeiter" (guest workers) whose labor was needed to bolster Germany's economic miracle. While separate agreements were made with Italy (1955), Spain and Greece (1960), Morocco (1963), Portugal (1964), Tunisia (1965), and what was then Yugoslavia (1969), Turkey provided the largest numbers and "the Turk" became the iconic foreigner who represented "the other." In 1973, the import of human capital was stopped, but one year later a new law allowed wives and children under eighteen to join their working husbands and fathers. Consequently, according to migration scholar Klaus Bade, the foreign, and primarily Turkish population grew "from 1960, the year before the building of the Wall, to 1990 the year of German reunification from 686,100 to 5,241, 801. At the end of 1992 around 6.5 million (at the end of 1993 there were approximately 6.8 million) of which 4 million (62 percent) came from the countries who provided guest workers. The proportion of foreigners (Ausländer) in the West climbed from 1.2 percent in 1960 to 8.2 percent in 1990."[2] Ever larger in numbers and more obvious (and perceived as threatening) in daily life due to their appearance, dress, and speech, Turks became a nagging sign of foreignness and had to bear the brunt of racism and xenophobia, especially in the 1980s and early 1990s. Stories abound of Turks being refused housing, jobs, or just being treated as second-class citizens. Drawing on their limited experience with a Turkish immigrant population that came from more backward rural Anatolia rather than sophisticated urban Istanbul, many Germans had a skewed impression of these Turks and viewed them as ignorant, uneducated, and criminally inclined. In response, the majority of Turks formed their own isolated ghettos; the best known of these is in the Kreuzberg section of Berlin. While not officially forced into these areas, as is typical for minority and immigrants groups, the Turks stuck together and maintained their own traditions, culture, and language. It was their children—another "second generation"—who would increasingly be caught between two cultures and two countries, neither fully Turkish, nor German, sometimes falling between the cracks and sometimes successfully becoming hybrids of both. Like the Jews in Germany, they laid the groundwork for a new identity, one that was much more difficult to achieve due to what the Germans regarded as their "exotic" physical appearance.

The Turk became the symbol for all that was foreign and different in Germany: dark-skinned, dark-haired Muslims who often dressed strangely and refused to change their habits to accommodate their hosts. The American German Studies scholar Leslie Adelson has noted, "The *Spiegel* cover article that responded to the devastating news from Solingen characterizes German Turks as 'icons of strangeness.'"[3] Adelson also cites Faruk Şen, director of the Center for Turkish Studies at the University of Essen, who in the same article declares, "Hostility against foreigners in Germany is hostility against Turks, because aggression is above all directed at those who look different."[4] The anthropologist Ruth Mandel deepened the discussion when she studied a major symbol of this "Andersaussehen" (looking different)—the Turkish headscarf as an insignia for the Turk's difference. In her words, "[On the left and on the right] we see the often conflicting meanings embedded in a single object as it becomes valorized in different spatial and temporal contexts."[5] In 2004 the headscarf debate emerged again in Germany and all over Europe, this time associated with political rather than only ethnic or national differences. However, except for devout Orthodox or Chasidic Jews who are recognizable by their beards, black hats, kippot (skull caps), and black garb, most Jews today, as were the predominantly secularized German Jews in prewar Germany, are not recognizable. Once Hitler's deportation policy took effect in September 1941, the Jews were marked with the yellow star, which, as the historian John Efron has pointed out, was to set them off from the German population as a recognizable group precisely because they were not different enough.[6] The distinguishing mark of Jewish males, the circumcised penis, is of course not immediately visible—the central theme of the 1991 film *Europa, Europa*—so the Nazis had to resort to pulling down a suspected Jew's pant to make sure. The Turks who are also circumcised, at thirteen according to their Muslim faith, are ethnically Caucasian but generally can be distinguished from the "Aryan" German population, who ostensibly are blond and blue-eyed. Both stereotypes are obviously false since, as any visitor to Germany or Israel knows, many Germans are dark-haired and many Jews are blue-eyed.

The visibility of the foreign is constructed in language and symbolic representation. German behavior toward Turks or Jews is not literally action taken against "real Turks" and "real Jews," but reflected in discourse and images that are based more in imagination than reality. It is a well-documented phenomenon that anti-Semitism develops even where very few or no Jews exist and sometimes the memory of a Jewish presence is enough for the seeds of this form of xenophobia to blossom. In fact, public life is dependent more than many in Germany are willing to admit on how Turks or Jews look, the ways they are represented, be it color, dress, or gesture. These facets of what sociologists call "habitus" are often identified with traditions that do not fit the norms of what it conventionally means to be German, that is white and Christian, even though these characteristics may not fit the reality of the German population. Germans are apparently as susceptible as Americans (Jews) to remaining fixed on a static notion of identity. It would be disingenuous here not to acknowledge that Jewish identity according to the Halakhah, as I discussed in chapter 3, is based as much on blood as the German identity that I question in this particular discussion. That the Jews are a different religion and Turks are usually Muslim is so obvious a marker of difference that not much more needs to be said.

Sephardic Jews and Turks have an intertwined history since the time when the Jews were expelled from Spain in 1492 and were granted sanctuary in the Ottoman Empire. At least from this specific connection, they are superficially often grouped together and viewed, at least in Western eyes, as dark and suspicious "Orientals." However, looking at Germany's Turks and Jews today, this is frequently a preconceived image. In 2002, some historical reality set in linking the two groups and putting both Turks and Jews in jeopardy. Turkey, as a non-Arab Muslim country, was not only the first Muslim nation to recognize Israel, but also continues to support the Jewish homeland, although this government position does not represent the majority of the population.[7] Turkey also opened its doors to Jewish refugees from Nazi Germany. In fact, it has been specifically pointed out in the debate on the new anti-Semitism that young Arab Muslim men, not Turks, have been the main perpetrators of anti-Jewish attacks in Germany, France, and other European countries. In Berlin, young Turks and Arabs have come to blows. Yet, Turks and Jews often have often become targets onto which Germans have projected their fears and anxieties. Jews are a constant reminder of a past that won't go away. Turks are the strange "guests" who were never really welcome and have overstayed their visit. Both groups represent to the German mind the "other," the one who does not fit static notions of German identity. In fact, to many Germans, the Turks have become "the new Jews." We must ask: are these comparisons linked to a heterogeneous rather than homogeneous German identity today as the nation comes to terms with its racial, ethnic, and religious diversity? How do historical notions of citizenship based on blood and its perversion by the Nazis continue to reassert themselves despite multicultural Germany's new understanding of itself that challenges static and racially based notions of identity?

Shortly after reunification, the serious attacks on Turks began. In the East unemployment and frustration that accompanied reunification spurred neo-Nazis, and in the West similar antisocial types out of pure prejudice attacked asylum seekers and Turks. In Hoyerswerda (September 17–22, 1991), asylum seekers were chased from their lodgings and pelted with stones as they drove away in buses. In Rostock (August 23–27, 1992), led by skinheads and neo-Nazis, frustrated and angry citizens, even more actively and in greater numbers than in Hoyerswerda, took out their resentment on the new scapegoats: Romanian Gypsies, Vietnamese, and Angolans. Even more frightening was the fact that ordinary citizens stood by and cheered as the temporary homes of these immigrants were set on fire, its residents attacked, and some even murdered. In Mölln (November 23, 1992) members of one family, a fifty-one-year-old woman, her ten-year-old grandchild, and her fourteen-year-old nephew, died in a fire bombing, and in Solingen (May 29, 1993), two women and three girls, four from the same family, were burned to death. Germany was shocked; comparisons were made to the Nazis; citizens marched in solidarity with the victims.

In the joyous afterglow of the country's reunification just months earlier, these attacks and other neo-Nazi and skinhead demonstrations against foreigners were all the more ironic and frightening. Some Jews in the former GDR, like Eva B., feared that the blatant attacks in the East might be a by-product of the new freedoms that they welcomed. Others, such as Ruth B., feared that these attacks would lead to renewed anti-Semitism.[8] Such demonstrations could no longer be explained away with communist slogans as minor aberrations in the socialist brotherhood. For the Jews, of course, such words and deeds were a reminder of virulent racial anti-Semitism and persecution during the Third Reich and its new political forms in Germany and Europe, largely inspired by hostilities in the Middle East. The distinctions in the various forms of anti-Semitism are, however, not always sufficiently recognized. While the comparative potential of these two groups should not be overdrawn, prominent Jewish and German politicians have acknowledged their common roots. Ignatz Bubis claimed in 1992 that there is no great difference between xenophobia and anti-Semitism.[9] Similarly, in 2002, in response to the anti-Semitic statements of politicians like Möllemann, Foreign Minister Joschka Fischer, regarded as a great friend of Israel and the Jews, also drew comparisons: "Anti-Semitism does not only threaten Jews but is a general threat to peace, freedom, and democracy. Racism is disgusting and politically very dangerous."[10]

Such sweeping comparisons that link anti-Semitism, xenophobia, and racism are understandably not as nuanced as is necessary for a historically grounded and socially founded explanation of both similarities and differences between Jews and Turks. It is also not appropriate or fair to use one group as a marker for the other. Xenophobia, literally the hate or dislike of something or someone different or strange, and anti-Semitism, irrational hostility toward Jews, are not always synonymous. However, when it comes to discussions of identity in Germany, Jews and Turks seem to have enough in common to raise doubts about who they are and where they belong in a Germany that for so long had understood itself as "pure German." Such language, of course, evokes the German past and references to a more pernicious version of how minorities fit into a common German national identity and the history of the German nation. These memories hang over any discussion of so-called foreigners in Germany. In 1992, a *Spiegel* journalist in fact bluntly noted, "The more positively one thinks about the Nazi regime, the more negatively one thinks about Jews and Turks."[11] Bubis has reminded us, as does this journalist, that Jews, the target of anti-Semitism, and Turks, who bear the brunt of xenophobia, are linked in people's minds and language, if not in real historical terms.

The urge to compare Turks and Jews also comes from international groups who feel a special responsibility to keep track of anti-Semitism in Germany, specifically from the United States, where the Jewish population identifies so strongly with the Holocaust. As the Holocaust fades into the past, Jews insist that new sites must be found to preserve the memory in the present. For Turks the move to Germany for the first generation and their children and grandchildren's lives away from home means constant attention to self-definition in an often unfriendly environment. Therefore, tensions and conflicts of individuals seeking to establish and erase boundaries in order to find their place in the German landscape often evoke opposition and aggression, as demonstrated in the attacks in 1992. Unfortunately, to make sense of this blatant racist aggression, many conjure up historical comparisons as a reference point for their anger. Consequently in 1992, the outrage expressed by (Jewish) Americans in particular seemed exaggerated and far out of proportion in relation to the acts themselves. While it is important for American Jews to be vigilant toward potential anti-Semitism in other countries, and especially Germany, their reaction transferred the emotional baggage too blithely from one historical event to the other.

At the time, for example, American Jews in particular and the American press in general reacted swiftly and forcefully to the attacks that reminded them of the 1930s and 1940s. Some people even used the word "atrocity" to describe Solingen, a term usually reserved for the magnitude and horror on the scale of the Holocaust. The conservative *Washington Times* writing about Rostock invoked Kristallnacht, the event that initiated the systematic persecution of the Jews in 1938.[12] And after the deaths in Mölln, the *Washington Post* writer Eugene Meyer stated, "The government of Chancellor Helmut Kohl has responded—belatedly, some say—to the rise in violence. But the Holocaust haunts descendants of the Nazi victims and troubles many Germans as well as the friends and relatives of Turkish 'guest workers' who live there."[13] Surveying German, Jewish, and Turkish opinion, Meyer's article, while reflecting the ambivalence of many, still seems fearful of Nazism's rising specter. Several local rabbis quoted in the piece expressed their anxieties in the language familiar to a Jewish-American audience unsympathetic to Germany. One rabbi, reminiscent of Goldhagen's thesis of "eliminationist anti-Semitism" inherent in the German population, declared, "The violence, ugliness, hatred of the foreigner and all the things we see emerging again really raise some terribly, terribly painful questions about the character of the [German] people."[14] Another rabbi, speaking more dramatically, stated, "It's horrendous. . . . These are shades of the Holocaust of Germany's past."[15] A. M. Rosenthal of the *New York Times* entered the fray with more fear and paranoia: "The attacks on foreigners, particularly those of dark skin, are not just sudden bursts of violence. They are as much a part of Nazi strategy as were the first attacks on the Jews."[16] And finally, a truly reactionary response by a respected law professor at Harvard, Alan Dershowitz, who asked "Why does the civilized world seem so shocked at the resurgence of nazism in Germany?"[17] He concludes, "Nazism will recur in Germany every time there is a crisis, unless the German leaders begin to speak the painful truth to their people."[18] Looking back at these statements from 2004, one might be more sanguine in reacting to these events, which have not proven to be as dangerous as some of these commentators once feared, although even ten years later, in response to recent anti-Semitism, a Boston newspaper reports, "Not since the Third Reich has there been anything like it."[19] Apparently, clichés and stereotypes do not disappear so easily.

At that volatile time, comparisons from Europeans were more sanguine and more critically minded in an attempt to avoid stereotypes. The September 10, 1992, *Frankfurter Allgemeine Zeitung* reported that one of Italy's leading journalists, Arrigo Levi, in an article about xenophobia in the *Corriere della Sera* entitled "We Are All Germans," warned his fellow Italians about xenophobia and the dangers of stigmatizing all Germans as Nazis. Levi complains that the Italians are too easy on themselves "by repeating the formula that the Germans are just the Germans, and therefore one sees the return to the dark past of National Socialism."[20] Are the neo-Nazis and skinheads like the Nazis and the asylum seekers and foreigners like the Jews? For the Italian Jew Levi, the explanation of today's xenophobia through yesterday's anti-Semitism apparently blinds his countrymen to their own fear of immigrants, in this case toward the Albanians who were sent back by the thousands. Here Levi compares the Italians to the Germans; he draws his fellow Italians' attention to the dangers of using the Germans as a metaphor for xenophobia, of using Nazism as the standard against which all evil is measured. This attitude can blind the public to right-wing or fascist tendencies even in democratic governments who couch such policies in benign terms.

Even if Jews and Turks are not directly linked, reports use evocative language and imagery drawn from the racial, ethnic, and religious prejudices in leftist or right-wing political ideologies. As seems appropriate, these positions can be used to discredit protest. The attacks on asylum seekers in Rostock were one such example. The left protested with antiracism demonstrations and the correspondent from the *Washington Post* emphasized how many of these protesters "sport[ed] pink or purple hair and nose rings."[21] "Many of the demonstrators were black-hooded anarchists known as 'Autonome' [independents] who angrily heckled the Lichtenhagen residents as racist."[22] These demonstrators "marched . . . waving Communist flags and chanting anti-fascist slogans such as 'East or West. Down with the Nazi plague.'"[23] The right-wing attacks were led by self-styled neo-Nazis wearing hob-nail boots and sporting Nazi insignias yelling "Sieg Heil" and "Germany only for the Germans."[24] In this news report, the protesters' efforts were cast as suspicious because of their appearance and behavior linked to a specific political stance.

Beginning with Hoyerswerda and intensifying later, references were made on both sides to Nazism, its racial ideologies, and its tactics. While Nazi vocabulary was constantly and consistently deployed in reports in Germany and especially the United States about attacks on foreigners, the meanings of these comparisons are rarely questioned. Words are loosely invoked, such as "Kristallnacht," "Pogrome," and "Judenverfolgung" (persecution of the Jews). Nazism or its competing political vocabulary of anti-fascism had become an all-encompassing metaphor. On the one hand, right-wing neo-Nazis can stir up their followers with well-timed shouts of "Sieg Heil," and on the other, left-wing anti-fascists can decry the "new Nazi plague." The continued success in America of films about Nazis, especially a purportedly Jewish one, such as *Europa, Europa, Schindler's List, Life Is Beautiful,* or *The Pianist,* makes it hardly surprising that the subject of Nazism should continue to resonate. This fixation covers the sometimes too facile references to Nazism as a shorthand for evil as well as the entertainment values of the movie industry and American media that capitalize on what Susan Sontag years ago quite accurately coined "fascinating fascism."[25]

A more compelling, albeit more slippery comparison, however, is the status of the Jews as "foreigners" in Germany. While there is the danger of eliding all those who are not German under the broad category of "foreign," it is the German translation of this term which complicates any discussion. Until the late 1980s, there were specific terms for each category of non-Germans: "Aussiedler," literally those who move out, for the "ethnic" Germans who came from Russia and other Eastern territories; "Übersiedler," literally those who move from one place and settle in Germany, for those from East Germany; the more politicized term "Flüchtling," meaning refugee, for those who came from the communist East; the very negative "Asylanten," asylum seekers; and finally, the well-known "Ausländer," literally those who come from outside, the most generalizing term for the "foreigner."[26]

However, increasingly today, Germany has become more diverse or multicultural. Those who are categorized by this pejorative term "Ausländer" may have come from outside of Germany, but now live permanently in the country, as one of the approximately 7.3 million foreigners making a home there, at whatever level of (dis)comfort. The infamous, now generic and international term coined by the Germans to delineate the particular economic immigrant class "Gastarbeiter" or guest worker, became synonymous with Ausländer (foreigner). They are, however, as is often cited, the "guests" who never went home. The word "Ausländer" itself distances these people "from outside" from the German population within whose midst they actually reside. The similar word "fremd/Fremder"—strange(r), those who are different or unfamiliar—more accurately describes those who are not part of the German racial/ethnic community, but may indeed live there and be subject to *Fremdenfeindlichkeit* (xenophobia or literally hostility toward foreigners or strangers). While Jews have been "Germans" for centuries and most Turks only recently, a survey analysis in *Der Spiegel* presented the problem in the mid-1990s: "In this country the basic attitude of most Germans toward the Jews is that strangers [Fremde] are most appealing to them when they are far away. Above all for this reason 'Jews in Israel' (with 1+ points) are more popular than 'Jews in Germany,' 'Turks in Turkey' more popular than 'Turks in Germany' (+1.4 versus +0.2 points). That in this respect there is no difference between Jews and Turks makes clear that the Jews [in Germany] are not fellow countrymen/women, but rather strangers [Fremde]. If someone does not like Turks, they probably will also not like Jews."[27]

The "foreigner," Fremde more than Ausländer, both Jew and Turk, is both alien and strange, especially when from farther away rather than closer. Such "strangeness" is appealing when it is distant, mysteriously transformed into the touristic and even exotic, which ironically often makes the Germans enthusiastic visitors in far-flung foreign, yet in this case appealing destinations, such as Turkey and Israel. Usually designating a citizen of another nation who now does in fact indeed live closer, Aus-länder (from outside, a foreign land) is not only a misnomer, but also less existential than the word "fremd," which connotes an estranged sense of being, whether one comes from *Inland* (inside) or *Ausland* (abroad). Such strangeness can be, as the article points out, the reaction of the Germans, as well as the foreigners' feelings about themselves. Jews today, even German Jews, may still feel as strange in their own country as anyone from abroad. Especially now, with the influx of Soviet Jews under the privileged status as *Kontingentenflüchtling* and the "naturalization" of more Turks into "Germans," neither of these two major minority groups are "native" to Germany or "naturally" Germans, making Russian Jews more foreign than their German brethren. Consequently, Jews and Turks often remain "foreigners" or "strangers" in Germany no matter what their citizenship or legal status. They are more *fremd* (strange) than *ausländisch* (from somewhere else), more alienated than misplaced. They simply feel that they do not belong. The more neutral term "non-Germans" for Ausländer was introduced in the 1990s, but it is not clear if this change in name will make much difference in the ways Germans treat those who are different.

The elision of Turk and Jew is only possible, in fact, by setting up false dichotomies that continue to further separate Germans from all other foreigners. The nebulous word "Ausländer," elides people from almost every country in the world into a dark, faceless mass and is so broad and undifferentiated as to include an American tourist, a Tamil asylum seeker, or an African diplomat, although clear, unspoken hierarchies have always existed based on class, race, and nationality. A white American is simply not the same as a brown Sri Lankan. Although both groups are officially foreigners, they are not both Ausländer.

After Hoyerswerda, protesters marched down German streets dissociating themselves from their German identity and identifying with the victims, proclaiming "I am a foreigner"[28] or "Dear Foreigners, don't leave us alone with the Germans."[29] During one Berlin demonstration against xenophobia, Rita Süssmuth, a prominent politician, called upon Germans "to make the day of German unity a symbolic demonstration against xenophobia, racism, and the perfidious spirit of anti-Semitism."[30] Again the Jew is invoked through an analogy to the foreigner, immigrant, asylum seeker, and while the comparison does indeed appear to work, it also reflects the tendency in Germany to operate in such absolutes.[31] These anti-German attitudes unfortunately encourage exoticizing the authentically foreign as objects to admire and celebrate, like displays in a museum, more than as people to get to know. It is not surprising that this leftist anti-German attitude includes the attraction of foreign restaurants, cultural festivals, and travels to third-world countries. For those who were not critical of Israel for political reasons, as was common among West German leftists at the time or now since the Second Intifada, it also has led to philo-Semitic enthusiasm for Jews and anything Jewish.

While the communist GDR underplayed the Jews and tried to create a different German identity tied to anti-fascism, the West German left tended to deny their (West) German national identity by making a too simplistic elision between nationalism and fascism. The right and even respectable conservatives had a different but also problematic response. Over-identified as they were with being German and the notion of a homogeneous and homogenized unified German *Kulturnation* (cultural nation), these people continued to speak of Germany as "kein Einwanderungsland" (not a country of immigration) until very recently, although approximately 15 percent of the workforce were migrants. More importantly, these attitudes focused the population's attention on xenophobia rather than racism with the implication that only changes in the law will solve the problem of foreigners in Germany. By proclaiming themselves to be "foreigners," the leftists wound up victimizing and patronizing those they wanted to help. By directing the focus on the foreigners, even leftists avoided dealing with the racism that spawned the violence from certain segments of Germans. Conservatives for their part, by adhering to an unrealistic image of an essentially white, Christian Germany, diverted attention to the foreigners and the laws to manage them, rather than to more deep-seated racist attitudes among the population. Because of its history and its different context of meanings in German, race has never been adequately acknowledged. A language exists for anti-Semitism and xenophobia that does not yet adequately articulate problems around race and racism.[32] Psychologist Birgit Rommelsbacher has noted, "In spite of the many attacks and in spite of Hoyerswerda, racism is rarely straightforwardly addressed. Instead, the President of the Federal Republic speaks of the 'crisis of human understanding,' social psychologists of the 'natural fear of the foreign' and 'normal reactions to stress.'" She claims that for Germans the notion of racism in itself is taboo and therefore ignored, just as are the problems of dealing with the Nazi past.[33] However, references to the Holocaust may be made freely because it has become an acceptable topic in German public discourse. Rafael Seligmann reaffirms this point when he reminds the Germans that they are better at commemorating "dead Jews" than taking care of their living ones.[34] Politicians conscientiously atone for their sins by invoking the horrors of the Nazi regime, but then can go on to do little about attacks on foreigners.

In East Germany, where much of the early violence against foreigners took place, the equation of xenophobia with the fascist Third Reich only supports those who now would like to characterize the former GDR as a fascistic state, as the inheritor of Nazism rather than its idealistic alternative that failed. However, one of the most powerful examples of dichotomizing positions that have affected Jews is the ideology of "anti-fascism" that was current in the GDR. It began as a legitimate notion that coalesced political efforts against the Nazis. But then it ballooned into a nebulous category that was discredited by its overuse by GDR politicians and ideologues who used it in their agenda of branding the Federal Republic as the inheritor of German fascism. The reification of the term came to overshadow and ultimately collapse important distinctions for understanding the Nazi period and the postwar years. As is well known, Nazism for the GDR had more to do with class warfare and imperialistic ambitions than racial ideologies underlying persecution and genocide. While some Jews in the GDR hardly acknowledged their Jewish heritage, especially those prominent in the Communist Party, others lived comfortably with multiple affiliations as Jews, Germans, and communists. Still others found it difficult to come to terms with the ways antifascism was turned against Israel as part of the general attacks on Western imperialism. Antifascist resistance against the Nazi regime, which included some Jews, still overshadowed Jewish suffering since these fighters' ideology suited the GDR's needs much better and made them more suitable examples for propaganda.[35]

It is clear that the GDR's program of antifascism and obligatory people's solidarity failed. The historian Konrad Jarausch has pointed out that the GDR historians "fixated upon the Nazi menace in the past, and failed to criticize the threat of Erich Honecker's police state in the present" and "did not engage the racial dimension of anti-Semitism and insufficiently inoculated youths against xenophobia."[36] Through the 1990s and even today, the economic and social inequities of the reunification process in fact sustain these citizens' hostility toward the foreigners in their midst, in addition to their own resentment at having been constituted as an "other" by the West Germans. The sociologist Nora Räthzel redefined the problem: "In the course of extended immigration, East Germans seem to have lost their Germanness and become the Other. Now they are not seen as embodying the typical characteristics of the true industrious German, but as possessing a number of negative attributes. . . . All of these negative characteristics, however, have to do not with their being 'German by blood' but with their being socialized in the Communist system."[37]

Frustrated at having been rejected by their German brothers and sisters, especially after the warm welcome they were given when the Wall came down, East Germans may well be longing to belong and to be taken back into the German fold. The presence of *Aussiedler* and Jewish *Kontingentenflüchtlinge* who are being financially supported by the government with subsidies, housing, and language courses is a slap in the face for many Germans, especially those that are suffering from the economic downsizing after reunification. Their "Sieg Heils" and chants of "Deutschland nur den Deutschen" (Germany only for the Germans) express the desires of demoralized youths with no hope and no future to be reintegrated into a secure social fabric. They also set their sights falsely on a utopian ideal of a pure German nation that was already completely discredited under Nazism and has no place in a German civil society today.

While Jews and "ethnic" Germans from the former Soviet Union are in the foreign mix today, as are other groups from southern and eastern Europe who have been free to move after 1990, it was primarily the influx of the *Gastarbeiter* to West Germany that changed the ethnic complexion of the country. The GDR had its own guestworkers as well, from Angola, Mozambique, Vietnam, and Cuba, who remained isolated from the natives even with all the platitudes about socialist solidarity. This international presence created a debate around a multicultural present and its German future. One forgets today that this migration of Turks and other guest workers came at the invitation of the German government. The burgeoning number of foreigners who followed the call took on jobs many Germans did not want and, as they grew more populous, threatened German identity. Ironically, in their view, it also challenged their economic futures, especially after 1990 in East Germany whose dire economic status had now become obvious.

While numbers alone cannot completely explain Germany's problems with foreigners, they do illustrate the stage upon which this multicultural drama is played out. Above all, it also has to be remembered that Germany's historical relationship to foreigners and to the modern concept of multiculturalism that developed in the 1970s and 1980s is quite different from the United States or Canada, which have traditionally been countries of immigration, or for other European powers such as France, Great

Britain, Holland, or Belgium who had large overseas colonies. Germany's problematic relationship to "others" in its midst emerges from the specifically German notions of community and nation which created a tradition unsympathetic to foreign elements: specifically, its citizens' relationship to the foreign (normative and prescriptive social attitudes), postwar Germans' difficulty of thinking of themselves in positive terms (rejecting any forms of national identification or pride), the lack of experience with foreigners (a limited colonial tradition), and the inheritance of Germany's systematic elimination of foreign or different peoples in the Third Reich (Jews, Slavs, Roma and Sinti [Gypsies], Jehovah's Witnesses, homosexuals). Berndt Ostendorf, an expert on comparative German and American multiculturalism, has stated categorically: "It is not surprising that the German 'crisis of multiculturalism' was first felt when the second generation, the *Gastarbeiterkinder* [guestworkers' children], came of age. This second generation did not enjoy the job safety of their parents and had no rights as citizens although, in marked contrast to their parents, they were born and raised in Germany . . . the second generation began to experience an identity crisis, that is, the dual pull of being de facto German, but de jure *Ausländer* [foreigner]."[38]

Lacking the American ethos inscribed in Emma Lazarus's words on the Statue of Liberty, Germany did not have immigration laws although it had immigrants categorized under other names. Above all, it did not have a notion of identity that was porous enough to accommodate such great differences. Germans felt overwhelmed; Turks felt ignored, despised, and even persecuted. Germany's liberal democracy was still being tested when it came to managing a diverse society that came to be understood under the term "multiculturalism." The attacks directly after reunification made many wonder how this drama was to end. The past hung heavily over the heated multicultural debate that followed and continues to this day. In fact, the discussion of *Leitkultur* is only one of many reiterations of questions of identity and belonging that still remain unresolved. Turks, like Jews, rejected the notion of one "dominant culture" to which they should conform. While it is legitimate to expect that new citizens learn the language, history, and culture of their adopted country, this should not mean giving up other identities they want to keep. As is the case in the United States or Canada, they wanted the option of maintaining multiple affiliations that would allow them the freedom of developing what citizens of these traditional immigration countries take for granted as a hyphenated identity. Turkish Germans, Afro-Germans, and of course, Jewish Germans or even new German Jews should be viable options.

For these people, of course, citizenship does not solve all the problems of being foreign or strange. There are ways of belonging that are not captured, for example, in the idea of homeland. "Heimat," the particularly German notion of homeland, is rife with nationalistic, ethno-racial overtones left over from the Nazi era and considered the exclusive territory of Germans, even today. In the 1990s German neo-conservatives tried to rehabilitate the term and make it acceptable in public discourse. Although such claims of national pride expressed in terms like "I am proud to be a German" might now be more acceptable, these words are still more closely associated with skinheads than with respectable politicians. Few Jewish or Turkish Germans would be comfortable uttering such a phrase.

It seems, as a *Spiegel* journalist has noted, "Germans like strangers best when they are far away."[39] Distance between Germany and their foreigners is not only about a place in the national homeland, it is also about social class, which leads to seeing foreigners only as capable of being fruit salesman and cleaning women with whom many Germans have limited social contact in their own neighborhood or office. The old-fashioned "Blut-und-Boden" (blood and soil) ideology reemerges here as an exclusionary tactic in nefarious though in less obvious and programmatic ways than it did in the nineteenth and the early twentieth century. A notion of German "Heimat," as it is played out in everyday life, allows increasingly for civic legal and political acceptance. However, it still makes belonging, as a social, psychological, or cultural issue, difficult to achieve. The confusion of being German in a civic sense and being "a German" as part of an ethnic German community—a new version of the old German notion of "Gesellschaft/Gemeinschaft" (society/community) debate—creates frustrated expectations on both sides. Many Jews are now citizens of Germany, because of German birth, new citizenship after the war (former DPs), and recent immigration from the Soviet Union. More Turks are applying for citizenship, although their numbers are lower than had been expected.[40]

These groups also continue to unsettle static notions of space and place. Just as "culture" itself, according to anthropologists E. Valentine Daniel and John Knudsen, is not "essential" or "fixed," but "a creative activity of symbol making and symbol sharing, . . . fundamentally dialogic,"[41] the relationship of Jews and Turks to their fellow Germans is also always in flux. It is always reconstituting new forms and meanings that to their German fellow citizens may seem to undermine the status quo of a permanent identity. Jews insist on remembering the Holocaust and Turks insist on maintaining their customs, as do Jews. The former continues to call attention to a past tragedy and a present responsibility some would like to put behind them. The latter foregrounds their blatant difference simply by outward appearance. As if to call the notion of "Leitkultur" constantly into question, these two groups are ciphers of difference and dislocation: they mark the relationship of history (the past to the present), ethnicity (German and foreigner), religion (Christian and non-Christian), and place (here and there). Thus, Jews and Turks are constant reminders of history and its import for contemporary identities that are intertwined and constantly shifting. Their mere presence unsettles the established notion of what it means to be German.

Many Jews and Turks find their identity within a collective because living in Germany presumes contradictions that are literally quite strange to Germans. Jews are not only non-Christian, but the distinction between ethnicity and religion is ambiguous and casts doubts on their ability to be really German, in other words, to have a coherent identity. Being Jewish does not only mean belonging to a religion, but also to a cultural and ethnic group that, of course, is dispersed in the Diaspora even with an official Jewish homeland. Known for their mobility and dislocation, the Gypsies, persecuted under the Nazis as today, represent in Europe a nomadic existence that makes them suspicious and untrustworthy to those who associate identity with a fixed home like Heimat and its rewards. Jews too are seen to have allegiances elsewhere. On the one hand, their special status can be interpreted conservatively as solidarity with Israel, or on the other hand, more liberally as Jewish identification with a notion of "Weltbürgertum" (secular world citizenship) carried on from their emancipation in the German Enlightenment. All Jews, even German Jews, are suspect because they represent these dual allegiances quite literally.

The Turks' ambivalence toward making Germany their home is not about whether they literally stay, but rather their insistence on questioning the dominant status of Germans who would control the conditions for their belonging. Even after two or three and in many cases even four generations, their desire to belong is also being questioned since many want to have a dual identity that would allow them to be simultaneously Turkish and German. The notion of multiple identities occupying the same subject position remains ironically "foreign," as one Turkish German feared, using the Jews as his reference, "Can I still return to Turkey, or am I a person, like the Jews before me, without a homeland?"[42]

Since German reunification and the creation of a "new Germany," the memory of the Third Reich has loomed large again. World Jewry repeatedly warned the leaders of the short-lived East German republic and then the new Germany that after forty-five years fears were reemerging about a militarily and economically dominant unified Germany in the middle of Europe. Germany's European neighbors also initially were reserved about this new German might in their midst. Subsequently, anxieties were quieted for a while until the resurgence of right-wing attacks on foreigners. Again the specter of Nazism seemed to be rearing its ugly head, especially for Americans who are quick to see Nazis around every corner. While the Nazi horrors need to be remembered, it is an injustice to compare the victims of both historical periods with each other. The Jews' tragedy was not only their persecution and extermination because they were different, religiously, ethnically, and according to the Nazis racially, but also the fact that in Germany their common ties through citizenship and nationhood meant nothing.

The comparisons for today's foreigners are even more unfair. Unlike the Jews who have the Jewish Community for support, most foreign immigrants are largely poor, uneducated, disenfranchised by their own country and without the protection of civil rights. They have come from economically disadvantaged countries and nations ravaged by war, some as legitimate political refugees threatened with death, torture, or imprisonment, and others as economic refugees, seeking a better future. To many, they were merely taking advantage of Germany's liberal asylum law (until it was changed in 1993), itself inspired by the Nazi past and its treatment of Jews and other minorities. However, above all they are not white and have less of a chance of being integrated into society than other minorities. These potential new Germans, based not on legal citizenship but on acceptance and belonging, are not given a chance to develop more complicated multiple identities as a Turkish-, Tamil-, or Angolan-German. Even an uneasy symbiosis, like the infamous German-Jewish one, is not possible for many refugees, some of whom now legally reside in Germany or have the equivalent of the American "green card." But, as has been proven repeatedly, German citizenship does not guarantee first-class treatment, as Turkish German former Green parliamentarian Cem Özdemir has often pointed out in interviews. As early as 1989, the anthropologist Andrea Klimt showed in her fieldwork with Portuguese guestworkers: "None of the migrants I knew, regardless of class, generation, or degree of 'integration,' considered the prospect of 'becoming German' to be desirable, realistic, or even imaginable. They, along with most Germans, understand that, 'being German' does not rest on such mutable characteristics as legal status, political loyalty, or acquired knowledge. Germanness is not perceived to be an open and permeable category, and Portuguese migrants feel that neither the color of their passports nor the degree of their cultural and linguistic fluency will ensure respect or acceptance."[43]

It seems that regardless of class, ethnicity, national identity, or skin color many Germans still see these original guestworkers as others. On a *Spiegel* title page, a more frighteningly contemporary commentary pictured quite literally exclusionary categories and stereotypes that are apparently still fixed in public consciousness. At the top of the page the words "Foreigners and Germans" are paired with the bright yellow letters "dangerously different" juxtaposed with incendiary stereotypes of what appears to be a Turkish woman (who looks black) leading a demonstration, Turkish girls studying in headscarves, and four Turkish boys holding weapons. The subtitle reads: "The failure of a multicultural society."[44]

If foreigners and asylum seekers from other parts of the world are to receive the humane treatment they deserve today in one of the richest countries in the world, then the so-called foreigner problem in Germany must be seen as a "German problem" deriving from residual racist attitudes as an economic and social dilemma. Germany hesitated to acknowledge officially that it is a "land of immigration" because once the problem is officially removed by legal and subsequent social recognition that might develop under more auspicious conditions of immigration, the underlying racism will become all the more evident. It will not necessarily disappear with "integration" into German life as long as both the left and the right are blinded by their inability to construct a new and more heterogeneous identity and to acknowledge the benefits of immigration.

Neither foreigners, Germans, or Jews can be made to fit into monolithic or universal categories; differentiation and specificity rather than uniformity and abstraction will contribute to a more nuanced and historically sensitive analysis. The comparison to Jews and the Nazi period may be a logical link. It may also serve as a kind of objective correlative to fears that have no analogue except in Nazism. But such historical invocations should at least be recognized as a questionable displacement of emotions from the object of hostility today to a mystifying past horror that continues to be exploited. The years 1989 to 1992 were not a replay of 1933 to 1945. Reunification was no more a completely new beginning than was 1945. When comparisons are taken out of context, they threaten to overshadow the injustices of both historical epochs.

Ten years after the Solingen incident, 2002 marked an unhappy anniversary for Turks as they commemorated what happened. May of that year also marked the inception of the new anti-Semitism. Turks and Jews were drawn together again, this time to form solidarities against renewed hostility toward those who were different. In fact, the leading secular Turkish-German association in Berlin, the TBB (Berlin-Brandenburg Turkish Federation) has explicitly been using comparisons between Turks and Jews to enhance their standing. As Gökçe Yurdakul and Michal Bodemann point out in their recent research: "Turkish immigrant associations show the similarities between the racism against Turks and anti-Semitism and argue that racism against immigrants in Germany today is an extension of previous anti-Semitic history. . . . Turkish immigrant associations (also) take Jewish associations as a master narrative and a political model for their own communities and also claim minority rights analogous to those of German Jews."[45] In other words, this powerful group of organized Turks recognizes how the Jewish story in Germany is connected to their own.

Now, the Turks in Germany have their own tragedy to commemorate. This event has been called "a turning point in the telling of time, a dividing line,"[46] in the words of "a defiant young woman interviewed in 1998 . . . for we say here; the time before the fire and the time after it."[47] Although the numbers of killed or injured were small, these bold attacks on Turks became symbolic moments of estrangement, persecution, and death. In the presence of leading figures from the Jewish Community and the Jewish Cultural Society invited to the commemoration,[48] the spokesman from the TBB stated, "This racist event in Mölln is similar to the anti-Semitic events in Germany."[49] He also went so far as to encourage German Turks who are residents of Germany "to shoulder this part [the Holocaust] of German history."[50] His point was that if Turks want to be residents of Germany, they are responsible for German history.[51]

This dramatic move points to an increasing solidarity between Jews and Turks not only through common suffering but also through utilizing their intertwining histories to promote political action. For example, the Berlin office of the American Jewish Committee meets regularly with Jewish and Turkish leaders to discuss common problems and mutual support. However, there are still yawning disparities between what the Jewish and Turkish communities receive. One German official admitted in 1999: "When you just look at the size of the population represented . . . there are about 10,000 Jews and roughly 150,000 Turks. If you compare the [respective] financial support for the Turkish and Jewish Communities, you would, of course, say this is unacceptably disproportionate."[52] The Turkish Community understands that there are historical reasons for this special status. However, this did not stop one leader of a Turkish group from remarking, "Every time a Jew opens his mouth, he has money and all sorts of things poured into it."[53] The numbers show that the Jewish Community, especially in Berlin, receives 45 million of its 48 million German Marks (DM) budget from the Berlin government and the Turkish umbrella organizations (around 35) receive only 1.5 million; the 40,000 member Türkische Gemeinde (Turkish Community), only 54,000 DM.[54] However, despite these differences, this work that is being done by the minorities themselves, the Jews and the Turks, must include and even be initiated by the majority Christian German population. This work must be accomplished not only in terms of financial support, but also through a change of attitude and perspectives toward those who are different. This participation is necessary if the dominant population wants to come to terms with the de facto heterogeneous society of the new millennium that acknowledges the multicultural character of the country and the changes in the nature of identity as Turkish, Jewish, or German.

Unfortunately, few people in Germany speak about Jews and Turks in the ways that I have here. Building on a tradition of various minorities seeking political solidarity, such as the Jews and blacks in the 1960s and 1970s, and later blacks and Latinos, American scholars of Germany have done much to draw attention to these two groups' potential relationship to each other. The only German scholar I know who addresses these topics seriously is Zafer Şenocak, who is, in fact, a Turkish German. He was born in 1961 in Ankara, arrived in Germany with his parents in 1970 and became a citizen in 1992. He is considered a second-generation writer like Seligmann, Honigmann, and the others. In one of his essays contained in a selection of his work published for the first time in English and appropriately entitled *An Atlas of a Tropical Germany*,[55] he addresses the

German-Jewish dimension as part of the problem of being "foreign" in Germany.

I have known Şenocak personally for many years. He is unusually sensitive to issues concerning Turks and Jews. Having spent increasingly more time in America as a resident author, he acknowledges the interest in America for linking the Turks and Jews through problems of history and identity. Şenocak speaks directly to this issue in his 1995 interview for the Berlin daily *Der Tagesspiegel* and published in his collection as "May one compare Jews and Turks, Mr. Şenocak?"[56] In fact, he often addresses minority issues dealing with home, belonging, and community. In Şenocak's terms a comparison is appropriate, but as Leslie Adelson, his translator and editor, points out, comparisons should not be "ready-made prototypes of sociological comparison,"[57] but rather the "imaginative project of *Berührungsgeschichte*, a history of Germans, Turks, and Jews 'coming in contact' with each other"[58] Adelson comments on how Şenocak, echoing the TTB's declaration, confirms that these groups must come to terms with the implications of their interactions with each other's histories for their own pasts, presents, and futures. Şenocak, a Turk living in Germany, must come to terms with a "vexed German history."[59] When he questions, "Doesn't immigrating to Germany also mean immigrating to, entering into, the arena of Germany's recent past? . . . Even the bitter experiences that led to the [near] annihilation of the Jewish minority must be reflected upon in the conception of a multicultural Europe."[60] Occupying the same temporal and historical space and confronting differential cultural norms and values means that Turks coincide with the traumas of German Jewish history, as well contemporary battles over identity and integration in a new Europe. Though he is critical of Germany (or at least was in 1995), Şenocak is optimistic, albeit guarded: "There is hope, in the fact that, fifty years after the nearly complete annihilation of the Jews in Germany, there are once more citizens of Jewish faith there. That there can be something like a Turk who is a Muslim and also a German citizen. The hope that people of Italian, Greek, Turkish, and Arab descent can communicate with each other in German in Germany and are citizens, from my perspective, is still a utopia."[61]

Now almost a decade later, the German immigration law has changed and a third, and even fourth, generation of Turk resides in Germany. There are 2.3 million Turks in Germany, 28 percent of the 7.3 million foreigners. Only a small number of them have become citizens. In 1999, there were approximately 298,000 Turks with German citizenship and 41,000 in Berlin alone.[62] Perhaps this is understandable when there are still German politicians like Jürgen Rüttgers who, in his 2000 election campaign in the German state of Nordrhein-Westfalen, used the rhymed slogan, "Kinder statt Inder!" (Children, instead of Indians) to raise fears of foreigners taking computer jobs away from Germans when the country's population is dangerously declining.

It remains to be seen how Jews and Turks will work together in the future, be it in political lobbying against discrimination or through multi-cultural events that demonstrate that there are different ways of being German. Today in the context of September 11 and the Middle East conflicts that might pit Jews against Muslim Turks in Germany, it is gratifying that the Turkish Community supported the Jewish Community during the Möllemann debate as well as in 2004 after the Istanbul synagogue bombing. They continue to reach out to the Jews just as Ignatz Bubis and Paul Spiegel appeared at Turkish rallies against discrimination. Increasingly, prominent conservative Jews such as Michael Wolffsohn are calling for more collaboration: "Germany's Jews need now an important strategic partner who stands outside of party lines. They would find such a partner in the German-Turkish community. As we are, they are a minority (substantially larger than us). Their orientation is pro-Western, market oriented, and they reject Islamicism, precisely because they are Muslims."[63] The Turkish Community also reaches out by organizing collaborative events such as "Das jüdische Leben in Istanbul. Das türkische Leben in Berlin" (Jewish Life in Istanbul. Turkish Life in Berlin).

As "Racism grows against Jews and Muslim," as reported by the *European Union Monitor* on December 12, 2002, Jews and Turks in Germany might unfortunately find common ground in increased prejudice against them both.[64] European efforts may be needed to counteract such hostile generalizing trends that go beyond the borders of Germany and stereotype "all Jews," "all Muslims," or all "others." The recent 2004 "Berlin Declaration" of the OSCE (Office of Security and Cooperation in Europe) Conference on Anti-Semitism and its active work against anti-Semitism was one such example. As the growing European Union goes into high gear to unify and harmonize policies, each country must examine its own historical treatment of minorities. Each will also have to find ways today to integrate disparate groups of immigrants, minorities, and other subjugated communities in their double national and European identities. This integration will have to recognize the "discourse of the other" in the terms of the Turkish-German scholar Şenocak: "Integration is not achieved when the differences of others are used to consolidate one's own image of the world. For real integration one must cultivate, in encounters with others, a sense for multiplicity and contradiction. In the process one would have to analyze sources of knowledge beyond preconceived opinions and identities. Disparate factors would have to be deciphered as a precondition for an encounter."[65]

Such encounters, like the one between Turks and Jews in Germany, will force these countries and their minorities to disentangle their individual histories from the dominant national narratives that, in many cases, are still being written and revised. We have seen Native and African Americans, as Jews before them, demand to be recognized as part of the national chronicle. Although these stories become increasingly complex and often contradictory, this difficult process will produce more open societies that understand themselves as composed of "others" who offer alternative versions of national and ethnic identities. We can only hope that there will be space enough for multiple stories to be told.

6

Creating a
Continental Identity

JEWS, GERMANS, EUROPE, AND
THE "NEW" ANTI-SEMITISM

In 1989–1990, the epicenters of Europe's profound transformation were Germany and the Soviet Union, the Continent's central powers. The fault lines that cracked open old regimes spread from East to West redefining the boundaries of citizens' relationships to their national, ethnic, and religious identities. As we saw, Russian Jews were now free to become both "Jews" and "Germans," or sometimes even both. In more recent years, far-reaching global events, such as September 11, 2001, the continued Middle East crisis, and the Iraq War have further unsettled European identity as the EU enlarged and simultaneously confronted the difficulties of a stronger, yet more contentious international position. Internal European disagreements about developing a unified foreign policy on these matters and dealing with its Muslim populations and anti-Semitism have also complicated the Jewish and German positions. As the EU debates its constitution (which is now failing), potential Turkish membership, and its relationship to Israel and the United States, the organization is becoming aware of how its minorities, both Jews and Muslims, will shape its future character and image. This range of issues also shows how complex and emotional the so-called Jewish question remains in Europe today, especially in a global scenario that cannot ignore the Arab Middle East, Israel, and European Muslims in its deliberations.

The infamous Jewish question in Europe today, however, concerns the future as well as the past. The reference points are security of the Jewish inhabitants in each country and their communal status in a more unified Europe, as well as the Holocaust and its legacy in Europe and Germany. Of course, the latter cannot be forgotten. As Serge DellaPergola, a prominent demographer of European Jewry, has flatly stated, "The chief single factor capable of explaining the variable patterns of three hundred years of Jewish demographic history—stronger than any other geographical, political, or sociological criterion—is the intensity of the Holocaust in each country."[1] In 1939, before the genocide, European Jews accounted for approximately 60 percent of the world's Jewish population[2] and by 2003 it was only 12 percent (1,550,800) of a total population of 12,950,000.[3] The traces of the Holocaust scar the new European identity aside from absent numbers. This is the case not only in Germany, the keystone of a future Europe that in 1945 had little future for a Jewish life. World Jewry even instituted a "ban" on Jewish life in Germany. Other factors such as fertility, intermarriage, mortality, and natural migration have also contributed to the dramatic drop in numbers. And as I have pointed out, the major migration from the former Soviet Union to Germany has changed the balance of European Jewry from East to West. However, as the story of the Jews in Europe unfolds sixty years after the conflagration that almost wiped out the entire population, the European Jewish community must also look ahead even with the mixed blessings of hope and concern.

Against the backdrop of anti-Semitic and anti-Israel sentiments, Europe is, in fact, caught on the horns of a dilemma caused by the surge of Jewish activity continent-wide and a diminishing population. Germany has always been a major European power, both in its more benign and more aggressive forms. Naturally, and also largely by design, this large country at the center of the continent also emerges as one of the strongest new players in the European future. At the same time, it also has the fastest growing Jewish community in Europe and has taken responsibility for its past crimes more than any of its European neighbors. Nevertheless, the picture today is not as sanguine as it was in the 1990s, when I would have presented a largely positive narrative of Jewish life in Europe. Half a decade into the new millennium, the situation is more complicated and ambivalent. My story must now take into account how we are to understand the conflicting signs of reinvigorated life and, in the extreme, the threat of potential death. What position do Germany and its Jews have in this new constellation? I want to look especially at the European Union and European Jewish organizations as they shape a European Jewish identity. Then I want to address how this identity affects notions of Germanness and German-Jewish identity for creating a positive European Jewish space, populated by both Jews and non-Jews and for combating anti-Semitism. We must bluntly ask What kind of European Jewish life will there be in the future and what might it look like?

Recent expressions of hate and prejudice mitigate the optimism of the revolutionary years of 1989–1990 and renew uncertainty about the safety, security, and for some, even the survival of Jewish life on the Continent. While these issues concern all Jews, prominent observers of Jewish Europe differ on the condition and future of Jewish life. Even before the recent outbreak of anti-Semitism, European historian Bernard Wasserstein in 1996 augured in his study, *Vanishing Diaspora: The Jews in Europe since 1945*, the complete disappearance of Jews due to a diminishing population.[4] Around the same time, another British scholar, this time a social anthropologist, Jonathan Webber, promoted a more socially constructed, fluid, and optimistic notion of Jewish identity in his volume *Jewish Identities in the New Europe*.[5] Taking a somewhat more controversial point of view, an American Jew, Ruth Gruber, who writes widely on contemporary European Jewish issues, bemoaned in her 2002 book, *Virtually Jewish: Reinventing Jewish Culture in Europe*, the prominence of what she calls "virtual Jews."[6] Finally, Diana Pinto, an Italian Jew living in France, who is a historian and consultant to the Political Directorate, Council of Europe, presented the most hopeful perspectives about what she calls the "new European Jewish space."[7] These various Jewish expert voices, to whom I will return, are acutely aware of the contradictions in Jewish identity and the complicated picture of Jewish life in the 1990s and in these early years of the millennium.

At the moment, of course, there appears to be a particularly European antipathy toward Israel and the upsurge of what is called the "new" anti-Semitism that raises serious concerns among Jews. The OSCE conferences held in Vienna in June 2003 and very prominently in Berlin in April 2004 are serious responses to the hostility directed toward Jews in the last few years. Significant attention has also been given to the link between anti-Semitism and anti-Americanism. This controversial position is prompted by the United States' involvement in Iraq and myths of an American-Israeli Jewish conspiracy that have reemerged, especially in the Arab world. Such hyperbole grows like bad weeds when questions of Jewish power and influence are used as weapons against the two countries that have the largest Jewish populations in the world and the strongest influence on German Jewry. Such exaggeration and prejudice have gone so far as to suggest that the Israeli intelligence service, Mossad, was behind the September 11 attacks in New York and Washington and that the Jews who worked there knew of the attacks in advance and stayed home. The infamous anti-Semitic text *The Protocols of the Elders of Zion* has become popular grist for the anti-Semitic mill in the Arab world and has been turned into a popular television series in Egypt. Even in Germany a book appeared implying that such conspiracies exist. European journalists, politicians, and academics in France, Britain, and other countries have added fuel to the fire by spouting anti-Semitic invectives, instituting boycotts of Israeli scholars, and publishing cartoons equating Sharon with Hitler.[8]

However, whether from vulnerability or paranoia, politicians and journalists, not only Jewish ones, have been making dramatic statements about the threats of anti-Semitism. In the midst of the current turmoil, an American ambassador to the EU, Rockwell Schnabel (a Bush political appointee), claims that anti-Semitism in Europe was "getting to a point where it is as bad as it was in the 30s."[9] Although American officials have dissociated themselves from this extreme position, such fears are voiced by European Jews as well. Among them is Cobi Benatoff, the president of the European Jewish Congress, who stated in ominous language: "The monster is here with us again."[10] Holocaust survivor and Nobel Prize–winning author Elie Wiesel called it "a European disease."[11] These remarks, expressed in vivid metaphors, are reminiscent of American fears I documented in chapter 5 when Turks were attacked and murdered in Mölln and Solingen. In contrast, another prominent Jewish official, David Susskind, honorary president of the Center of Secular Jewish Communities of Belgium, tempered these frightful indictments by pointing to Europe's liberal democratic traditions: "We Jews who live in Europe live in states governed by the rule of law."[12] A prominent German journalist asked more judiciously in the title of an article in the esteemed newspaper *Die Zeit*: "Why this fear? New distrust shapes German Jewish debates in recent weeks."[13]

This range of feeling and opinion implies either the possibility of a new European Jewish genocide and naiveté or over-optimism. Roman Prodi, the former president of the European Union, finally stated he would encourage EU states to fight against "all manifestations of racism, xenophobia, anti-Semitism."[14] Prodi, of course, was also accused of anti-Semitism by world Jewish leaders for censoring an EU-sponsored study on the topic which claimed that Muslims in Europe were primarily responsible for attacks on Jews. He cancelled and then reinstated a proposed EU conference on anti-Semitism when Jewish officials accused him of being anti-Semitic. A major report, "Manifestations of Anti-Semitism in the European Union," sponsored by the European Monitoring Centre on Racism and Xenophobia (EUMC) and written by scholars at the highly regarded Center for Research on Anti-Semitism, Technical University Berlin, also suffered this fate.[15] Despite the controversy aroused, such conferences and reports continue to focus attention on anti-Semitism, as another OSCE meeting held in June 2004 in Paris on hate speech on the Internet and one in Brussels in September 2004 on racism, xenophobia, and discrimination demonstrate.

Aside from the OSCE's action on anti-Semitism, perhaps the most positive development has come from the European Jewish communities themselves as they work together to set up strategic plans for building cooperation and influence. The most important group, the broad-based European Council of Jewish Communities (ECJC), reflects the changes in the last fifteen years in the council's mission and in European Jewish needs. In May 2004, it published a detailed plan from its Commission on Strategic Planning for the period May 2004 to May 2008. Aside from presenting a mission statement and operational guidelines, the document substantively recommends that the ECJC focuses on what they call "six main tracks": education, social welfare, culture and heritage, Jewish contributions to civil society, community capacity development, and representing Jewish interests in Brussels.[16] Significantly, issues of racism and anti-Semitism are included in the last point that is identified with communal politics at the inter-European level. This represents the shift toward increasing political action and influence in the organization's agenda and a change from its orientation in the early 1990s when it was merely called the European Council of Jewish Communal Services (ECJCS).

The unification of Europe forced the organization to reconfigure itself. It grew from a bridge between West and East with fifteen national affiliates who primarily worked in the area of education, social welfare, and culture into approximately seventy member organizations in forty-one countries by 2003.[17] They represent approximately 2.5 million Jews in thirty-seven countries. France, with 600,000, Britain, with 340,000, and Germany, with 100,000, are the three largest communities, with smaller numbers in all other European countries, from Turkey with 26,000 to Poland with 10,000 and Bosnia Herzegovina and Luxemburg with 1,000 each. Increasingly, the ECJC is working internationally by collaborating with American Jewish organizations, such as the American Jewish Committee, American Joint Distribution Committee, the Conference of Presidents of Major American Jewish Organizations, B'nai Brith International, and Agudat Israel. It holds seats on the Claims Conference and World Jewish Restitution

Organization[18] and works closely with the European Jewish Congress and has sponsored all-European meetings in Madrid, Prague, and Budapest. These meetings, in the words of one commentator, are part of efforts "to create a pan-European Jewish entity that can take an active part in the formation of a democratic Europe."[19] Other events have also been organized, such as European Days of Jewish Culture and Heritage initiated by B'nai Brith Europe and even Chanukah Olamit (global Chanukah) sponsored by the Agency for Jewish Education, which links Jewish day schools around Europe. Children lit Chanukah candles and sang Maoz Tzur as a web camera focused on the Western Wall in Jerusalem. The second Bet Debora conference of European female rabbis, cantors, and interested Jewish participants from primarily Reform, but also Conservative and Orthodox congregations, met in Berlin dedicated to the theme "Jewish Family—Myth and Reality."[20] These events reveal the political, social, and religious involvement of the European Jewish communities with diverse issues. They have also organized political protests against anti-Semitism, such as an organized march of nearly ten thousand people in Brussels, the home of the European Union, on May 29, 2002.[21] Clearly, Europe's Jews, as is reflected in the discussions at their meetings, seek to coalesce around both serious and joyful events.

A closer look into particular meetings sponsored by ECJC reveals both the confidence and turmoil of the time. Nineteen ninety-five was an optimistic moment to see European Jews constituting a "third pillar" in world Jewry between the two largest communities in the United States and Israel. Michael May, then executive director of the ECJC and now executive director of the Jewish Community of Berlin, made this point forcefully at the first such meeting since the end of communism called "Planning for the Future of European Jewry." European Jewry, he stated, is in the process of asserting itself as the third bloc within the world Jewish community: "Both America and Israel are, to some extent, living off European themes and transitions; however, the Europeans are seen as the poor relatives. We wish to change this perception and this conference is the first step in this direction."[22]

In 2002, another ECJC Prague conference took place. A journalist in an article not coincidentally titled "New chapter in Jewish history emerges in Europe," also characterized the Jewish community very optimistically. Yet he added some specific new qualities: "What's happening is that the size and composition of the Jewish communities in Europe are changing in ways that reflect the era of globalization, Internet communication, the broadening culture of the soon-to-expand European Union, and the search of personal identity."[23] In fact, many participants at this Prague meeting, while recognizing the grave dangers of anti-Semitism, consider Jewish life "flourishing," according to Julian Voloj from the 200,000-strong European Union of Jewish Students (EUJS). He continues: "There's a lot going on. We should not just focus on negative things, but on the future."[24] As Ruth Gruber reports, panelists and audience members also debated "how to prevent legitimate concern over current events from blurring into paranoia."[25] A Portuguese participant, Marta Mucznik, executive director of the EUJS, voiced this view: "We are concerned how to build a positive Jewish identity that is not just based on the Middle East. This is part of our identity, but it should not be all."[26]

For Voloj, the former president of the German student group and a former leader of EUJS, the work of European Jews that spans the Continent is even more powerful than that of the European Union. Their initiative is also supported by the regularly sponsored pan-European Summer University where five hundred young Jews gather. Voloj is proud of their youthful accomplishments: "We are much further than the EU. We have thirty-two member countries—all of Europe from Finland to the Balkans, from Portugal to the eastern part of Russia. We experience the problems of European integration up close in our organization."[27] In short, European Jewish collaboration achieved what the EU has not yet accomplish. This younger generation, represented by Voloj and his associates, seems to be more strongly European than even their elders.

However, not immune from immediate events, in April of 2004, Voloj also expressed concern about the new wave of anti-Semitism, especially on European university campuses: "It's not politically incorrect anymore to speak against Jews."[28] He is working to educate Europeans about Israel and anti-Semitism and is even trying to pass a resolution at the European Youth Forum condemning anti-Jewish violence in Europe. According to his interviewer, Voloj "will coordinate a leadership training conference for European Jewish student leaders." He added, "If you're a Jewish student leader on campus in Europe, you have to know how to fight."[29] For Voloj, his organization, with 200,000 members, is the future of a new European Jewish identity, although sometimes he must fight stereotypes of European Jews toward German Jews like himself and Michael Friedman, the former director of the European Jewish Congress. Consequently, Jews in Germany, who lead important European organizations, must fight the same kind of prejudices that American Jews still feel for Germany. As part of a European organization of Jews and especially of Jewish young people, Jews in Germany can gain status and support for their fast-growing community that has brought Eastern and Western Jewry together again in an unexpected way.

The European Union itself represents opportunities for Jews who see that it offers support for Jewish unity and protection from discrimination under the Copenhagen Accords. Touching both sides of Jewish concerns, the EU stands for integration Europe-wide and for security within individual countries. Sharp conflicts between Prodi and prominent Jewish leaders following the EU expansion agreements in December 12–13, 2003, therefore, were a setback for EU-Jewish relations. Shortly after the EU expansion on May 1, 2004, which included Poland, the Czech Republic, Hungary, Slovakia, Slovenia, Latvia, Lithuania, Estonia, Malta, and Cyprus, a Polish Jewish activist said, "I doubt that there are any Jews in Poland or among our neighbors who are not in favor of us joining the EU." He continued, "The main thing is that we will be one body. For Jews this means that the idea of forming 'European Jewry' will be easier to explore. The national differences . . . will remain, but there will be an administrative background to European Jewish identity."[30] The well-known Polish Jewish journalist Konstantin Gebert made similar claims: "EU enlargement brings European Jews even closer together and will enable us to test out the 'third pillar' premise." He also sees membership in the EU offering to Jews "protection of E.U. laws on minorities."[31] Others, among them Salomon Korn, a vice president of the Central Council of Jews in Germany, have voiced concerns about new Eastern European member states which bring ingrained anti-Jewish sentiments to their political and economic opportunities.[32]

The concerns of these European Jewish leaders even after 2002 illustrate some of the tensions for European Jews in the continuing debate on internal Jewish communal issues, such as leadership, pluralism, structure, training, and the impact of outside political forces such as the Iraq War and Middle East politics in general. Although traditional anti-Semitism or anti-Israeli attitudes have come from the extreme left or right, it was noted at the Prague meeting how conventional political affiliations are being questioned. These changes are exemplified, for example, when in Germany, the strongest support for Israel and the Jews comes from the leftist Greens in the person of German Foreign Minister Joschka Fischer and in Italy from the rightist Berlusconi government.[33] Apparently political realignments in European politics are also challenging conventional assumptions of who supports the Jews or Israel.

Internal and external shifts within Jewish communities that are subject to European and international policies and national interests intensify the complex picture of European Jewry that must be seen as part of the new Europe itself as represented in the European Union and its myriad of institutions. Even with all of its problems and changes, the EU has surpassed the greatest expectations of postwar European leaders' hopes for a peaceful future with economic, political, and social cooperation. The issue of the Iraq War, its relationship to the United States and to Israel continues to be difficult. Although the EU is Israel's biggest trading partner, the organization has been sharply criticized for its pro-Palestinian and anti-Israeli stand by the United States, Israel, and Jews worldwide. Yet it is still unclear how the Jewish populations of the new Europe or individual European countries will ultimately benefit from the changing relationships that enlargement brings. While Russian-Jewish immigration to Germany is the largest, there are other movements such as Israeli emigration to the Czech Republic, Poland, and Norway. Some American Jews are also moving to Europe, as in the case of a New York lawyer who moved to Prague in 1990 to be part of the rebuilding process.[34] However, the Middle East crisis and the strong Muslim presence in particular European countries, such as Germany and especially France, have complicated the status of Jews in Europe and made both Muslims and Jews the object of racist attacks, especially since September 11.[35] In other words, the new unrest in the Middle East since September 2000 and September 11, 2001, have infused world politics into the "domestic" agenda of Jewish life in Germany and Europe. It has created different stakes for what Europeanization may mean in a world divided by religious and cultural rather than just political ideologies. In short, it reminds the world that culture matters.

My focus on discourses and activities rather than just facts and figures points to a reevaluation of the debate about a future for European Jewry since my own optimism about Jewish life in Germany or on the Continent counters statistics and demographic data that show decreased numbers. In his study, Wasserstein paints a dismal picture and concludes his book ruefully by comparing the fate of European Jews to those in China, "The Jews in Europe now face a similar destiny. Slowly but surely, they are fading away. Soon nothing will be left save a disembodied memory."[36] Fortunately (or unfortunately) benefiting from more tolerance, openness, and assimilation possible in an open Europe, Jews are marrying gentiles (estimated at almost 50 percent), having fewer Jewish babies, and not maintaining their spiritual and religious lives. For Wasserstein, as for Nahum Goldmann whom he cites, this process seems natural and should be accepted, "Peoples disappear in history by suicide, not by murder."[37] Wasserstein interprets further, "If the Jews of Europe do, in the end, disappear, it will be because, as a collectivity, they lost the will to live."[38]

Such extreme pessimism is limited only by demographical standards. Webber, Gruber, and Pinto offer other perspectives on European Jewish life that present more upbeat and current approaches. Gruber is not, as her book's title might indicate, interested in the virtuality of Jewish identity constructed through technology and the Internet, a topic I address in chapter 8. Rather her notion of "virtuality" underlines the contradiction between the surge of Jewish activity and interest in Jewish history, ritual, culture, and practices and the relatively few "real" Jews participating in these efforts. She names, for example, the explosion of Jewish museums in Europe, especially in Germany, the popular cafés and restored synagogues of Cracow, the burst of enthusiasm for Eastern European Klezmer music throughout Central and Eastern Europe, and generally the expansion of tourism to Jewish sites:

> Today in Europe the public idea of a Jewish culture—or what is "Jewish"—is shaped very much from outside as well as from within the Jewish community. Likewise, the wealth of performance, instruction, talk, and exhibition that today consciously advances an idea of collective Jewish identity as often as not ends up advancing it in the minds of non-Jewish rather than a Jewish audience. Given the post-Holocaust lack of flesh-and-blood Jews and visible social, cultural, and religious Jewish environments in much of Europe, the resulting collective vision is quite frequently the product of literary imagination—"Jewish style," perhaps, rather than "Jewish." This virtual Jewishness or virtual Jewish world is a realm, thus, in which Jewish cultural products may take precedence over living Jewish culture; a realm in many senses constructed from desire rather than from memory or inherited tradition. "Jewish" thus becomes a label with a life of its own.[39]

Admitting a "lack of flesh-and-blood Jews" might be interpreted as was Rafael Seligmann's call for attention to living rather than dead Jews. However, it seems that Gruber turns the discussion toward "real" Jews when she recognizes the limitations of creating an "authentic" Jewish culture after the Holocaust. Although she does not define her criteria, her argument is based on a notion of Jewish authenticity that is hard to defend today, especially from an American perspective, unless one stands by halakhic definitions that would eliminate many Jews who are dedicated to either the faith or the culture, as is the case in Germany, without having a Jewish mother. Clearly, at stake here is a definition of who is Jewish, which is one of the central issues in Israel as throughout Diaspora Judaism. In the latter case, especially in Europe, Webber rightly sees that the labeling of contemporary Jewish identities merely represents the attempt to signpost the way amidst the bewildering confusion of too much meaning being compressed into too small a space.[40] Reminding us that the only place where Jews met "as one undifferentiated people" was Auschwitz, he and others recognize how identities shift depending on definitions of context, peoplehood, community, family, values, and even the imagination. While being a "Jew" may only be defined through Jewish law and Judaism by religious belief or observance, "Jewishness" is more of an ethnicity or cultural definition, a sociological and anthropological category that is fluid, socially constructed, and open to interpretation. Ultimately, according to Webber, "the territory of the Jews . . . remains what it always has been—a disputatious concern with the fulfillment and meanings of their identities."[41] With attendance down at synagogues worldwide, many Jews declaring themselves nonbelievers, and Jews wanting to affiliate with communities no matter if they are halakhically Jewish or not, the implication of Webber's point must be taken seriously.

Ultimately, Gruber does not address the various ways that define Jewishness and she remains ambivalent about the upsurge of interest in "things Jewish" in Europe. Behind her claims is an implicit privileging of "real Jews" who are somehow better at playing Klezmer or serving food in a Jewish café than gentiles. Following only religious halakhic rules, mixed marriages with a Jewish father and gentile mother and their offspring will not be accepted as part of the Jewish community. What about conversions performed by non-Orthodox religious authorities, gay or lesbian Jews, or any person who wants to be part of the Jewish community and doesn't fit the religious standards? This problem is particularly acute, as I have shown, in the German case.

After suggesting that Europe benefits from this resurgence of interest in things Jewish, Gruber still remains skeptical and even fearful that Jewish life may become "hijacked." "Without a living Jewish dimension, the virtual Jewish world may become a sterile desert—or a haunted Jewish never-never land. Some Jews have begun to take positive steps to help chart future development of this phenomenon by making sure that there is actual living Jewish input, and Jewish organizations are trying to develop strategies."[42] Ironically, she concludes her book with Webber's interpretation, whom she, however, misinterprets. In my reading of his work, he reaffirms a broader rather than a narrower, fixed definition of Jewishness. "There is a difference," he says, "between official, established Judaism and how Jews actually live. And there is an imagined Judaism, created ex nihilo. . . . Representation is a moving target. Jewish culture is undergoing such changes that to pin it down to one representation is an illusion."[43]

For European Jewry to survive, a radical rethinking of categories must take place about identity and the construction of Jewish identity. Closest to my own approach is the historian Diana Pinto and her notion of the European Jewish space. Controversial because of her optimism about the future and, at the same time, pragmatic about declining numbers of European Jews, she states, "Rather than perceiving this numerical reality as an impoverishment, Jews should consider this structural condition as a major positive challenge, indeed as a challenge unique to Europe. For if Jews now live in Europe in a voluntary manner it means they share a series of complex affinities with 'others' and it is this link that must be deepened and turned into a creative dialogue, starting with non-Jews who choose to enter the Jewish space."[44]

While her notion of a positive European Jewish space may sound abstract, behind it is an optimistic vision for European Jewry that is inclusive rather than exclusive and acknowledges the realities of political and social life in contemporary Europe. Her vision is future oriented, as is mine. It acknowledges the horrible past on the continent of Europe, instigated by Nazi Germany, and by many other countries from West to East. Revelations in the last decades about the complicity of nations like Switzerland and Sweden, long thought to be innocently neutral, make the case for a Europe that is both guilty and responsible for positive changes toward its current Jewish populations. The publication of Polish historian Jan Gross's discovery of details about the massacre in the town of Jewabne carried out by Poles in 1941 reminds us that Germans were not alone, and as demonstrated in the Kielce massacre in 1945, anti-Semitism did not abruptly disappear once the war was over.[45] Many assumptions about guilt and responsibility as identity are still unresolved.

Nevertheless, as Pinto points out, precisely because of this closeness of European Jews and their gentile neighbors, who both persecuted and saved them, the Jewish "coming home," as she calls it, "not only has lifted an oppressive silence but has permitted long-needed national debates to take place, thus liberating and enriching political and cultural agoras throughout Europe. . . . European Jews in this context offer the living proof that the Holocaust, while never being forgotten, can be transcended, and this stance more than any other, may set them apart from their Israeli or American cousins, for whom the Holocaust has become a frozen memory."[46]

The future she envisions for a European Jewry therefore works not only in spite of, but also because of these many fractured Diaspora histories. Of course, this perspective refocuses attention from the two largest and most powerful Jewish populations, the United States and Israel (a topic that I will take up in the next chapter), to the European continent itself. As the scene of the genocide, European countries and its inhabitants have a special responsibility for the massacres of millions that took place on their soil. But as Europe struggles to establish a new profile on the global stage, especially after the conflict produced by the war on Iraq, the Jews of Europe, British or German, Italian or French, see themselves forced to take sides in a highly politicized environment. Jews always have hybrid identities that cannot only be defined religiously, as we know from the secular population of the Jewish homeland whose Israeli identities often overshadow "being Jewish." As being Jewish has become "natural" in the case of Israel and more "ethnic" than religious in the case of the United States, it has complicated the definition of what it means to be Jewish in other parts of the world. It is not surprising that the German Jews I met around the country were of different minds whether to define themselves as Jews, as Germans, or as Europeans.

I welcome the expansion of the European Jewish identity to include all types of Jews with their different experiences and identifications and all kinds of non-Jews who sincerely appreciate and contribute to the building of Jewish sites. It is very important to realize that Jewish activity cannot be measured only by statistics, but must include discourses about Jewish "things," as Gruber herself calls it. What I mean here is that Jewish museums such as those in Berlin, Vienna, or Prague, Jewish cafés and restaurants, or Jewish cultural festivals, while not "really Jewish," that is, produced by "real Jews," create sites for Jews and non-Jews alike to experience Jewish history, ritual, and tradition. Just as branding an automobile as "made in America" whose parts are imported from around the world and assembled by immigrant labor, a state of pure "Jewishness" is no longer achievable. The statements and images, even imaginary ones, of a Jewish novel or film, therefore, enhance public consciousness about Jewish life. They include more people in a Jewish space and in a Jewish discourse community. They educate people to Jewish issues and concerns and expand understanding of differences and Jewishness as well. In a recent collection of articles about the first ten years of the Berlin Jewish Film Festival, ten Jewish critics came up, not surprisingly, with ten different answers for the question What makes a film Jewish?[47] Even the advertising slogan of years past, "You Don't Have to Be Jewish" reminds us that a "Jewish experience" can mean enjoying lox and bagels, as well as studying Jewish theology or even attending a Sabbath service. Each has its own value and significance; some require more knowledge, while others demand official sanction. However, they all enlarge the Jewishness of Europe in various ways, if Jewish identity is based as much on Jewishness as it is on Judaism. In short, religious belief is no longer the only criterion for Jewish identity.

The pluralism Pinto promotes supports my thesis. She sees that Jews in Europe have had, especially since 1989, an opportunity to take advantage of the changes. A convinced Europeanist, Pinto sees a new self-consciousness and self-confidence in Jews throughout Europe who are establishing more open relationships with the nations in which they live.[48] However, as much as Pinto would like them to give up their "iconic" or symbolic status, Jews are still, in my opinion, a gauge of democratization and religious freedom for the outside world. During my research, the international affairs director of the AJC told me about his high-level meetings in the Baltic states as these prepared for admission to the European Union. Treatment of the indigenous Jewish population was an important criterion for those who would evaluate these countries' human rights' records and potential as a condition for full membership in a European community. In other words, the treatment of Jews in Europe is the measure for acceptance and success.

In fact, as the European Union experiences growing pains, especially with the addition of new members, change does not only mean the additional numbers of Jews to be included in an official definition of Europe. As transnationals as well as citizens of individual European nations, Jews offer, as Voloj claimed, links among disparate national, ethnic, or regional communities within and between nation-states. They can also be symbols in Europe and especially in Germany for tolerance and diversity. This special status may remain with us for a long time, even as Europe, and especially Germany, moves toward some version of "normalization."

But can normalization be achieved when events and statements targeting Jews and Israel have created a significant shift in public discourse that has come to be called the "new" anti-Semitism? For many Jews and Germans, longstanding taboos have been broken that permit prominent politicians and cultural figures to cross sensitive boundaries of discourse which was not possible before. Within Germany, it started in May 2002. Jamal Karsli, a member of the Green party, was expelled because of inflammatory statements comparing Israelis to Nazis and accusations of a "Jewish lobby" at work. Jürgen Möllemann, a high-ranking FDP politician publicly sympathetic to Arab causes, accepted Karsli, who was born in Syria, into the party. Möllemann was then criticized by Michel Friedman. Möllemann, a long-time critic of Israeli policy and Ariel Sharon, then attacked Friedman by stating, "The intolerant and spiteful handling by Mr. Friedman of any critic of Sharon unfortunately is liable to awaken anti-Semitic resentments."[49] Hoping to win votes, Möllemann distributed a flyer before the election in which he further intensified his reproach. Shortly thereafter, he was accused of shady financial dealings. In June 2003 he committed suicide. At the same time, author Martin Walser's latest novel *Death of a Critic* was called by the literary critic of the *Frankfurter Allgemeine Zeitung* (FAZ), Frank Schirrmacher, "a document of hate" as well as a symbolic "execution" of Jewish media commentator and literary critic Marcel Reich Ranicki who closely resembles the main character.[50] Walser had not been forgotten for his invocation of Auschwitz as a "moral cudgel" against the Germans and subsequent combat with Bubis, who castigated Walser for what he called "spiritual arson." In November 2002, during the event in Berlin Spandau, marking the renaming of Kinkelstrasse to its pre-Nazi name, Jüdenstrasse, Alexander Brenner, the head of the Berlin Jewish Community, was greeted with cries of "Juden, Juden" (Jews, Jews). Brenner and others present heard such inflammatory statements as "Juden raus! (Jews, get out) or "Die Juden haben Jesus Christus gekreuzigt" (The Jews have crucified Jesus Christ); the police claimed that this had yet to be proven.[51] And just as a reminder from chapter 1, in October 2003, Martin Hohmann, a CSU MP, laid out the history of the Jews during the Bolshevik Revolution as proof of how they too have been perpetrators. Using precise data, he presents a litany of the percentage of Jews among the Soviet revolutionary council, the Central Committee, the Soviet Secret Police, and on and on. In Germany, he seemed pleased to be able to mention similar high percentages of Jews in the socialist movement. By calling the Jews in the Bolshevik revolution a "Tätervolk" (a people of perpetrators), a term reserved for Nazis, he implicitly equated Jews with Nazis that support anti-Zionist progaganda.

This series of coinciding events set the stage in Germany for yet another contentious debate that has parallels, it is important to note, in France where there have also been well-publicized incidents. Attacks on synagogues, Jewish cemeteries, and Jews themselves prompted calls by the World Jewish Congress for a Jewish boycott of France. However, in Germany, where no boycott has been threatened, such events overshadowed by history make the German situation unique and more fraught with concerns.

Of course, anti-Semitic statements objectively illustrate deep-seated prejudices and mindless stereotypes that persist about Jews and are dragged out whenever necessary to coalesce the support for one cause or another. There is no question that these statements or events must be monitored and addressed firmly and quickly. However, more subjectively, they also demonstrate a situation that emerges when the newspapers, television, and the ever-present public discussions exploit serious events and statements for their emotional value. American print media have also taken their turn. The *Boston Globe* reports "Kristallnacht Returns."[52] In Germany, Paul Spiegel matched the newspapers' invectives by calling Möllemann's comments "the worst insult" against Jews since World War II.[53] Fortunately, less extreme, and perhaps less political than from a public Jewish leader, numerous articles analyzed and tried to place these outbursts in an historical context, to define what they mean, and to understand their repercussions: "End of a Healing Period,"[54] "Anti-Semitism with a New Face,"[55] "The New Old Anti-Semitism Debate,"[56] "Anti-Semitism without Anti-Semites,"[57] "A Modern Anti-Semite."[58] Many other titles illustrate the problem that is as much about the discourse on the status of Jewish life in Germany and Europe as it is about the people and events themselves. In the political sphere, German Foreign Minister Joschka Fischer has been the most vocal, balanced, and wise in responding forcefully and publicly to recent anti-Semitic statements: first, in response to Möllemann, "Germany, Your Jews—Again a New Silence in the German Jewish Relationship"[59] and more recently, at a conference sponsored by the Anti-Defamation League in New York (November 1, 2002) on "Global Anti-Semitism."[60]

Statements like Fischer's have been lacking from other German political elites, in attention to content, form, and context. A language of excess and exaggeration on both sides of the German debate has obfuscated rather than illuminated the problems facing Jews and other minority groups. And I would like to emphasize the "other" in minority groups, just as Fischer has linked anti-Semitism with racism. There is no question that Germany's commitment to dealing with its difficult history is laudable and exemplary, as is its dedication to democracy. However, a certain satisfaction and even arrogance can mask resentment and frustration with a past that does not go away and a present that offers ever new pitfalls for intolerance and relativizing of German guilt. Right-wing populism generally and hostility toward immigrants specifically that have been central planks of political platforms in France, Holland, Belgium, and Austria are fortunately absent in Germany. Nevertheless, German parties and politicians do use xenophobia and ethnic stereotyping to gain votes. In Germany, covertly in Walser and Hohmann, overtly in Möllemann, the " 'new' anti-Semitism" illustrates how easily one can extrapolate from an individual—for example in the case of Michel Friedman—to a collective negative identity of "all Jews."

Most troubling has been the response by many Germans to the Israeli-Palestinian conflict. To criticize Israeli politics or Ariel Sharon may be legitimate, but to attribute Nazi behavior to Israeli methods is as imprecise and dangerous as when American Jews use the term "Nazi" loosely to describe any strict enforcement of law or discipline, even in comic forms such as Seinfeld's "soup Nazi," or simplistically compare Turks to Jews. Similarly, not all criticism of Israel can be labeled anti-Semitic, although as is obvious from the debate, the lines are often very difficult to distinguish. The use of simplistic formulas on either side of the conflict leaves little room for differentiation, underplays the specificity of historical situations, and diverts attention from explicit and specific uses and meanings of terms and images to banal generalities. Whether or not a bystander actually yelled "Juden raus" during the renaming ceremony of the Jüdenstrasse, the problem of prejudice or intolerance cannot be solved by naming it "anti-Semitic" or labeling the entire series of events in Europe as the " 'new' anti-Semitism."

How do we then approach this issue that seems to suffer from its categorization as a German evil whose naming has become a cliché and instituted stereotype rather than analysis? The statements in December 2002 of Hessian Minister President Roland Koch in which he equated the law singling out rich Germans for a special inheritance tax with the Nazi decree that made the Jews wear a yellow star and its repercussions seem a sad example of how such language can play out in Germany. While these kinds of actions or statements might be seen as the breaking of taboos leading to "normality," they are not the best way to approach the problem. Where a discourse of intolerance and prejudice exists toward different people—Jewish, Turkish, or any other—normalization cannot take place. There must be an atmosphere in which Jews and Germans together can navigate this new state of affairs. It must be a situation that does not cause pain or suffering to one group or the other and does not deteriorate into name calling and cliché that do not address the real problems.

Still, there is no question, as proven by the OSCE conferences, that hostility toward Jews in Europe is a serious issue that has burgeoned in recent years. The conference, as well as the well-attended NGO meeting sponsored by AJC the day before, was full of typical well-meaning speeches emphasizing action. Speaker after speaker addressed prominent issues concerning legislation, law enforcement, monitoring and data collection, education, the media and best practices for combating anti-Semitism, as well as racism and xenophobia. Just one week before the celebrated admission of ten new countries to the EU, the OSCE and Europe had obviously taken on a more somber topic. Some people were concerned that aside from the joy of expanding Europe there might also be the problem of expanding anti-Semitism in those countries that had not dealt squarely with their past. But most importantly, the symbolic value of the conference confirmed that Europe had gotten the hint that anti-Semitism was a serious problem. While it is difficult to avoid programmatic statements and clichés at such gatherings, the important message was loud and clear: Europeans must do more to combat this dangerous prejudice. The subject of the Middle East was prominent as was what role Muslim youth in Europe, as well as skinheads and neo-Nazis, had on the rise of hostilities toward Jews. It was a major success of the conference that this point was recognized and that the Middle East conflict should not be an excuse for anti-Jewish actions. The "Berlin Declaration" at the end of the conference proposed by the Bulgarian chairman, who is also Jewish, spelled this out clearly.[61]

In addition to featured speakers who were prominent representatives of the fifty-five OSCE member states, time was allotted for other interested parties to voice opinions and concerns. They all condemned anti-Semitism and many denied that such sentiments existed in their individual countries. However, Michael Posner from Human Rights First, one of the most articulate spokespeople, enumerated the countries—some of which were present—where monitoring, legislation, and responsibility was lacking. His frankness countered the unavoidable generalities of many speakers. Prominent Americans were present, such as Colin Powell, Elie Wiesel, the executive director David Harris and the international relations director Rabbi Andrew Baker of AJC, as well as leaders of other American Jewish organizations. Of course, there were disagreements whether what Europe was now experiencing was the "old" anti-Semitism or a "new" incarnation, or whether the phenomenon should be understood as part of or separate from racism and xenophobia in general. Nevertheless, there was uniform agreement on the need to disconnect criticism of specific Israeli politics or policies from the "demonization" of the country, as Israeli scholar Yehuda Bauer put it, "as the collective Jew." He warned against anti-Semitism as a core conception of radical Islam and called it a "genocidal ideology," yet also counseled fellow Jews "to stop presenting [them]selves as ultimate victims."[62] From most reports the conference was considered a success, precisely because of its European emphasis and concern. Other conferences were planned, such as one on hate speech on the Internet in Paris in July 2004 and in Brussels in September 2004. In addition, as of August 2004, the OSCE office in Warsaw hired more staff specifically to turn the declaration's suggestions into action.

At the conference in Berlin, the memory of the past was, of course, not forgotten; in fact, it was a part of the symbolism of the location. Israel's President Moshe Katsav was in the city and held meetings and dinners with Jewish leaders who were in town for the conference. He was joined by Natan Sharansky, the Israeli minister for Jerusalem and Diaspora Relations, and the director of Yad Vashem, Avner Shalev. The links between the Holocaust and current anti-Semitism were certainly not lost on Israel. In fact, Sharansky presented a report on Anti-Semitism 2003 and announced at the Holocaust Memorial Yad Vashem in Jerusalem on January 25, 2004, that January 27 would be the first Israeli "National Day of Solidarity with the Jewish Communities of the World to Fight Anti-Semitism."[63] On the German-language website of the Israeli embassy in Berlin, it was noted that January 27, the day of the liberation of Auschwitz-Birkenau in 1945, was chosen to coincide with the commemoration of the Shoah in fourteen European countries. As the web newsletter reports, "During the opening ceremony at Yad Vashem, Minister Sharansky spoke of the necessity to create a day to fight anti-Semitism since Israel wanted a link between the memory [of the Holocaust] and the current aggressive acts (*Herausforderungen*)."[64] The author goes on specifically to quote the minister's exact words: "When synagogues and cemeteries are trashed and burned and this takes place not in a dark corner of the world but in the heart of enlightened Europe, then this is a problem that concerns us all."[65] Avner Shalev added dramatically, "It is becoming increasingly legitimate to criticize Jews and Israel in such a way that the Jews as a whole are de-monized and de-humanized. This sickness is a serious threat not only for Jews but for all of Europe. This threat touches the basic questions of our self-understanding in relations to our societies, nations, and civilizations."[66] While this event is obviously significant for Israel and for Germany, few Americans are aware of this special day or this European commemoration although there has been a great deal of publicity about the rise in attacks on Jews and Jewish establishments in Europe.

But the Jews do indeed stay, continue to emigrate from the former So-viet Union, and choose Germany over Israel as a place to make their home. Interviews with prominent leaders of the Jewish Community in Ger-many and with American directors of important Jewish institutions now lo-cated in Berlin, which I detail in the next chapter, convince me that Jewish life, even with its many problems, including "new anti-Semitism," offers optimism and potentially a vehicle for improving transatlantic rela-tions. The sheer presence of a Jewish population with a variety of religious orientations, as well as opportunities for Jews who are culturally identified rather than affiliated according to Orthodox Jewish law, paints a picture of a thriving and vibrant community. It is one populated by a mixture of Ger-man, Polish, and primarily Russian Jews with Israelis, Americans, Canadi-ans, and others from around the world complementing the mix.

The Jewish Community also has a symbolic value beyond the numbers. Although this new community may not be enough to guarantee that Jews will never be the targets of prejudice or attack—since anti-Semitism does not need Jews to flourish—its mere presence carries weight and makes a powerful statement. It represents the defeat of Hitler's Final Solution, a future for a new Jewish life in Germany, and hope for acceptance of diversity in a country that, unlike the United States, defined itself for a long time as only white and Christian. Perhaps it is not surprising that the German Jewish organization Gesher-Forum for Diaspora Culture held a colloquium in Berlin in December of 1989 and has published a book entitled *Galut 2000—Toward a European Jewish Identity*. In this pan-European and North American collection "leading Jewish thinkers from across Europe examined the nature of a common European Jewish identity which might complement those of Israel and the U.S., while recognizing the great differences between European Jews, both as Europeans and as Jews."[67]

Transatlantic relations might be improved if more Americans, especially Jewish Americans, knew more about the complexities of Jewish life in Germany and the role of German politics and culture in European-wide relations. During the OSCE Conference in Berlin, its location, as the capital of Nazi Germany and now the location of such a conference on anti-Semitism, was cited by almost all of the prominent participants, including Fischer himself. "The German government has invited you all to this conference in Berlin—in our capital, in the city, in which almost seventy years ago not far from here the destruction of European Jewry was decided, planned, and instituted. We, as hosts, want to acknowledge the historical and moral responsibility of Germany for the Shoah. The memory of this monstrous crime against humanity will also influence German politics in the future."[68]

Unfortunately, Germany is still often identified in the United States exclusively with past Nazi horrors rather than with its postwar democratic and liberal successes. The site of the OSCE Conference was to demonstrate dramatically Germany's commitment to combating anti-Semitism even though Jews have not been targets there as frequently as in France. In fact, some Jews in Germany seem to be less fearful than their American counterparts. For example, Cilly Kugelmann, program director for the Jewish Museum, who has lived in Israel and criticizes the German left for its "anti-Semitism cloaked in anti-Zionism," still finds "the alarmism about an apparent new anti-Semitic danger greatly exaggerated."[69] The German government, Israel's best friend in Europe, as many on both sides claim, continues to maintain an unquestioned "special relationship" to the Jewish state, no matter whether it criticizes Sharon's policies or does not support the war in Iraq. Fischer has become one of the leading politicians from a member state of the entire European Union, who consistently speaks out for Jews and for Israel. Fischer represents the special attention that Germany pays to its Jewish citizens and new Jewish immigrants. As he reminded Jews and non-Jews alike at the OSCE Conference, "For every active attack against a Jewish citizen, every desecration of a Jewish cemetery, indeed, every single anti-Semitic expression threatens not only Jewish people and Jewish communities in Germany and elsewhere, but also and precisely our open and democratic society as a whole."[70]

The focus on Berlin, Germany, its commitment to fighting anti-Semitism, as well as the significance of the German-Jewish Community, also points to most Americans' ignorance about their allies and the Jewish communities that live in the Diaspora, especially this particular one. Only by increased information and contact between the United States and Germany/Europe can Americans understand how they are still often encumbered by myths, stereotypes, and clichés of the "old Europe" that describe all Germans either as militaristic Nazis or, more recently, as wimpy peaceniks. According to this interpretation, Jews should be afraid to live in a country with either of those dangerous alternatives that could mean attack from the inside or vulnerability to attack from outside. It is time for Americans to see Germany not in such black-and-white terms and to understand the importance of increased knowledge for improved transatlantic relations. Compared to other European countries, however, Germany—its government and its institutions, as well as the majority of its population—has shown its ability and willingness to face the past and to support through its growing Jewish Community the creation of a potential bulwark against a threatening future. This new Germany, however, is only visible if we look beyond stereotypes to see opportunities that might otherwise be missed. Clearly, a new Jewish community in Germany is not enough by itself to prevent acts of hatred against Jews in Europe. However, it can be a bridge, ironic as this may be, between the United States and Europe, and more importantly, an example of how breaking down stereotypes and generalizations can lead to understandings never before thought possible.

Still, one wonders about a European Jewish future, even as the Continent assumes a new role alongside the United States and Israel. With an estimated 3 million Jews in the European Union, 1.5 million in the former Soviet Union, and an equal number in the rest of Europe, European Jewish life can become the third pillar so many European Jewish leaders seek. Clearly, the new German Jewry, because of its country's past and present, has to become a central part of any European framework, much in the way that the organized Jewish students are creating links across the Continent. While Jewish cooperation in Europe may be stimulated by activities or policies of the European Union, organizational activity cannot be left up to political organizations, although one should expect that they would welcome any cooperation among (Jewish) Europeans that would contribute to the harmonious relations they themselves seek. Europeans and European Jews will have to develop their own resources and not be dependent on the United States and Israel. These sentiments are echoed by Gideon Bolotowsky, president of the Jewish Community in Finland, who states, "It's time for European Jewry to get its act together and start really rising up to the task of becoming the third pillar of world Jewry, alongside American Jews and Israel, that everyone is talking about."[71] In the next chapter, I examine how the role of the two superpowers for Jewish life in Germany—the United States and Israel—influence domestic and international relations among Jews and Germans, Israelis and Americans. Berlin is the most interesting stage for examining this cross-fertilization and hybrid identity building. Germany, and especially Berlin, the symbolic site of destruction and regeneration of Jewish life, may offer possibilities of a more developed Jewish American dialogue with Europe, a continent that must be grasped in its complexity and difference, even as it tries to form new domestic and international ties. Precisely because of its history, its sensitivity to the past, and its new Jewish community, Germany may indeed be America's best link to Europe.

7

The United States and Israel

SUPER-POWERING GERMAN JEWISH IDENTITIES

Although the growing European Jewish community is ambitious, it still lives in the shadow of Israel and the United States. The internal development and sustainability of Jewish communities on the Continent are dependent on these two powers, even as European Jews establish themselves as a larger and more diverse community, unified through their commitment to a new Europe. The strength of the United States and Israel lies, of course, not only in their numbers. It is also maintained by America's singular global political and economic status and Israel's historical and moral role as the homeland of the Jewish people. But what influence do these "super-powers" have specifically on Germany's Jews, a diaspora that has a special place in the minds of the Jewish world?

In 2001, *New York Times* columnist Roger Cohen quoted former Israeli ambassador to Germany Avi Primor in an article entitled "Israel's Ties with Germany Elude U.S. Jews." "[Primor] travels regularly to the United States to tell American Jewish groups how good Israeli-German ties have become; 'Their reaction . . . is often one of shock, pain, and indignation. They want to preserve Germany in their minds as a negative nation.'"[1] Although the Iraq war has tarnished the alliance, Germany has traditionally been America's best friend in Europe. However, most Americans do not know that Germany is also Israel's best friend on the Continent. Highlighting Primor, this article by a prominent Jewish-American journalist seems, in fact, to reproach American Jews for their inability to follow Israel's lead in recognizing Germany's positive relationship to the Jewish people. In short, if Israel can appreciate Germany then why can't American Jews? Although the United States periodically criticizes Israel and even makes political suggestions that are unpopular in Israel, America's commitment to Israel is a given, no matter which political party is in power. For Germany, the same holds true.

This triangular multilateral relationship of the United States, Germany, and Israel, of course, has many dimensions, some of which often burden their rapport. For example, the Second Intifada plays out in Germany and on its Jewish population. This is especially the case when Jews in Germany are literally made surrogate whipping boys for Israel or when criticism of Israel turns anti-Semitic by using the vocabulary and symbolism of German Nazism to describe Israeli politics or the prime minister himself. German-American relations have also been affected by Germany's stance on the American-led war in Iraq that has stirred up the Middle East and hinges on Israel's security.

If Israel, along with the Holocaust, has indeed become a kind of "civic religion" for many American Jews, as some observers claim, then obviously Germany and its Jewish population must figure prominently into this equation. For one side, they represent a betrayal, and for another, proof of Hitler's failure to eradicate the Jews. Since its defeat in World War II, and subsequent rebuilding economically and politically with American aid, Germany has also developed a complicated yet committed relationship to Israel. Its policy of providing military and economic assistance has obviously largely been shaped by a sense of moral obligation. An agreement on restitution, known as "Wiedergutmachung," literally "making good again" (in Hebrew *shulumim*) was concluded by Germany's first postwar chancellor, Konrad Adenauer, with the State of Israel and the Conference on Material Claims against Germany in the Luxembourg Reparations Agreement of 1952. This plan initiated what would come to be known as the "special relationship" to Israel. But it is also clear that this financial plan was pragmatically orchestrated to prove Germany's commitment to the Atlantic Alliance and rehabilitation as a worthy future democratic ally. Lily Gardner-Feldman has noted: "To Adenauer the key foreign policy goal was the return of German sovereignty on the basis of equality."[2] Germany and Israel, even before diplomatic relations were established in 1965, have been thickly intertwined since the 1950s at all levels of exchange, not only militarily. This was the case, no matter whether individual personalities were particularly close, such as Adenauer and Ben-Gurion, or Golda Meier and Willy Brandt, the latter through international socialist links, or if they were at odds, such as Helmut Schmidt and Menachem Begin. Germany remained committed to Israel's security, often operating quietly behind the scenes, even as they publicly refrained from support.[3]

The oft-quoted claim by John McCloy—"The world will carefully watch the new Germany and one of the tests by which it will be judged will be its attitude toward the Jews and how it treats them"—became a gauge for Germany's future.[4] This standard has remained in force in the immediate postwar period, in 1989–1990 as Germany reunified, and is still the norm today. More than fifty years later, the special relationship holds firm, as the German embassy in Israel proudly notes in its website's "Background Papers." "Since [the close relationship between Chancellor Adenauer and Prime Minister David Ben-Gurion in the 1950s], a growing network of governmental and parliamentary contacts have been established between the two countries. . . . [After diplomatic relations were established in the mid-sixties] state visits stand as highlights . . . President Roman Herzog's first official visit outside of Europe was to Israel in 1994. Prime Minister Ehud Barak was the first foreign leader received in Berlin after the German government's relocation from Bonn in the fall of 1999." Chancellor Schröder also visited Israel.[5] More recently, German concerns or criticisms of Israel's policy on Gaza settlements in April/May 2004, for example, might have suggested a change in the relationship between these two countries. However, in expert Gardner-Feldman's words, "If . . . one takes a broader approach by considering other statements by German leaders [Joschka Fischer, for example], and by focusing on Germany's quiet actions, the historically determined 'special relationship' appears more vibrant. Moreover, this 'unique partnership' with Israel could well enable Germany to play an intermediary role in both the Middle East and transatlantic arenas."[6] Germany's support of Jewish immigration from the former Soviet Union, even as they choose it over Israel, with all of the difficulties for the immigrants, is also a reminder of Germany's commitment to having a Jewish community on its soil and the security that Germany provides that is unfortunately absent in Israel today.

While German-Israeli relations have prospered, world Jewry, especially in the United States, has kept a keen eye on the development and behavior of Germany toward its own Jews, albeit not without some skepticism toward Jewish life there. Unlike the general Jewish public, however, American Jewish organizations saw early on the benefits of developing institutional ties with West Germany. The American Jewish Committee (AJC), for example, already in the 1950s, established ties with the new democracy and saw the benefits of a dialogue based on commitment and trust for a better future. The longstanding complex history of the American Jewish community and Germany has involved the AJC, the B'nai Brith Anti-Defamation League (ADL), the World Jewish Congress (WJC), and other organizations. In his detailed and comprehensive study *Ambiguous Relations: The American Jewish Community and Germany since 1945*, the Israeli scholar Shlomo Shafir chronicles this complex, and as he himself terms it, this "ambiguous relationship."[7]

Although America's attention on Germany focused on the latter's position on the front line of the cold war, German elites understood how important it was to be accepted by the American Jewish community. Any real power Jews may have had was often overestimated, as it sometimes still is in wild conspiracy theories of Jewish-American world domination. However, German politicians still courted American Jewry for its presumed influence on American foreign policy toward the new democracy which had to bear such a heavy historical burden. This is still the case today, as was illustrated in the debate about a neoconservative Jewish influence in the Bush White House that encouraged war with Iraq at any cost, on the one hand, and the commitment of German political leaders and party representatives to American Jewish institutions and causes, on the other. At any AJC annual dinner these Germans are present in full force, as are representatives from the American administration both in and out of power. Symbolically, at least, American and German political elites pay homage to Jewish institutional clout.

German reunification brought the question of American-Jewish trust in Germany to the fore once again. According to Shafir, "For a great many American Jews, the unforeseen rapid unification was an emotionally painful experience. . . . They had come to regard the partition of Germany as a kind of historic punishment for Hitler's war of aggression and genocide."[8] Although some Jewish organizations were initially skeptical about this transformative moment, "AJC, B'nai Brith, and ADL . . . endorsed unification on the basis of West Germany's record and Jewish concerns such as antisemitism, reparations, Israel, and Holocaust education."[9] Still, other Jewish organizations and individuals remained reserved and even hostile. However, it was clear that American interests would be served by this historic event according to polls in November 1989—67 percent of the American public supported reunification, growing in March–April 1990 to 76–77 percent, and in May 1990 to 84 percent.[10]

The choice of Berlin in particular as the new capital may have re-minded Jews of the Nazi past, but also signaled the beginning of a new Berlin Republic. The country's center was moving east to accommodate the shift in European realignments and the distinction of this new capital for a different Germany. Since the end of the war, this special city drew American presidents to demonstrate by their presence the U.S. commit-ment to Germany's security and partnership in the Western alliance. This was especially acute in the cold war environment in which the Russians and their Warsaw Pact partners were breathing down the Allies' necks just a few kilometers away. The partitioned city of Berlin was a symbol of di-vided Germany and the bipolar world that seemed destined to remain in this tense balance between liberal democracy and communism. Presi-dents John F. Kennedy at the Schöneberg City Hall in 1963 and Ronald Reagan in 1987 made dramatic pronouncements at symbolic locations in Berlin. The first President Bush, while not appearing in Berlin, spoke forcefully in May 1989 in Mainz with Chancellor Kohl at his side about "this brutal wall."[11] Both President Clinton and the current President Bush visited Berlin as well, the first to a groundswell of enthusiasm at the Brandenburg Gate on July 1994 and George W. Bush in May 2002 at the German Bundestag to a less overwhelming response. The historical con-texts and responses by Berliners to these two American presidents could not have been more different.

On July 12, 1994, then-President Bill Clinton and German Chancellor Kohl stood together at the Brandenburg Gate in Berlin. Both spoke of "culture," as if now that the cold war was over, there was finally space for a subject that had been overshadowed by the importance of politics. Clin-ton, speaking in German, drew on the now infamous tradition of a Demo-cratic president whom he greatly admired and a predecessor who spoke some decades before and in relative proximity to the site of this speech. To be sure, the global political situation was decidedly different ten years after the fall of the Wall, the reunification of Germany, and the disappearance of the communist threat that had brought Kennedy to declare: "Ich bin ein Berliner" [I am a Berliner]. In fact, the global political situation had never been better, nor had German-American relations. Clinton, who walked from the Reichstag to the Brandenburg Gate, gave his speech fac-ing east, as does the Quadriga on the top of the monument. While Clin-ton's words were not as poignant as Kennedy's (although his German pronunciation was deemed much better), the president was able to draw on a historical and symbolic moment that has been ingrained in the political culture of Americans and Germans, East and West. Clinton spoke to the Germans "from the East" who especially appreciated his mention of their "gentle revolution." At a time when racist and xenophobic acts were on the rise in Germany, Clinton spoke to these themes as the leader of the multicultural society par excellence to warn his German friends about the dangers of not understanding the foreign.

Clinton made another visit while in Berlin, less publicized, but equally important in the context of cultural values and symbolic acts of the acceptance of difference. With Chancellor Kohl and his wife he visited the Neue Synagogue Centrum Judaicum (New Synagogue) on Oranienburgerstrasse. While Kohl had rarely been seen in a synagogue, the American Baptist Clinton and his wife were much more comfortable in this "foreign" venue, but also in general in diverse religious and racial settings, a hallmark of Clinton's presidency. Living, growing up, and being educated in the United States had given the Clintons, like all Americans, certain advantages in dealing with different races, ethnicities, and religions. This was the import of his speech at the Brandenburg Gate. This is what an American president, even with the problems that still exist in the United States, could say to the Germans. While Clinton's words did not have the impact of the words by his hero JFK, his visit to the synagogue was the closest he came to emulating the former president. His presence at this particular synagogue, visible symbol of Jewish Berlin that was desecrated by the Nazis and destroyed in Allied bombings, and its ruin later torn down by the East Germans, rather than other more controversial sites that were being considered, was an expression of solidarity with those who are persecuted for any reason. What Kennedy performed linguistically, Clinton affected symbolically in a rather different discursive form and in what might have seemed to some as an out-of-the-way site with less political import.

The voices of the twenty thousand who gathered for George W. Bush's visit to Berlin on May 22, 2002, less than a year after the terrorist attacks on New York and Washington, were not raised in support, but rather in protest. Bush was only to be in Berlin for a nineteen-hour stopover on his way to Moscow for three-day talks with Vladimir Putin. The president spoke at the German Bundestag and in front of the new Chancellery Building across the street from the famous Reichstag, and not far from the Brandenburg Gate itself. Called a warmonger rather than a peacemaker, Bush would not outdo his predecessors, as one journalist drawing on the presidential tradition of visiting Berlin notes, "There won't likely be any lines like 'Ich bin ein Berliner.'"[12] The reception of Bush's speech at the German Parliament, the first ever by an American president, was greeted cordially; only a few PDS [former GDR Communist Party] parliamentarians walked out. In the more contained environment of the Parliament, Bush's remarks, which were billed by the Americans as a historic speech, concentrated on the war on terrorism and the importance of the transatlantic alliance for security. He described the September 11 attacks in their magnitude as "a deep dividing line in our history—a change of eras as sharp and clear as Pearl Harbor, or the first day of the Berlin Blockade."[13] Using historical markers signaling both America's entry into World War II, which ultimately led to the defeat of Germany, and one of the dangerous moments of the cold war, Bush emphasized how the war on terror falls in line with these grave moments in history. From the perspective of the Iraq war and the havoc it has wrought on American-European relations, Bush's words may have sounded like the usual politically symbolic rhetoric of such moments, but at that time the good will of Europe was still behind the United States. He emphasized the commonalities of Europe and the United States as a "house of freedom" and "heirs to the same civilization."[14] Consequently, he applauded the European Union, the inclusion of former Soviet satellite countries and even of Russia itself in this future European alliance. Against this American-European civilizing force, which holds "the same ideals," are those who remained as yet unnamed, except that they are our enemies, "beyond Europe [where there are] gathering dangers and important responsibilities . . . dangers originating far from Europe . . . that thrive on violence and the grief of the innocent."[15] Bush's invocation of Dietrich Bonhoeffer, the Protestant pastor who left America "to stand against Nazi rule" and ultimately gave up his life was poignant.[16] It not only invoked this Western symbiosis, but more importantly, it illustrated a moral choice for good over evil by a German against the singularly most-recognized crime, Nazi rule and by implication the Holocaust. Although Bush did not make direct reference, except in brief allusions, to the destruction of the Jews or the rebirth of their community as Clinton had done by visiting a synagogue, he recalled the genocide through the figure of Bonhoeffer to legitimize the U.S. fight against terrorism.[17] Bush did not visit a synagogue until he was in Moscow, and it was only in 2002 that he visited Auschwitz.

Germany's Jews watch such events closely; public figures are judged on their attention to Jewish concerns such as anti-Semitism or the symbolic visit to a concentration camp. For the great majority of Germany's Jews, especially for the older generation who lived through the war, Germany's postwar recovery and largely amicable American occupation, the United States is a liberator, a friend, a protector, as well as a refuge if necessary. Certainly for this group, America remains a dominant presence in their imagination. Many of Germany's Jews have lived in the United States, have relatives or friends there, and travel there often. It is, in fact, linked in their minds with Israel as one of the two secure homes for the Jewish people. The exceptions are perhaps those Jews on the left whose anti-imperialist and anticapitalist politics mitigates their unqualified support for either the United States or even Israel. These attitudes were mirrored in the overwhelming support for the Iraq war by the Jewish Community and those who questioned and even protested against it.

The last ten years have brought reaffirmed alliances, but also new tensions to the German-Jewish community's relationship with Israel. Unfortunately, a highly negative tone was cast in 1996 that continues to be a reference point. Israeli President Ezer Weizman came to Germany, the first visit by an Israeli of his status. Weizman's own family participated in the writing of the heroic Israeli history as a nation whose new existence tragically emerges from the ashes of Nazi Germany.[18] He comes from a respected Israeli line; his uncle Chaim was one of the founders of the state of Israel and its first president. Unfortunately, Ezer Weizman is now remembered by his questioning of how Jews could live on this tainted soil. Unofficially, he even said at one point during his visit that he would be afraid to live in Germany since every time he turned his back, he would fear he was being called a dirty Jew.[19] In fact, he incurred the critique of Ignatz Bubis, then-president of the Central Council, who was obviously offended by the president of Israel's blunt questioning of the very community in Germany that Bubis himself was trying to build and lead. He retorted, "There is no reason to say that Jews cannot live in Germany."[20] While a proud Jew, he was also proud to be, as the title of his book emphasizes, "a German citizen of the Jewish faith."[21] But as Israelis like Weizman tried to isolate German Jews, Bubis often had to remind non-Jewish Germans that he did not want to be turned from a German into an Israeli simply because he was Jewish. An oft-cited example occurred when he was handed a copy of German President Roman Herzog's speech in

Hebrew or was greeted by Günter Reichert, president of the Federal Office for Civic Education, after Herzog's speech to Weizman with the comment, "Your president gave a good speech."[22] The ignorance on the part of gentile Germans of calling Weizman Bubis's president illustrates that not only Jews themselves from outside Germany, like Weizman, have difficulty acknowledging a German-Jewish identity that can have multiple loyalties. Whether from Christian Germans or other Jews, Jews in Germany are constantly being questioned about their right to exist or their ability to govern or represent their own interests. Apparently, being Jewish, whether American or Israeli, transcends national boundaries, except in the case of Germany, whose Jews retain a national affiliation that won't disappear. Just as the German Jews who went to Palestine during the 1930s were treated rudely by their fellow Ashkenazim, Jews living in Germany still continue to be subjected to harsher standards than Jews elsewhere.

In response to Weizman's 1996 declarations, a group of Jewish students living in Germany gave a variety of responses. On the one hand, we hear, "One should decide for oneself where one lives,"[23] and on the other, "I think it is understandable that Weizman said such a thing. We Jews who live here in Germany ask ourselves the same question. Weizman's statement describes one of my own vulnerabilities."[24] While normalization remains questionable, Alice Brauner, one of a group called "The Young Jews of Berlin" and author of the article, exemplifies the more positive attitude: "I won't emigrate. On the contrary, our roots in this country cannot be broken."[25] The daughter of film producer Arthur Brauner, who returned to Germany after the war, calls herself "a Jewish Berliner with German citizenship."[26] And as Michal Bodemann points out, "to feel they should identify themselves as a German or not is avoided."[27] Yet Brauner calls Germany home. "Nevertheless, we stay. We stay because we are at home here and feel at home here."[28]

For these young Jews in Germany in the mid-1990s, as today, their identity is subject to constant repositioning, trying to find a place from which to speak and act as Germans and as Jews simultaneously. Such a situation requires a delicate balance and mutual recognition of how being a non-Jewish German, a Jewish German, or an American Jew influences understanding of where one belongs in the constantly shifting historical, political, and now religious contexts in Germany. Jews especially feel vulnerable to these vicissitudes, yet not only young people are susceptible to changing realities. To be Jewish or Christian, German, Israeli, or American are very important criteria that profoundly shape interpretation that cannot be ignored. In short, Jewish identity is constructed as much by position as by blood. The new generation of Jews in Germany, older second- and third-generation children of Holocaust survivors, while they express some of the same ambivalence of their parents and grandparents, still give the impression that they are in Germany to stay.

In December 2002, a more recent visit to Germany of an Israeli president, Moshe Katsav, revealed a change in tone and attitude by an Israeli leader. He spoke at the dedication of a new synagogue in Wuppertal during a three-day visit with Chancellor Gerhard Schröder to discuss the Middle East. Taking note of the more positive attitude by an Israeli leader, Paul Spiegel, the president of the Central Council of Jews in Germany, called Mr. Katsav's visit "a historical moment for Jews in Germany and for Germany itself."[29] He continued, "This visit is a confirmation that the Jewish community is also finally respected in Israel."[30] Both he and President Katsav, nevertheless, reminded Germany of the need to fight anti-Semitism. This point was clearly articulated even against the positive backdrop in German-Jewish relations that had been affirmed a month earlier with the signing of the federal contract granting the Jewish Community 3 million euros, three times more than previously. Michel Friedman, vice-president of the Central Council, called it "extraordinary," and said "the country is taking an institutional responsibility toward the welfare of the Jewish life in this country."[31]

In 2004, on the occasion of the Berlin OSCE Conference, President Katsav visited the capital again and met with political leaders, such as Chancellor Schröder and Foreign Minister Fischer. Signaling two important issues for Israeli-German relations linked to anti-Semitism— immigration and Holocaust remembrance—he was accompanied by Nathan Sharansky, minister of Diaspora affairs, and Avner Shalev, the director of Yad Vashem. Aside from meetings, Katsav dedicated a street across from the Bundestag to the assassinated Israeli Prime Minister Yitzhak Rabin. At a reception given by the chancellor for the participants of the OSCE Conference at which Katsav was present, Schröder framed this conference in Berlin within German history: "The fact that we are hosting this international conference in the very same city [where little more than half a century ago, inconceivable crimes against European Jews were planned and orders given to carry them out] is symbolic of the enormous progress that has been made in the fight against anti-

Semitism."[32] Unlike his predecessor Chancellor Kohl, Schröder spoke to broader themes about tolerance related to the concerns of the conference that were left up to Clinton years before. "We need an open dialogue, one that will bring people of different cultures and religions together. A spirit of tolerance and identification with one another that will keep minorities from being marginalized."[33]

The Central Council of Jews in Germany's own relationship with Israel was accented in July 2003 when a five-member delegation, among them Paul Spiegel and Vice President Charlotte Knobloch, traveled to Israel. From the Jewish Agency's 1948 ban that threatened to "excommunicate" Jews who did not leave Germany up until Weizman's visit, Israeli policymakers have been generally skeptical of Jewish life in Germany, even as they developed their close "special relationship" with German governments and their elites. However, Germany's Jewish community looked toward Israel, in German Jewish journalist Richard Chaim Schneider's words, as an "Ersatzheimat" (surrogate homeland).[34] Typically, Jewish families in Germany up through the nineties sent their children to Israel or to other countries like the United States or England for education or even for a permanent future. Natan Sharansky, in an interview with the *Jüdische Allgemeine Wochenzeitung,* still claimed, "Of course, in point of fact, I see it as a problem that only one generation after the Holocaust, Jews are settling in Germany." He balances this point, however, with affirming diplomatically the importance of working together with the Central Council.[35] Obviously, this statement, which coincidentally appeared next to a prominent front-page article entitled "With Guarded Hope" about the visit of the Central Council to Israel, recognizes again the ambivalence on both sides, especially strained by the immigration of so many Russian Jews to Germany. Traveling to Israel to donate $250,000 for needy children, this "trip for solidarity and information" obviously worked for public relations as well since, as the journalist Judith Hart emphasized, in contrast to the reporting in the Israeli media there was no difference of opinion about the *aliyah* of Russian Jews between the Central Council and Jerusalem.[36] In short, according to Spiegel, "There is no divergence between us and Israel. . . . But now that they [the Russian Jews] are here, . . . it is our humane Jewish duty to help them."[37] Spiegel also expressed his hope for approval from the Supreme Rabbinate for conversions by German rabbis so "there are not Jews in Germany of first and second class."[38] In his own article on the trip, Spiegel made the obligatory gesture toward balancing

German-Jewish commitment to the country that they now increasingly call their own and their commitment to Israel. Since, as he says, "anti-Semitism will never be completely stamped out . . . with all of the loyalty that we have for Germany to which we stand self-consciously without a bad conscience or feelings, the existence of Israel equally gives us a sense of additional certainty [*Sicherheit*]."[39]

This final word, which can mean both physical and emotional security or certainty, reminds us that the former may be less "certain" than the latter since terrorist attacks in Israel undermine one side of this term. More than other nations in the Diaspora that have an unbroken tradition of dual loyalties, Spiegel and the Jewish community of Germany still stand uncomfortably between two superpowers who continue to shape the domestic agenda of Jews today, not just in Germany, but all over the world. However, strides have been made in Germany for claiming a stronger, more identified, and more independent community whose relationships to these two countries will mature toward a more equal relationship.

The attention to tolerance and the protection of minorities has not been left up to German elites alone, even in this more favorable environment. A major factor contributing to this improved relationship, although not without tension, is the presence of "non-state actors" such as the AJC, the Ronald Lauder Foundation, and the Chabad Lubavitch on German soil. Such non-governmental organizations (NGOs) function in two ways to affect foreign policy by, according to Gardner-Feldman, "attempting to influence government policy in the home country, or directly building a relationship with the government of the other country."[40] Acting with similar moral and political intentions, the AJC, founded in 1906 by German-Jewish immigrants, played the major role in facilitating relationships between Jews in the United States, the German government, and the Jewish community in Germany since the end of the war. The opening of its Berlin office in 1998 was a major watershed. After being the first managing director of the office for two years, Eugene Dubow, who had orchestrated bringing an American rabbi to the fledgling East Berlin Jewish Community in the eighties, retired and Deidre Berger, a former newscaster for National Public Radio and a journalist for the Jewish Telegraphic Agency, took charge after a stint as associate director. These years have seen the office grow in size and stature. In a city like Berlin, where spaces are so replete with meaning, its location adds to its status. It is literally situated between two significant sites of German history—between the supposed Hitler Bunker on the north and the remnants of the Wall on the south—and headquartered in the symbolic Mosse Palais across the street from the new Potsdamer Platz. When the office, one of the first in the neighborhood, opened, the square was filled with cranes and construction sites. Now it is the center of the new Berlin with postmodern skyscrapers and pedestrian zones filled with business people on their lunch hour. Potsdamer Platz is the closest Berlin comes to looking like a major American metropolis; still Berliners are ambivalent about this redrawn skyline and redeveloped city quarter.

For the AJC, the location represents its cosmopolitan role in international Jewish relations. Members from the organization itself, as well as other Jewish and German dignitaries, pay frequent visits to Berger, an attractive, petite, and stylish manager of a very complex organization. Supported by a small but dedicated staff and interns, the office bustles with activities that inevitably bring together diverse constituencies from various national or ethnic affiliations (Jewish, German, Christian, Turkish, American), diverse professionals (important government officials such as foreign ministers and presidents, scholars, teachers, students, AJC members), or some combination thereof. These groups focus on education, domestic and international relations, tolerance, and Jewish life in Berlin.

Simultaneously, the AJC has also grown in importance as German-American relations have become more intricate. High-level administrators, like Executive Director David Harris or Director of International Affairs Rabbi Andrew Baker, often function as ambassadors around the world on important Jewish issues. Consequently, the Berlin office has become something of a German outpost for international Jewish affairs; these Jewish leaders are their official emissaries. The newly opened AJC Transatlantic Institute in Brussels will complement the other European offices in Warsaw and Geneva as the organization focuses on European and European Union issues. Slave labor reparations, anti-Semitism and the Möllemann affair, the Second Intifada and the war in Iraq are only some of the topics that have occupied the Berlin office and for which the director is called on to speak publicly. For the recent OSCE Conference on Anti-Semitism, AJC Berlin organized an NGO Forum preceding the official meeting and shortly before that convened a task force on education and anti-Semitism.

As an American, as a Jew, and as representative of a premier American Jewish organization, the director of the AJC is a spokesperson whose status and power often transcends what one would expect from an NGO. Yet, such organizations, especially such a non-state actor that is both Jewish and American, have become conduits to segments of the German elites—government, armed forces, churches, intelligentsia—that are unreachable, inaccessible, invisible, or merely inappropriate for serious conversations with governments.[41] In a sense it is the concern and responsibility of Jews in America, the largest Jewish Diaspora population in the world not represented by the United States government, which necessitate such an unofficial organizational linkage.

This kind of Jewish influence contrasts with presumptions about so-called Jewish power that have sounded increasingly anti-Semitic, such as a link between America's war in Iraq and American support of Israel supposedly instigated by the neo-conservative, and above all, Jewish influence on the Bush administration's foreign policy by people like Paul Wolfowitz and Richard Perle. While there is no question that Jews have power and influence, as any group does that coalesces around a cause, it is more likely that we see this played out in the non-ideological policies of an NGO such as AJC, than in a presumed Jewish cabal in the White House. Precisely, these stereotypes of international or cosmopolitan Jewry have fed into the rise of anti-Semitism in Europe. While American policy toward Israel is at center stage, these two countries' attitudes toward Germany and its Jews play out in largely symbolic and sometimes material ways. The growth of a new indigenous German-Jewish identity will also be stimulated by reactions both for and against such international interventions that should not be cast in old formats and clichés.

The fifth anniversary of AJC in Berlin in March 2003 showed how important this NGO had become for German-Jewish-American relations. Looking back to the opening event of the Berlin office in February 1998, it was clear that this was a major event for American Jewry, German Jewry, and the German government. It was celebrated by the AJC, the local Jewish Community represented by Ignatz Bubis, and Andreas Nachama, president of the Berlin Jewish Community at the time, and major German political leaders, such as President Roman Herzog, Foreign Minister Klaus Kinkel, and Berlin Mayor Eberhard Diepgen. Chancellor Kohl declined the invitation citing other obligations, but instead wrote a warm letter of welcome to the AJC. As reported by Dubow, there were over three hundred articles about the event and every radio and television station in Germany covered it. More importantly, he outlines the reasons for the establishment of the first office of this kind on German soil: "It will put us in closer touch with the growing Jewish community in Germany, help support Germany's important relationship with Israel, and give us an outpost in Central Europe to watch all the developments that affect world Jewry in this region. The opening of AJC Berlin is a logical step in helping to extend the reach of American Jewry in an increasingly smaller and global world."[42]

After five years and subsequent souring German-American relations because of the Iraq War, the AJC has become an important conduit for discussion. Coinciding with the anniversary at the end of March 2003, the war brought David Harris and Deidre Berger among other AJC officials to meet with Chancellor Schröder and Foreign Minister Fischer. As with Katsav's two visits, the tone was positive. Reporting on the comments of American Jewish leaders, a journalist noted: "Germany's commitment to Israel and the United States remains strong despite divisions over Iraq, but anti-Americanism on the street is a 'worrisome' trend that German leaders should address."[43] In the exact words of AJC President Harold Tanner: "Germany is very important for the United States, for Israel and for the Jewish people. . . . We feel we can better serve our relations by being here, and we are proud this is our fifth anniversary."[44]

While American and Israeli relationships are clearly central for the Jewish community in Germany, the ties are not always simple, as Weizman's visit had shown. Similarly, while the AJC continues to cultivate its relationship with German-Jewish leaders, with important German government officials, and the major German political foundations, such as Konrad Adenauer (CDU), Friedrich Ebert (SPD), and Heinrich Böll (Greens), collaboration with the Jewish Community has not always been easy. However, the foundations are more than willing to partner with the AJC around issues such as anti-Semitism and tolerance education, as well as sponsoring trips of young parliamentarians to the United States to meet American Jewish officials. However, where Israel was once the watchdog on internal Jewish matters in Germany, the worldwide NGO network of the AJC, the benefit of its German expertise in its Washington and Berlin offices brings it in close contact with the Central Council on matters important to all of Diaspora Jewry such as anti-Semitism and the Middle East crisis. The 2004 OSCE Conference in Berlin was a pointed example of how American-Jewish and German-Jewish organizations can work in tandem with German and European supporters to create an international meeting that attends to a universal scourge, especially today. More domestic issues, such as tensions over Russian-Jewish immigration to Germany, pull the German-Jewish community once more toward Israel. It remains to be seen what kind of delicate balance the local community will establish for itself between these two super-powers.

As the Jewish community in Germany has grown and acquired strength in numbers and political influence that enhances its status, it has publicly a very positive, and privately a somewhat ambivalent attitude toward its American brethren. For the future of a German-Jewish community, it will be important that the two "super-powers," when it comes to Jewish matters, have to respect the independence and authority of German Jewry. They will have to conduct their own business and develop their own policies vis-à-vis the German government, as well as religious, social, or cultural matters domestically and internationally.

To be sure, tensions sometimes arise during collaborative projects about aims or objectives; egos are often bruised when this or that person in the Community is not adequately consulted or invited to an important public event. Relations seem to have improved from the time when the Jewish Museum's gala opening included few members of the local Community whose vision for the museum was different than the one actually realized. However, strains will persist because of political and economic differences or inter-Jewish conflicts that welcome the solidarity of American Jews on one side or the other. For example, tensions still remain between Jews from the former East Germany and the former West Germany, demonstrated in the overwhelming participation of former GDR Jews and Russian immigrants in the Jewish Cultural group that was started in the East before 1989. In the latter case, the Community's very public battle with the World Union of Progressive Judaism about recognition and resources also can draw the Americans into the fray.

Individual American Jews also have a leading presence in Berlin in intellectual and cultural life. Michael Blumenthal, the secretary of the treasury in the Carter presidency and now the director of the Jewish Museum in Berlin, is perhaps the most prominent. Another major cultural organization, the American Academy in Berlin, which is directed by Gary Smith, an American Jewish scholar of the Frankfurt School of Critical Theory, sits in the high-class suburb of Wannsee. In a luxurious villa, the Academy, which opened in 1988, brings together writers and poets, painters and sculptors, curators, anthropologists, German cultural scholars, economists, historians, theologians, legal scholars, journalists, architectural and cultural critics, composers and musicologists, and public policy experts.[45] Following Smith in his important function as director of the Einstein Forum, Susan Neiman, an American Jew and a former professor of philosophy at Yale and Tel Aviv, organizes these international intellectual discussions that draw substantial public audiences. She is also the author of a memoir about life in Berlin in the 1980s called *Slow Fire: Jewish Notes from Berlin* (1992).[46]

Along with the AJC, the Lauder Foundation, now housed in its own *Lehrhaus* (learning center) — named after an institution founded by Franz Rosenzweig in the 1920s — in the Rykestrasse synagogue in the trendy section of eastern Berlin called Prenzlauer Berg, adds another dimension to the American Jewish mix in the city. Unrecognizable as what Jews in Germany might think of as an Orthodox rabbi, the young and dynamic Josh Spinner, who was born in Baltimore and grew up in Hamilton, Ontario, directs the Lehrhaus. I visited his offices on a cold, blustery winter day in January. I remembered that this was the synagogue in which I celebrated Rosh Hashanah services in 1990, at the first unified service of East and West Berlin Jews. Adorned with its prominent stars of David wrought in iron on the gates, the building looked the same although the surroundings had changed dramatically. Now Prenzlauer Berg, according to many, is the best place to live in Berlin. The sign of the Lauder Foundation stands out on the red brick exterior wall, although I would have had no trouble finding the foundation since a policeman stood outside. A young woman unlocked the gate and led me up a flight of stairs to renovated offices whose newness marked the ever-present extinction of the less modern insides of former GDR buildings. As I waited for Spinner, I also remembered my visits to the first very modest Lauder office in the early 1990s when the director, Joel Levy, had just arrived and the Lehrhaus was only an idea.

My conversation with Spinner, whose only religious marking was his kippah (yarmulke), lasted two hours. He was lively, engaged, energetic, and clearly committed to the future of Jewish life in Germany. He felt that God had brought the Jews to Germany and it was his job to do what he could to make a Jewish life possible, no matter where it might be. His intense commitment is reflected in his powerful words: "Wherever there are Jews, there should be a Jewish life."[47] What he called "the pariah status" of Jews in Germany for so many years since the war's end should not hinder the development of Jewish life that is active and in the world, being German as well as Jewish. Rather than demonstrating Jewishness through symbolically attending a Klezmer concert, remembrance of a lost world that did not even belong to German Jews, Spinner offers substantive Jewish learning through full- or part-time study. While not training Jewish "officials" such as rabbis and cantors, Spinner is training, in his words, "what to look for in a rabbi or cantor."[48] In other words, Lauder's goal is to create a knowledgeable, educated, and integrated halakhic and secular Jewish life from within, wherever Jews live, be it Germany or elsewhere. Then they can show their fellow citizens, as well as non-practicing Jews, the real existence of a Jewish life based on the skills of "any observant Jewish man."

Like Berger of the AJC, Spinner is aware of the tensions within the Jewish Community and the ways that external organizations are often regarded as competitors. For Spinner, as for Brooklyn-born Rabbi Yehuda Teichtel who heads Chabad Lubavitch, they offer alternatives and satisfy needs that the Jewish Community cannot provide. Teichtel, unlike Spinner, looks like any Chabadnik in the streets of Crown Heights or Jerusalem. Located in an apartment on a quiet street in the former West Berlin, Teichtel's multifaceted and cramped office/shul/kitchen/meeting area has, unlike Spinner's quarters, the feel of a typical Berlin apartment, which it actually is. Oblivious to the disarray, Teichtel seemed more than happy to tell me about his work. His energetic enthusiasm typified Chabad's goals to win over Jews to their brand of pious and dedicated Judaism that focuses on the teaching of Torah, recognition of the Creation, and the importance of each creature. This philosophy guides "each person to refine and govern his and her every act and feeling through wisdom, comprehension, and knowledge."[49] A curious mixture, but not atypical for Chabad, of both entrepreneurial and spiritual attitudes, Teichtel came to Berlin in 1996 with his wife as the emissary of the Lubavitcher Rebbe who had had a special interest in Germany for more than twenty years. Pointing out that Chabad came at the invitation of the Jewish Community, he smiles as he tells me how the past seven and a half years have been so successful. Through personal connection to Jews, Teichtel sees Chabad responding especially to the unaffiliated Russian immigrants. He proudly enumerates that there are 4,800 families connected to Chabad, 1,000 actively involved with four to five hundred children. Aside from the education programs such as schools and camps and social assistance, Teichtel gleefully tells of some of his public projects to make Jewish life more visible, for example, organizing 1,000 people with sparklers on the main boulevard in western Berlin to celebrate Chanukah or four hundred children celebrating Purim publicly on the Kurfürstendamm. For Teichtel, this is "the best sign that Judaism is happening."[50] He also prides himself on bringing in people to Shabbat services with his "Shabbat package" where, for a minimal amount, individuals receive Shabbes food or teach children how to bake matzeh or how religious scrolls are written. Following his dictum to "go where the people are,"[51] Teichtel even visits Jewish inmates in Berlin prisons. Teichtel's organization has stimulated private functions as well, holding weddings (one had just taken place the night before I visited him), bar and bat mitzvahs, and home visitations. Surprisingly unprejudiced and open, he emphasizes that he has never experienced anti-Semitism from Germans, but rather from Arabs, a situation that he emphasized could take place anywhere. He looks forward to continued good relations with the city—he is proud that Klaus Wowereit, the mayor of Berlin, has visited Chabad. Albert Meyer, the new head of the Berlin Community, is a big supporter. Teichtel's plans for an enlarged Chabad Center in a new building testify to the future he sees for a flourishing Jewish life in Germany and he is actively raising money. This optimism illustrates his fervent belief that the greatest service to six million killed is the establishment of Jewish life on German soil to prove Hitler wrong. Apparently, the suspicions from the Community and other Jewish organizations that greeted Teichtel and his wife when they arrived have disappeared and he looks forward to his continued work in Germany.

These three representatives of major American Jewish organizations do not, of course, represent the mainstream of American Jewish life, but are institutional proof of serious American Jewish engagement in Germany. Numerous other Jewish institutions have brought rabbis and lay leaders from the United States, in addition to German organizations that bring young gentile Germans, Jews, and sometimes Israelis together, such as "Bridge of Understanding" and "Action Reconciliation Service for Peace," both directed by non-Jewish Germans. Since 1961, the latter has brought approximately 2,500 young people to work in Israel in social welfare and hospital programs. In fact, youth exchanges between Germany and Israel are numerous and organized "by political foundations, churches, universities, or different cities directed to the German public."[52] There are also many German-Israeli sister city programs and exchange programs, especially for young leaders, political elites, journalists, and opinion makers, such as the Federal Office for Political Education, the Federal Press Office, the Foundation for Science and Politics, and importantly, the German-Israeli Parliamentarians group. Apparently, according to the Foundation for Science and Politics, "Israel is—after the USA—the most visited country by German politicians."[53] The major German political foundations have offices in Israel, as well as strong links with Israeli political parties, as that between Mapam (Israeli Labor Party) and the SPD, enhanced through the Socialist International. In addition, American Jewish and Israeli scholars and students participate in exchange programs.

Thus, Berlin, aside from its demography and numbers, holds memories that will continue to resonate precisely because of how history and those who have made and written these stories have created meaning for this special place. Each new generation reshapes these memories, such as the hundreds of young Jewish Americans and Canadians living, working, and studying in Berlin who are drawn to this site, even unconsciously, because of its special meaning. Like Paris in the early postwar period, Berlin has become a home for temporary and permanent expatriates, many of whom are Jewish. In the artistic, cultural, intellectual, financial, and technology milieus, there is energy and excitement only possible in a city that is literally and metaphorically transforming itself constantly and stands as a model for the entire country and the Continent.

One hopes this cosmopolitan city will continue to be populated by new German Jews, as well as other new kinds of Germans or non-Germans from different countries, whose future is linked to a positive depiction of a multicultural society. North American organizations whose representatives and citizens are more familiar with diversity are contributing significantly to understanding among various constituencies, both religious and ethnic. More pronounced than in North America, Israel, of course, provides its own complex picture of diversity among Orthodox and secular, Sephardim and Ashkenazim, as well as Jews from places like Yemen and Ethiopia. Still, with the help of outsiders and the perspectives such as those from the United States and Israel, German Jewry will begin producing its own future leaders. There will be more German Jews to direct and lead the Community, the synagogues and religious, educational, and social programs. Many Jews in Germany would prefer producing their own rabbis rather than having to import them from abroad since lack of familiarity with the tradition and history of the Jewish community in Germany has repeatedly caused problems. If German Jewry is to continue to grow and thrive, it will have to become one Diaspora population among others, yet special because of its history and unique because of its new dynamism, evolution, and population. In short, it must look backward and forward at the same time. While German Jewry was once thought to have literally been destroyed for the present with no future, its growing new community may now ironically be the site for rethinking not only Jewish German life, but also a redefined notion of the Jewish Diaspora for years to come.

8

Toward a New German Jewish Diaspora in an Age of Globalization

The preceding chapters have contributed to my thesis that the dramatic fall of the Berlin Wall in 1989 and its geopolitical repercussions precipitated the creation of a new Jewish and Diaspora identity in Germany. The movement of peoples and ideas, as well as their representations in public spheres—in literature, journalism, and museums—support this viewpoint. Film and television are, of course, other examples which I do not address here. A new Diaspora community is forming, one that has a "German-Jewish" identity rather than, as in postwar terms, being made up of "Jews in Germany." In time, the notion of a new German Jew may come to dominate the more evasive categories that tried to represent the complex identities of postwar Jews in Germany in so many different terms. This transformation is shaped by the domestic, continent-wide, and international (especially American and Israeli) influences that are part of a globalized environment which must be taken into consideration if we are to understand changing notions of Diaspora today.

The Jewish literature on the subject of Diaspora (voluntary exile) and the Galut (involuntary exile) is quite extensive and complicated for English speakers. Howard Wettstein notes in his introduction to the volume aptly titled *Diasporas and Exiles: Varieties of Jewish Identity* (2002), "the term 'exile' rather than the more modern Diaspora better translates Galut, the traditional Hebrew expression for the Jew's perennial condition. . . . To be in Galut is to be in the wrong place; it is to be dislocated, like a limb out of a socket."[1] From the biblical expulsion of Adam and Eve to the historical destruction of the Second Temple in 70 C.E. and the defeat of Bar Kokhba in 135 C.E., dispersal, defined as "galut[,] became not an exception, but the rule for Jewish life."[2] In the opinion of the scholars in this volume,

Galut and Diaspora need to be distinguished because the first, defined as exile, suggests "anguish, forced homelessness, and the sense of things being not as they should be"[3] and the latter "suggests absence from some center . . . [but] does not connote anything so hauntingly negative."[4] These distinctions are very important not for merely semantic or pedantic reasons. Rather they offer the possibility to differentiate the potential positive and negative meanings of displacement, commonly connoted with the word "diaspora" and applicable to all peoples who are not in any so-called center associated with the homeland, but rather in the "periphery." Like Sander Gilman, whose notion of the "frontier" seeks to avoid such absolutes that ascribe only positive or negative characteristics to one or the other, I am seeking to highlight the fluidity of meanings traditionally associated with Israel and the Diaspora.[5] This developing new Jewish identity and the new German Jew will have an altered relationship not only to a potentially positive Diaspora rather than Galut in its strictest sense, but also to German Jewry's prewar past, to its collective memory of the Holocaust, and to its future in Europe.

But diaspora and the movement of peoples associated with a phenomenon that has become all the more pervasive since 1989–1990 cannot be disentangled from the international processes of globalization mediated by advances in technology and mass communication. As the anthropologist Arjun Appadurai has aptly noted: "Electronic mediation and mass migration mark the world of the present not as technically new forces but as ones that seem to impel (and sometimes compel) the work of the imagination. Together, they create specific irregularities because both viewers and messages are in simultaneous circulation. Neither images nor viewers fit into circuits or audiences that are easily bounded within local, national, or regional spaces."[6]

In short, images and ideas are on the move as much as people. Global technology has created communication, dialogue, and exchange irrespective of time and space. Obviously, Jewish identity has also benefited from these new kinds of links as borders are crossed or redrawn, be they of nation-states or in virtual cyberspace. There exists a "virtual Jewishness" created, for example over the Internet, much different than the one Ruth Gruber fears is being created on the ground in Europe by non-Jews. New theories about identity, belonging, community, and home, all notions that one could call "virtual" in a radically different way central to this study, are also being rethought when boundaries of all kinds no longer confine movement as they once did. Beyond what I have demonstrated in this book, under the influence of Benedict Anderson's now classic notion of "imagined communities," Jewish identity and diaspora is thus being constructed and "imagined" in a myriad of new ways especially for the paradigmatic Diaspora people of the last two thousand years. In the words of the classicist Erich Gruen in the lead article on "Diaspora and Homeland" in the aforementioned volume: "Diaspora lies deeply rooted in the Jewish consciousness. It existed in one form or another almost from the start, and it persists as in integral part of the Jews' experience of history. The status of absence from the center has demanded time and again that Jews confront and, in some fashion, come to terms with a seemingly inescapable concomitant of their being. The images of uprootedness, dispersal, and wandering haunt Jewish identity throughout. Jews have written about it incessantly, lamented it or justified it, dismissed or grappled with it, embraced it or deplored it."[7]

Today, of course, all peoples are marked by global processes that create the shifting identities that Appadurai described above, especially the modern-day diaspora peoples—black Africans, the Chinese, the Armenians, the South Asians, and in new ways, the Jews. In the words of Jonathan and Daniel Boyarin, the former an anthropologist of the Jews and the latter a radical Talmudic scholar, in their book *Powers of Diaspora: Two Essays on the Relevance of Jewish Culture*: "Diaspora, partaking always of the local, but by definition never confined to it, thus suggests itself as a place where that interaction can be grasped. . . . There may be something to be gained from thinking about diaspora . . . as a positive resource in the necessary rethinking of models of polity in the current erosion and questioning of the modern nation-state system and ideal."[8]

As we know, the Jews of Europe, and especially those of Germany, as a prominent yet destroyed diaspora population, have a rich and tragic history. The Jewish Museum in Berlin, as I described earlier, traces the two-thousand-year Jewish presence in the geographic area that comprises modern-day Germany. We know as well that our remapped globe is inhabited, however comfortably or uncomfortably, by refugees, exiles, immigrants, or tourists. These various iterations of people on the move are simultaneously defined legally, socially, and theologically (often by others in power) as to where they belong in the social order and their specific relationship between their origin and their destination. Studying globalization in general and the new German Jews in particular has taught me that we must pay more attention to those "travelers" who make up increasingly larger portions of the world's population and that the diaspora zones they create often do not necessarily coincide with the formal borders of nation-states. Historically, in the Jewish tradition, the Boyarins make a strong case for the condition that most diaspora peoples and probably all global citizens find themselves in the twenty-first century: "diaspora identity is a disaggregated identity. Jewishness disrupts the very categories of identity because it is not national, not genealogical, not religious, but all of these in dialectical tension with one another."[9]

The Jews in Germany, like the Turks, are one such example of a group whose identity is constantly changing with the dramatic shifts in migration in the global tug of war of Jewish identity politics between the United States and Israel, and now Europe. As I have shown, the year 1989 altered the face of Jewish life in Germany. This historic turning point cast that country once again as a nation of immigrants as far as Jewish life was concerned, even if the official policy of Germany stated categorically that "Germany is not a country of immigration" and Jews from the Soviet Union were legally defined in a privileged category as "Kontingenten-flüchtling" and not immigrants. These "new" German Jews have become the quintessential hybrid diaspora people. This is the case in a European environment that has both persecuted them and now in many cases welcomes them as a "litmus test" of democracy and liberalism, especially as Eastern European countries, freed from the Soviet yoke, legitimize themselves as acceptable for entry into the EU and NATO. In fact, in the Boyarins' and Diana Pinto's terms, the Jews can ironically be seen as holding the key to the future of Europe. Where once a "new Europe" meant a continent without Jews, it now means a continent with new Jewish communities and a strengthened Jewish self-consciousness. In the words of Jonathan Boyarin: "Jews are thus examples of different notions of Europe. In addition to specifying Jews as a uniquely and unequivocally demonic force, Hitler made an example of them as well. They were the example of what had to be eliminated in order to produce a New Europe. Anti-fascists and other liberals . . . also take the Jews as exemplary Europeans, those without whom there can be no 'Europe as such.'"[10]

Thus, the Jews of Europe and especially of Germany reflect not only the demographic shifts, but also the constantly transforming identities of the new Europe in the individual histories of these nations to "their Jews." These domestic and international relationships are now even more confused because of ruptures in the transatlantic alliance caused by tensions in the Middle East and the Iraq war.

Increasingly, the relationship between Israel and its Diaspora is being altered due to religious, political, or social differences and the changing Jewish culture in both the traditional Jewish homeland and Germany. Many citizens of the homeland seem more Israeli than Jewish.[11] Consequently, Jewish Diaspora existence may well become more de-centered and self-assured. Historically, this balancing act goes back to the State of Israel's earliest years. In 1950, the correspondence between David Ben-Gurion and Jacob Blaustein, the president of the American Jewish Committee, made clear that the allegiance of American Jews was to the United States, home of the largest Jewish Diaspora, and not to Israel. This understanding continued to be confirmed years afterward although it was valid only for American Jews and not the rest of the Diaspora.[12]

In his study of seven Diaspora cities, four of which are in Europe, *Home Lands: Portraits of the New Jewish Diaspora* (2001), journalist Larry Tye extends the dimensions of this new relationship when he states: "The Jewish diaspora is as critical to the survival of Israel as Israel is to the survival of the Jewish people."[13] Four years earlier, another Jewish American journalist, Mark Kurlansky, affirmed, more cautiously at that earlier phase of European integration, the new weight of the European Diaspora in his book *A Chosen Few: The Resurrection of European Jewry*. But even Israelis have weighed in on the subject, as Yossi Beilin, minister of justice in Ehud Barak's cabinet stated, "We are equals, that's the new covenant."[14] And in the words of Israeli political scientist Yossi Shain: "Thus, it seems that Jews inside Israel cannot separate themselves fully qua Jews from the Jewish community abroad, just as diaspora Jews cannot escape the realities of the modern state of Israel."[15] History bears this out as well. The relationship of the Diaspora to Israel, and one must add to the Holocaust, especially for American Jews, changed with the 1967 war when "Israel gained active diasporic support and, in turn, legitimized the normalized status of the Diaspora and provided it with a much-needed sense of community identity."[16] Recent immigration data show four times as many Israelis live in the United States as American Jews in Israel. Another surprising statistic indicates that the number of Israelis of German descent applying for German passports has increased dramatically in the two years since the start of the Second Intifada. The German embassy in Tel Aviv is currently issuing some 250 passports a month, more than double the number of the 1990s, and is expected to top 3,000 this year, compared to 1,751 in 2001.[17]

A lawyer who represents many of these dual citizens claims that many Israelis regard a German passport as "an insurance policy" in case times get harder.[18] And perhaps even more surprising is the fact that in 2002 more Jews from the former Soviet Union immigrated to Germany (19,262) than to Israel (18,878).[19]

The Diaspora's changing attitude toward Israel, which Tye chronicled in his book that concludes with a chapter entitled "Israel, A Partnership of Equals," acknowledges more detachment and increased willingness on the part of even Jewish organizations to consider other Jewish populations as important as Israel's. The existence of a Jewish state, while central to world Jewry's notion of community, may no longer be, according to Tye, the place they call home, as even Israelis realize that *aliyah* (Hebrew: ascent) or immigration to Israel of all Diaspora Jews is neither realistic nor efficient. Other Jewish scholars also present this dilemma, among them Jerold S. Auerbach, *Are We One? Jewish Identity in the United States and Israel* (2001),[20] Deborah Dash Moore and S. Ilan Troen, editors of *Divergent Jewish Cultures: Israel and America* (2001),[21] and Steven T. Rosenthal, *Irreconcilable Differences: The Waning of the American Jewish Love Affair with Israel* (2001).[22] The recent statistics of immigration from the former Soviet Union to Israel cited above were tempered by the hope of the Jewish Agency that Russian Jews who immigrated to Germany might go to Israel. However, the agency now recognizes that the development of a strong Jewish community in Germany cannot be halted and rather than fighting this reality, it now plans to foster a spirit of Zionism in this population to "encourage Jewish roots and Jewish Zionist education . . . to create the opportunity that at least the younger generation will believe that their place is in Israel, not in Germany."[23] Such Zionist goals in the German-Jewish community are an interesting counterargument in the face of my own interviews with Russian Jewish students who, while clearly ambivalent about living in Germany, for the most part still plan to make their home in their new host country.

Tye may purposefully have split the word "Home Lands," in the title to his book to represent the literal breaking and questioning not only of this conflicted term, but also of a conflicted identity, as is the case for many of these German Jews who want to remain. While most feel more at home in their new country than expected, in fact, some much more than in Israel, the specifically German notion of "Heimat" is still inflected with the semantics of racial exclusion identified with the Nazi era and may therefore never take hold. Current debates in Germany about who should be included in the German Holocaust memorial, specifically named "Memorial to the Murdered Jews of Europe," and the possible addition of one for the *Heimatvertriebene* (Germans forced out of their homes in Eastern Europe at the end of World War II) are recent attempts to rehabilitate the notion of Heimat as it acknowledges German as well as Jewish victimhood. For Jews in Germany, homeland in any of these particular forms remains, perhaps more than for any other Diaspora Jewish population, an unachievable or at least an ambiguous goal. As I have tried to show in this entire study, the shadow of German history to this day darkens even the most optimistic efforts toward reconciliation.

Precisely because "diaspora" defines itself by the constant migratory and semantic flow between a contested notion of home (where one belongs), and domicile (where one lives), the study of diaspora must go beyond merely empirical data. I refer here to the numbers and status of the people after migration as well as the processes of movement. In other words, a closer examination of how these shifts in mobility take place and what they mean for our understanding of evolving identities is needed. The transformation of Jewish identity in Germany—from pre-1933 German Jew to post-1989 German Jew—represents such a reality in German history. While Heimat may not fit the Jewish experience in Germany today, it does not mean that Jews in Germany are not making a different kind of home. This diaspora process affects both the self-definition of Jews, indigenous and newly arrived, as well as the German non-Jewish populations' perceptions of the minorities and themselves. And for both sides it means a changing conception of Germanness, Jewishness, and home itself.

Diaspora, according to political scientist Itty Abraham, has stimulated in the nation-state "a foundational trauma . . . [namely] the desire to identify unambiguously who belongs within the state and who does not."[24] What at first glance seems a clear-cut either-or for defining diaspora is being complicated by the literature on diaspora in which there is a growing emphasis "on the dual orientation of diaspora communities; on the one hand, to fight for citizenship and equal rights in the place of settlement, often alongside other ethnic groups; and, on the other, to continue to foster transnational relations and to live with a sense of displacement and of loyalty to other places and groups beyond the place of settlement."[25]

As they confront an evolving and dynamic notion of identity, Russian Jews in Germany have become increasingly aware of their "Russianness" as well as their Jewishness. They may want to stay in Germany's comfortable surrounding that provides financial and personal security, although they will never quite feel that they belong, that is, that they are Germans. The fixed definition of "Heimat" equated with "Germany" may be changing as "Germany" and "German" lose some of their nationalistic and even racial overtones. At least, the Russian immigrants feel, according to some surveys, that there is more stability in their new host country than in the shaky states of the former Soviet Union.[26] Like the Turks, they remain a hybrid group, the constant presence of foreignness, in the eyes of a Germany that is itself still uncomfortable with an evolving notion of German identity. While the presence of these Jews reinforces the integrative, progressive, and above all civic power of a German democracy to accept difference as part of German identity, their effect is countervailed by the conservative retrenchment articulated in the debate on German *Leitkultur*, an exclusive ideology that advocates circumscribed ethnic criteria for who may belong in a German Heimat. As described earlier, these criteria seemed to many Jews too reminiscent of exclusionary policies against those without the proper racial or ethnic pedigree.

The new German Jew is evolving, made up primarily of Russians—subsumed here are Ukrainians, Byelorussians, Georgians, Latvians, Lithuanians, and Estonians—but also of Israelis, Americans, and other nationalities settling in the future site of one of the largest Jewish settlements in Europe. Berlin, the new capital of a reunified and rehabilitated Germany, is becoming, above all, the cosmopolitan European capital at the crossroads of East and West, North and South. Writing in 1998, the journalist Neil Ascheron confidently proclaimed: "In twenty years' time the very epicentre of European gravity will have shifted eastwards to a point nearly half-way between Moscow and the Atlantic. That point is called Berlin."[27]

Michal Bodemann places similar emphasis on the cosmopolitan role of Berlin when he asks at the conclusion of his last book: "What are the consequences for the Jewish Community now that Berlin is the new capital?"[28] His answers are important and reflect his professional expertise as a sociologist concerned with ethnicity. He reminds us of the centrality of Berlin as cosmopolitan metropolis that must have ethnic minorities, such as the Jews, to give it such status. Jewish life has assumed a new, if different role in the city that is now home not only of the largest Jewish population in Germany, but also of the headquarters of major German-Jewish and international Jewish organizations as well. Jewish life is now centered in the same space as Jewish memory, both prewar, East German, and post-reunification. Finally, Bodemann correctly grants Berlin its place for the future of Jewish memory in Germany: "Memory [of the Shoah] will continue to survive, even get stronger, with or without artificial monuments, as long as Berlin is the capital and German identity remains a topic of discussion."[29]

Consequently, a new Jewish identity and even an evolving future German identity would find common ground in the global migration of peoples that transcend borders of states and demarcated regions. Local specificities always necessarily intrude in broader global shifts and vice versa, as the Jewish and the German or as in the culinary metaphor, bagels become almost as common as Turkish döner kebabs and even Berlin's favorite curry wurst. Perhaps they will all be served at the German table. Such changes, be they in culinary or in Jewish-American culture, mirror the struggle between the particular and the universal characteristic of global culture as it countermands any steadying of the constantly shifting foundations that undermine fundamental mutually exclusive categories of "German" and "Jew." The process of unseating static notions of identity, be they German or Jewish, follows the path of the Jews in Germany on their road to becoming a new German Jewry, an identity based on civic rather than ethnic values. Jews in Germany who acquire citizenship and participate in the democratic processes of the state will express their German Jewishness as citizens, be they religious or secular, and not as ethnically or nationally identified "Germans."

"Cosmopolitanism" may be a fitting term to describe this rehabilitation of the notion, especially in the diaspora context. The Soviet and other communist regimes once used this term pejoratively to mark Jewish citizens as too worldly or too closely affiliated with interests incompatible with the state's goals. Now it may well be acquiring more positive meanings for global Jewish life. More generally, but applicable to Jews, according to Mike Featherstone, it described "dabbling rootlessly in a variety of cultures. This view of the cosmopolitan as voyeur, parasite, or some sort of cultural tourist emphasizes this incapacity to form lasting attachments and commitments to place and others, the inability to participate in a community for which one feels obliged to make sacrifices."[30] However, in a new more positive cosmopolitanism, less ideologically laden as in the Soviet sense and increasingly more cognizant of the benefits of multiple cultural experiences, identities have more room to expand to include varieties of affiliations simultaneously. Of course, they remain in constant flux, never normalized or prescriptive, but this constant repositioning and interaction provides an essential moment for critical reflexivity, as unsettling as it is liberating. This in-between or third state may be the only constant in the coming years as part of what many would, in fact, identify as the postmodern condition. This "space," to use a term I have referred to earlier, may be the new kind of "home" that exists for Jews in Germany. It may be one that cannot be situated in a single place, but rather is one that does not bear either the pain of rootless diaspora existence in Germany or the desire to be in the longed-for homeland of Israel. What for a long time were mutually exclusive alternatives now seem to be giving way to alternatives, in representations of the German Jewish population in literature and in daily life. Rafael Seligmann's character Jonathan, Barbara Honigmann's heroine Sohara, and Wladimir Kaminer's own authorial voice could be interpreted as different versions of what might be called a "third way."

A notion of such a hybrid home and hybrid identity, beyond the security of an "either-or," raises more difficult questions. In the words of one diaspora scholar, "Diasporas, it seems, are both ethnic-parochial and cosmopolitan."[31] Therefore, we have to ask: Does a diaspora community, such as that of the new German Jewry, distinguish itself from other Jewish Diasporas today? What kind of German-Jewish home will exist? Globalized and cosmopolitan, or local and provincial? How will it be evaluated? What will this mean for German Jewry in particular and Diaspora Jewry in general?

Some expert commentators on diaspora and its German Jewish iteration take different viewpoints on these questions. Not surprisingly these observers are German Jews who make their home in Canada, Israel, and the United States, rather than Germany, as if to acknowledge that an outside perspective is necessary to understand what is at stake in a discussion that is so deeply imbedded in German and Jewish assumptions. Reversing conventional ideas, the "periphery" here adds perspective to the "center," rather than the reverse. Bodemann describes a globalized or cosmopolitan German-Jewish consciousness as part of what he calls a "re-ethnicization": "The new media may have brought everyone closer together, but political and social realities remain as far apart as ever, with each ethnic Diaspora conjugated by the realities of its unique social and political environment. What the new media have . . . accomplished is the continuous infusion of new ethno-national, cultural influences from abroad, often from the country of origin; re-ethnicization, yes, but not de-ethnicization."[32]

Bodemann goes further to suggest that any globalization process will have to take place "within the confines of Europe, although this has not yet materialized."[33] Nathan Sznaider and Daniel Levy, two sociologists who prominently figure in a debate on cosmopolitan memory and the Holocaust, are more optimistic and positive than Bodemann about diaspora and its potential for cosmopolitan identity: "Jews, particularly in Europe, were a 'people' and at the same time they were cosmopolitan—sometimes not of their own free will. Jews chose to live in the tension between universalism and individualism, but this tension today is not a purely Jewish existence, which had represented 'otherness,' today increasingly resembles the concrete experiences of many ethnic and religious groups. The term Diaspora has a positive connotation and its metaphoric qualities extend beyond territorial boundaries. Diaspora is not to be mistaken for total universalism. Diaspora is precisely the tension between universalism and individualism."[34]

This positive cosmopolitanism, which is not a universalism in a re-ethnicized German-Jewish context, addresses precisely the status of the new German Jewry presented here.[35] Resembling other diaspora peoples structurally, yet retaining the specificity of the Jewish experience in Germany and Europe before, during, and now almost sixty years after the war, the new German Jews represent a revised notion of Diaspora Jewry and contribute to a new notion of home. In Pnina Werbner's words: "As diasporas gain historical depth, they acquire alternative sacred centers, either complementary to or in tension with the original homeland."[36] In short, Israel is no longer necessarily home for all Jews even as it remains a source of identity and kinship.[37]

In fact, American Jewry, well integrated into American life, feels that their country is the most secure homeland today for Jews, a place where they can be free of anti-Semitism in its most pernicious forms. Leon Wieseltier states this bluntly when he claims that the United States is "a Diaspora that is not an exile."[38] The United States, and Canada for that matter, can afford its constituents the freedom of dual allegiances that present more of a problem in countries with small Jewish populations or virulent anti-Semitism. It can also play an important role for Israeli identity by legitimizing

Conservative and Reform Judaism in a homeland beset by contentious divisions between secular and ultra-Orthodox factions.[39] It is a harsh debate for which the infamous German term "Kulturkampf" (cultural struggle) has even been invoked.[40] However, German Jewry's relationship to either a real or imagined homeland is constrained by its unique link to its own conflicted notion of "Heimat," Jewish ambivalence toward Germany as home, and Israeli dissent over the boundaries between national and Jewish identity, in other words between political or religious Judaism. Germany is developing, albeit more slowly and more carefully than the United States, a positive notion of Diaspora that neither excludes Israel nor makes the Jewish state the only site of Jewish belonging or identity.

These redefined notions of Jewish identity are being played out in a global arena that fosters movement and creates a unique stage upon which this new identity dance can be performed. However, according to some critics like Daniel Goldhagen, in his article "The Globalization of Antisemitism,"[41] or the historian Simon Schama, globalization is also engendering anti-Semitism in new virulent forms.[42] Like globalization and the debate it spawns, Jewish life and Jewish identity can be both nourished and impoverished by the whirlwinds that plant seeds all too indiscriminately around the globe. Schama, persuasively, and Goldhagen, less so, make a case for the dangers of the Internet in disseminating hate speech and anti-Semitic diatribes that are, in Schama's words, "verification and adjudication free."[43]

Other Jewish voices welcome the benefits of the worldwide technological revolution for the creation of identity, even a Jewish identity. After subscribing to a listserve called "CyberJew," Mark Poster, a prominent intellectual historian and leading theorist of the Internet, posed the provocative question Is a Cyber-Jew possible? in a book chapter entitled "Virtual Ethnicity."[44] The emergence of a "CyberJew" should not be surprising among the increasing technological means to exchange information and, in this case, construct identities and build new Diaspora consciousness. Jewish newspapers and news agencies, such as *The Forward*, *Der Aufbau*, the Jewish Telegraphic Agency, as well as websites such as hagalil.com or the juedische-allgemeine.de for European and German news, are only the most obvious of such opportunities for Jews around the world to access information and connect with each other. Other examples include Jewhoo, "a site devoted to cataloguing the Jewish identity of various celebrities in multiple categories, such as the arts, business, entertainment, and government,"[45] and ClickonJudaism, sponsored by the Union of American Hebrew Congregations or Reform Movement, which seeks "to get people engaged through the quality of the content online and to use that engagement as a doorway to the synagogue."[46] According to Harry Chauss, the Reform, progressive, or unaffiliated Jews "are most in search of an identity" and therefore are the target audience for these sites as well as Orthodox Judaism's "Aish haTorah," which also aims at this Reform group. Orthodox Judaism too has its sites, such as the Orthodox Union, which simply describes what is kosher and what is not. Chauss interprets this more "dispassionate" information as reflecting that Orthodoxy "means having chosen to accept certain axioms about life" and therefore not as much in need of identity building.[47] In the romantic realm, where Jews can create both sacred and profane bonds, there is even www.jeurope.net, initiated by Russian Jewish immigrants to Germany to help young Jewish singles around Europe to meet through the American example of "speed dating." The organizers have a dream, reports the journalist for the *Jüdische Allgemeine Wochenzeitung*, where the article appeared, "to create a virtual community for Jews living in Europe."[48] Let me add another, more serious example about a website itself. Hagalil, as described by Thomas von der Osten-Sacken, is "a private German Jewish portal which has become one of the largest in the German language, with over 140,000 entrants monthly. The idea of this portal stemmed not only, and not primarily, from the need to combat anti-Semitism and the anti-Semitic sites on the Internet, but to utilize the net for communication between Jews and to deal with Jewish topics. In as much as few Jewish centers are left in Germany, in contrast to the U.S., France, and England, and because only a small number of Jews are scattered throughout Germany, this medium seemed ideal."[49]

Such websites, listserves, newsgroups, chatrooms, and MOOS devoted to building "ethnic community" or "virtual ethnicity" on the Internet can be both unsettling and utilitarian, especially in the case of a positive diaspora identity that necessarily denies a place to traditional significance for Jewish identity. In Poster's words, "For many CyberJew participants: the Internet, far from dissolving ethnicity, enables all Jews, wherever they are on the planet, to connect with one another."[50] One provocative example introduces Poster's book *What's the Matter with the Internet* (2001) and reaffirms Chauss's contention above about Orthodoxy. An Orthodox Jew at the Western Wall in Jerusalem holds a cellular phone up to this sacred site to enable a distant friend to pray.[51] As Chauss points out, this kind of Jew is affirming an already established identity. Calling this "a new configuration of the virtual," Poster points to the possibilities of globalized technology detailed in the following by anthropologist Barbara Kirshenblatt-Gimblett: "The upsurge of Jewish networking, its rapid growth, scope, and ambitions, highlights the power of the medium to sustain an already diasporic formation." She cites rich examples from Jerusalem One, which seek to "build and maintain a professional, accessible system . . . to the Jewish world," Lubavitcher Chasidim who "coordinate the dispersed followers of their leader (rebbe)," and Chabad-Lubavitch in Cyberspace which "extends to tens of thousands of subscribers . . . where there are little Jewish resources . . . almost all the religious instruction they might need."[52] There is even a list serve called "Trek-Cochavim" "for those who want to discuss the Star-Trek World from a Jewish or Israeli perspective," as well as a virtual shtetl.[53] In other words, Jews as the diaspora people par excellence now employ both the connectedness and disconnectedness of the Internet to further break down boundaries and create alternative virtual notions of place in order to build rather than destroy Jewish identity.

Opportunities that may seem to go from the sublime to the ridiculous betray, however, a profound desire for contact and belonging through community, as we saw in Seligmann, Honigmann, and Kaminer as well. Created here is precisely the community that is "a place without a location."[54] As Kirshenblatt-Gimblett phrases this issue in a question about electronic communication in general: "How is locality produced in a medium dedicated to the seamless flow of data through a network of nodes that are addresses but not places?"[55] As Jews in a new globalized space, the Internet, understood as Poster and Kirshenblatt-Gimblett posit, makes it a symbol for all of Jewish Diaspora life today. The new Jewish Diaspora identity I describe here, while having the markings of conventional affinities of tribes based in blood, becomes a different kind of civic, political community constructed in many of the same terms as the global electronic communication network that is re-forming all identities today.

The global flow and movement of people, ideas, and commodities, as Poster reminds us, illustrates how much more important identity has become in our contemporary age than it was even twenty years ago before the Internet and electronic communication took off. But we should not forget that "cultural meanings and attitudes circulate the planet as well."[56] Facilitated by technological means, be it supersonic airplanes or e-mail, the significations that we associate with certain definitions and identities, such as "Jewish" or "German Jew," "diaspora" or "homeland," are in a constant process of change and realignment. As part of the postmodern turn, these re-articulations of what were once thought to be secure terms and meanings challenge our belief in the constancy and consistency of time and space for providing a fixed context of meaning. Who would have thought that post-Holocaust Jewish life would create the possibilities for a new German Jew or that a conservative Israeli government would be negotiating the existence of a Palestinian state? History has not only taught, but also learned that even hard facts offer reinterpretations of issues, terms, and ideas, and peoples that once seemed fixed and static. Mobility in all of its forms has become the motto of our day.

Perhaps Americans, and particularly American Jews, can also recognize that long-held assumptions about Germany or Palestine/Israel, for example, also deserve reconsideration in precisely the same way that "German Jew" has come to mean a different identity than before. It is understandable that American Jewry would remember and commemorate the two most important benchmarks in modern Jewish history, the Holocaust and the creation of the State of Israel. But its preoccupation with these two moments to the exclusion of less sensational and dramatic events that have come to be known as the "Shoah business" in the former and more politely named in the latter "a civic religion" contributes to reflecting on a new American Jewish identity as well. This could be one that is not based narrowly on victimhood, suffering, persecution, and death. Living in a Jewish community more secure than any in the world, American Jews might do well to rethink the meaning of life over death, as Jews in Germany have been compelled to ponder because of profound movements and shifts in their worlds on both sides of Europe. At the root of all this is the question of identity: who we are, where we belong, what is home in a world, especially in the United States since September 11, which no longer holds the certainty we once took so much for granted.

On such shaky ground, Americans, as Germans, Europeans, and Israelis have, may come to recognize that the future may offer only possibilities and risks, especially in view of these tragic events in the United States, the Second Intifada in the Middle East, the rise of anti-Semitism in Europe, and the Iraq War. There will certainly be more events that will unsettle Jewish identity, security, and belonging. Up until 2000, Israel powered the juggernaut of Jewish identity. According to Shain, "Whereas previously Israeli Zionism demanded a privileged Israeli voice in defining Jewish interests and identity, now, not only does the Diaspora largely determine its own way of life in America, but it has also demanded and gradually gained a voice in Israeli Jewish affairs. This new Zionist vision of reciprocity strengthens both pillars of world Jewry today in America and Israel, while simultaneously encouraging kinship solidarity."[57] After 2000, "the failure of the Oslo peace process and the waves of violence that ensued dramatically shifted the focus from Jewish identity back to existential security."[58]

With the emergence of the European third pillar in world Jewry, buttressed by the new German-Jewish population and the addition of Eastern Europe Jews, the relationship of Jews worldwide will shift again. In the future, even with small numbers, further expansion of their numbers will bring added strength to the Jews in Europe and certainly as well unforeseeable pitfalls. Even as it has become depleted of large numbers of its Jewish population through mass emigration to Israel, the United States, and Germany, Russia too is experiencing a rebirth of Jewish life and identity. Nevertheless internal Russian political problems that could always affect its Jewish population leave the situation for Jews there uncertain. However, a major issue for Jews, and for that matter for the rest of the world, is an end to the Palestinian-Israeli conflict, preferably in a two-state solution that brings peace and security to both sides. As we saw in the pre-2000 internecine battles between universalists and particularists, secular and religious Jews, and between the Diaspora and Israel, the cessation of external hostilities ironically is likely to bring with it heated internal Jewish battles. The end of the Middle East conflict will surely affect the entire Jewish Diaspora's concern about Israel's well-being, the war's resonance on national domestic political matters that touch Jews around the world, and the identity of Jewish life again as a diaspora issue.

The German-Jewish Community's own internal battles with Progressive Judaism, which emerged again in the spring of 2004, focusing on Diaspora identity there, remind us how grateful we should be that a community now exists in "the land of the murderers."[59] New questions will hopefully emerge from Germany and Europe, if not on the Holocaust itself then on current issues concerning international relations, especially after 1989 when Germany, and particularly Berlin, has become a new center of Jewish life in Europe. Can or will the Holocaust continue to be the touchstone or the gauge for articulating or representing moral good or absolute evil? Will the vocabulary of the Holocaust remain appropriate for describing atrocities elsewhere or as a universal metaphor? What will be the relationship between the universality of this position accessible to any taker and the particularity of the Jewish experience of genocide in Europe? How do international media affect Jewish memory of the Holocaust or other specifically Jewish historic experiences? In other words, what will the Jewish voice be in a new globalized Jewish environment such as Berlin, a city so saturated with cultural memory for Jews and so much the product of movement, transformation, and reconstruction for all citizens? In the absence of absolute truth, there must be at least an ethic of memory encompassing our many interpretations so that Holocaust deniers will not be able to take advantage of these fluid boundaries and spread their negative propaganda.[60]

In a world of intertwined global politics marked by wars, disasters, and human tragedy, as well as more positive futures, can we imagine a new role for what we might call "the Jewish voice" worldwide?[61] Rather than having to be, as so often before, the watchdogs for hostility, hate, and persecution, as well as its victims, might Jews not mediate between centers and peripheries and transcend boundaries of national politics in order to fulfill a transnational role imbedded in their traditional Diaspora identity as I have suggested above in the German case? This does not mean that Jewish commitment to Israel should diminish, only that the benefits of new Jewish communities in Europe and elsewhere in the Diaspora might play a stronger role as Diaspora-Israeli relations are recalibrated between the universals and particulars of globalized society today. Perhaps the Jewish voice can exemplify the positive aspects of a future globalized society that is characterized by hybridity and difference, rather than by purity and sameness. This would mean focusing on the interaction and production of voices and the identities that produce them, rather than on absolute or exclusive positions—either being only "for" or "against," or "one" or the "other."

These questions about the Jewish voice represent, to my mind, both the future of all minority voices in and between both political systems—for example, the Muslim voice in Europe or the African-American voice in the United States, as well as the Jewish—and the recognition of how nations come to terms with their diverse religious, racial, or ethnic diaspora populations of all kinds. How will the memories of these peoples' suffering—the competition of what Eric Langenbacher calls "memory regimes"[62]—affect domestic politics, foreign policy, and international relations as they do in Germany, the United States, and the Middle East? This situation is already the norm and it will continue to advance as the transfer of ideas and images increases, even more quickly through information technology than the large migration of people from country to country.

Globalization flattens experience as much as it expedites information flow and transfer. Identities are exchanged, assumed, and constructed at will, creating an insecure basis—even for those skeptical of absolute truth or authenticity—for substantive contact and communication. Mobility of various kinds will create a push-and-pull that will reshape cultural identities into new forms that will, in turn, challenge traditional notions of nation-state, ethnicity, race, or religion. Unfortunately, there are risks involved with such movement, as we saw so dramatically on September 11 when borders, once thought impregnable, were crossed in real and virtual space to both create the catastrophic events and make it possible to experience their horror simultaneously anywhere on the globe. Now "transnationals" or "non-state actors" terrorize friends and foes alike, making it even more difficult to know the boundaries of security and trust that guide us in distinguishing those who would do us harm from those who would not. Friends have become "enemies" and "perpetrators" are called "victims." In this frightening new system of relations, the United States and Germany, the former a traditional immigrant country and the latter new to this club, should draw more deeply on their long-term friendship and common values to support the positive aspects of movement inherent in new global networks, even as they recognize in post-1989 and again post-2001 that each has taken on a new role that in some way precludes the secure ties they once both had with each other.[63] These new pathways on land and in space are not a panacea but a reality of a new world order whose destabilization can be used for our benefit or disadvantage. Should we not harness these new arrangements positively for creating space to construct new identities that defy what we think we know and we have yet to learn? The developments in Germany I have discussed here may indeed offer some new perspectives on this problem.

POSTSCRIPT

I want to believe that the disturbances in Jewish life in Germany that have occurred since 2000 and have been described as the "new" anti-Semitism will be a passing phenomenon. Without undercutting the seriousness of recent events, I have seen bouts of such antagonisms emerge, be discussed seriously, and diminish. In fact, reviewing newspaper articles over many years for this book about Jewish life and anti-Semitism in Germany reminded me that anti-Semitism has always been present in various guises and with varying intensity. By the same token, there has always been discussion about its manifestations in Germany. However, today these expressions of hatred and prejudice emanate from different groups than before and are spurred by international events that demonize Israel and the Jews of Europe. If that is indeed a "new" anti-Semitism then this description may stand, but it should neither overstate nor underplay what constitutes Jewish life today. This observation is not meant as an apology or excuse, but rather my attempt in this book to take a longer and wider point of view that goes beyond the moment of its writing and presents a perspective imbedded in history and a broader political, social, and cultural context. As the author, I want this study, of course, to survive current events. I know too many German experts who never would have imagined the reunification of Germany and Russian specialists who were taken completely by surprise when the Soviet Union collapsed like a house of cards. I would also not want to be accused some years after the publication of this book of glib or naïve prognostications. So I have refrained from making sweeping judgments or definitive pronouncements about the future. In fact, I hope that the approach I have taken here, as well as the subject itself—the "new German Jew"—reflect how tentative and modest a scholar or critic must be today.

But I have traced here a new chapter in Jewish life in Germany: the creation of German-Jewish identities whose existence carries historical remnants of memories, language, and images reframed into what I hope will be a new narrative, in fact, what might turn out to be a hopeful and even positive story. Such a possibility recently seemed to be presented in one of Germany's most popular weekly television programs featuring one of Germany's primetime icons—*Tatort* (Scene of the Crime) with masculine, rough-hewn star Götz George playing Detective Schimanski. This installment took, at least in the eyes of a television critic, a step forward in the depiction of Jewish life.[64] Schimanski, with his usual cunning, comes to the aid of an Orthodox Jew who thinks he is about to be murdered by another Jew. Schimanski takes a job in a kosher restaurant to shadow the potential criminal. The critic emphasizes in his review in the prominent conservative daily *Frankfurter Allgemeine Zeitung* an interesting and provocative change from the typical obligatory and overly pious German knee-jerk response to Holocaust victimhood and guilt that took a female police detective to Israel in an earlier episode. In this installment, he writes, "While the Jewish religion may seem strange, also comical for those who do not hold these beliefs, [t]his [attitude] is not [presented] as a crime (*Verbrechen*). Religion, in this case the Jewish faith, is offered with dignity and is not ridiculed. It is shown [rather] as a possibility (*Möglichkeit*)."[65] Schimanski can be titillated by "the unfamiliar (*fremd*) ritual of circumcision, including its strangeness, fascination, and promise," when he hears how it improves sex, an act that is as profane as the ritual is sacred. Schimanksi confronts a Jew as criminal as well as victim; a gentile detective talks about a Jewish ritual with humor, irony, and even some excitement. However, even these incidentals in the plot that present advances that would be interpreted as significant only in Germany for what it might mean about German attitudes toward Jews, the critic acknowledges how important such collective identities have become for our imagination. Yet, he must still admit, "how difficult it still is to say the word 'Jew' without somehow having the vague feeling that you are anti-Semitic."[66]

We might wonder if the accomplishments of *The Cosby Show* for African Americans in America from 1984 to 1992 (and then in years of reruns) might give us a hint of things to come in Germany. In fact, perhaps as a portent of new attitudes, in early 2005 a film appeared, the first postwar German Jewish comedy, entitled *Alles auf Zucker!* (Bet it all on Zucker!) by Swiss German Jew and filmmaker Dany Levy who now lives in Berlin. *Spiegel* journalist Jody Biehl headed her review with the claim "Germany Breaks a Taboo" and noted that the film has blossomed into a surprise box-office hit and that the film's director says he's tired of seeing Jews portrayed only as victims . . . laughter could be the best medicine for ever tense German-Jewish ties. What Biehl calls their (the Germans') "stereotypical heaviness" toward Jews might be tempered by the humorous Jewish stereotypes Levy himself uses to portray his characters. Levy has made seven other films, including one about German-Jewish relationships which he called *Meschugge* (English title: *The Giraffe*). About his new production Levy states bluntly, "Germans no longer have any experience or relation to Jews and that creates a natural discomfort. Combine that with Germany's bad conscience over the Holocaust and you get an irrational fear. I want to change that. My film is not a film about Jews. It's a film about people caught up in everyday chaos who happen to be Jews." Indeed, Levy hopes, "Germans can laugh with these Jews . . . [and] start to see how human they are . . . Maybe then Jews will lose a little of their foreignness. And maybe, just maybe Germans will lose a little of their fear."[67]

Representing Jews in new ways, as demonstrated here, may contribute to changing the perception of Jews in the public's consciousness. These portrayals might make it possible to imagine a different relationship between non-Jewish Germans and German Jews by way of a popular German television show that shows Jewish rituals and traditions or a fictional film that exaggerates Jewish characteristics to make people even laugh at Jewish jokes. I gave one controversial example of this problem in chapter 2 concerning the Berlin Holocaust Memorial. Whether these examples indicate "normalization" in the future remains to be seen, where the word "Jew" or its cognates might cross Germans' lips a little more easily to describe a neighbor, friend, or colleague neutrally rather than either in an overly respectful or an insulting way. Extremes of philo-Semitism, more prevalent in Germany than anywhere else, or anti-Semitism both inhibit the normality that is hinted at in this television program and emphasized in the film. I hope that these and many other examples I have offered throughout this book point to the evolution of a "new German Jewry" whose comfortable and productive presence will contribute to a more optimistic future for all of Germany.

Notes

Chapter 1. A New Jewish Life in Germany

1. Ruth Ellen Gruber, *Virtually Jewish: Reinventing Jewish Culture in Europe* (Berkeley and Los Angeles: University of California Press, 2002).

2. "Interview with Julius Schoeps," *Das Parlament* (July 28/August 4, 2003).

3. Andrew Roth and Michael Frajman, *The Goldapple Guide to Jewish Berlin* (Berlin: Goldapple Publishing, 1998), 3–4.

4. Lara Daemming, "Berliner Synagogen im Wandel," hagalil.com (November 12, 2002), http://www.hagalil.com.

5. Bill Rebiger, *Das Jüdische Berlin: Kultur, Religion und Alltag gestern und heute* (Berlin: Jaron Verlag, 2000), 26.

6. Ibid., 26.

7. Jeffrey M. Peck, "East Germany," in *The World Reacts to the Holocaust*, ed. David S. Wyman (Baltimore: The Johns Hopkins University Press, 1996), 447–472.

8. Paul Spiegel, *Was ist kosher? Jüdischer Glauben–Jüdisches Leben* (Berlin: Ullstein, 2003), 285.

9. Ibid., 286.

10. Ibid., 299.

11. Cornelia Rabitz, "Der Bubis Faktor: Für viele Bundesbürger prägt der Zentralvorsitzende das Bild von Juden," *Jüdische Allgemeine Wochenzeitung* (July 2003): 1.

12. "Die Jungen Juden von Berlin," *Tip* (December 14, 1995): 26–30.

13. "Die Juden leben," *Der Spiegel* (November 16, 1992): 75.

14. "Die historische Rede" (November 11, 2000); *http://www.hagalil.com/archiv/2000/11/spiegel.htm.*

15. Dominik Cziesche and Barbara Schmid, "Schlag ins Wasser? Deutsche Muslime distanzieren sich von Jürgen Möllemann," *Der Spiegel* (June 10, 2002).

16. Robert Leicht, "Am Ende nirgendwo zu Hause," *Die Zeit* (1999); *http://www3.zeit.de/archive/1999/34/1999/34.bubis_xnet7.term=Am.*

17. Roger Cohen, "Uneasy Peace," *New York Times* (August 6, 2000).

18. Jeannie Marshall, "Suddenly in Germany, It's Cool to Be Jewish: History's Strange Circle," *National Post Magazine* (July 29 and August 5, 2000).

19. Micha Brumlik, ed., *Zuhause, keine Heimat? Junge Juden und ihre Zunkunft in Deutschland* (Gerlingen: Bleicher Verlag, 1998), 116.

20. Ibid., 183.

21. Ibid., 179.

Chapter 2. Shadows of the Holocaust

1. Jeffrey Herf, *Divided Memory: The Nazi Past in the Two Germanys* (Cambridge, Mass.: Harvard University Press, 1997)

2. Ibid., 13.

3. Alan E. Steinweis, "The Legacy of the Holocaust in Germany and the United States," in *The United States and Germany in the Era of the Cold War, 1945–1990*, vol. 1:

1945–1968, ed. Detlef Junker (Cambridge, U.K.: Cambridge University Press, 2004). This citation refers to the English version of the two-volume handbook listed in the bibliography.

4. Andrei S. Markovits and Beth Simone Noveck, "West Germany," in *The World Reacts to the Holocaust*, ed. David S. Wyman (Baltimore: The Johns Hopkins University Press, 1996), 426.

5. Herf, *Divided Memory*, 336–337.

6. Edward Linenthal, *Preserving Memory: The Struggle to Create America's Holocaust Museum* (New York: Viking, 1995), 7.

7. Ibid., 7.

8. Ibid., 9.

9. "Raoul Hilberg Interview," in Linenthal, *Preserving Memory*, 11.

10. Text of executive order found in Report to the President: President's Commission on the Holocaust, Washington, D.C., 27 September 1979, 20, as quoted in Linenthal, *Preserving Memory*, 23.

11. For further discussion of the East German reaction to the Holocaust, see Peck, "East Germany," 447–472.

12. As quoted in Geoffrey Hartman, ed., *Chronology, Bitburg in Moral and Political Perspective* (Bloomington: Indiana University Press, 1986), xiii.

13. As quoted in George P. Schultz, *Turmoil and Triumph: My Years as Secretary of State* (New York: Maxwell Macmillan International, 1993), 546.

14. Quoted in Hartman, *Bitburg*, 45.

15. Richard von Weizsäcker, Speech to the Bundestag during the Ceremony Commemorating the 40th Anniversary of the End of the War, 8 May 1986, in Hartman, *Bitburg*, 265–272.

16. Ibid., 265–272.

17. Ibid., 265–272.

18. Ibid., 262–272.

19. Markovits and Noveck, *The World Reacts*, 435.

20. Charles Maier, *The Unmasterable Past: History, Holocaust, and German National Identity* (Cambridge, U.K.: Cambridge University Press, 1988), 3.

21. Ibid., 3.

22. "Beware Lest the Nightmare Recur," Jewish Community Publication, 1988.

23. Frank Stern, *Dann bin ich um den Schlaf gebracht: Ein Jahrtausend jüdisch-deutsche Kulturgeschichte* (Berlin: Aufbau-Verlag, 2002), 212.

24. Alvin Rosenfeld, "Another Revisionism: Popular Culture and the Changing Image of the Holocaust." In Hartman, *Bitburg*, 90.

25. Michael Berenbaum, "The Americanization of the Holocaust," in *Bitburg and Beyond: Encounters in American, German, and Jewish History*, ed. Ilya Levkov (New York: SPI Books, 1987).

26. Rosenfeld, *Another Revisionism*, 91.

27. Fred Kempe, "Die alten Rituale müssen enden," *Der Tagespiegel* (March 3, 1997).

28. As quoted by Karen Remmler, "Reclaiming Space: Jewish Women in Germany Today," in *Writing New Identities: Gender, Nation, and Immigration in Contemporary Europe*, ed. Gisela Brinker-Gabler and Sidonie Smith (Minneapolis: University of Minnesota Press, 1997), n 3, 190.

29. Daniel Jonah Goldhagen, *Hitler's Willing Executioners: Ordinary Germans and the Holocaust* (New York: Alfred A. Knopf, 1996), book jacket.

30. Goldhagen, *Hitler's Willing Executioners*, jacket copy.

31. Marc Fisher, "The German Question: Is This Holocaust Theory an Ugly Truth or a Blood Libel?" *Washington Post* (April 26, 1996).

32. Goldhagen, as cited in ibid.

33. Goldhagen, *Hitler's Willing Executioners*, 582, n38.

34. Ibid., 582, n38 and 593–594, n53.

35. Martin Walser, "Erfahrungen beim Verfassen einer Sonntagsrede." Speech on acceptance of the Peace Prize for the German Book Trade in Frankfurt, 1998.

36. Ibid.

37. Bubis's response was reported prominently in all of the major German newspapers and magazines such as *Der Spiegel*, "'Moral verjahrt nicht': Ignatz Bubis über die Auschwitz-Debatte und seine Auseinandersetzung mit Martin Walser und Klaus von Dohnanyi" (November 30, 1998).

38. "Nachtkultur," WDR Fernsehen Online; www.wdr.de.

39. Cited in *Die Welt*, online (March 8, 2004); *http://www.welt.de/*

Chapter 3. Russian Immigration and the Revitalization of German Jewry

1. "Lied'l fum goldenen Land," *Der Spiegel*, 50, 40 (1995): 135.

2. Emma Thomasson, "Germany Still Draws Jews Despite Anti-Semitism Dispute," Yahoo! News Canada (June 26, 2002), http://ca.news.yahoo.com.

3. Toby Axelrod, "Russian Emigrés Breathing Life into German Jewry," *Jewish Bulletin of Northern California* (December 3, 1999); http://www.jewishsf.com.

4. Robin Ostow, "From Victims of Anti-Semitism to Postmodern Hybrid Representations of (Post) Soviet Jews in Germany," *East European Jewish Affairs* 33 (2003): 54–70.

5. Susanne Spülbeck, "Wissenschaftlicher Lauschangriff auf ein Dorf," *Süddeutsche Zeitung* (July 4, 1997).

6. Jeroen Doomernik, *Going West: Soviet Jewish Immigrants in Berlin since 1990* (Aldershot, England: Avebury, 1997).

7. Robin Ostow, *American Jewish Yearbook 1992*, ed. David Singer and Lawrence Grossman (New York: The American Jewish Committee, 1992), 378.

8. Ibid.

9. "Jewish Immigrants Promised Help," BBC News (January 9, 2000); *http://news .bbc.co.uk*.

10. "Lied'l fum goldenen Land," *Der Spiegel*, 135.

11. Herman Simon, personal conversation with the author, Berlin, 1995.

12. Charles G. Hawley, "Germany Boosts Judaism," *Christian Science Monitor* (February 6, 2003); http://www.csmonitor.com.

13. Candidate list for Jewish Community Elections. See website of Berlin Jewish Community.

14. Introductory Speech at the election of the Executive Council, Berlin Jewish Community, 2004.

15. Ibid., 2004.

16. Michael May, personal conversation with the author, June 25, 2003. I am greatly indebted to Michael May for his knowledge and perspectives on the situation of Russian immigration to Berlin.

17. Hawley, "Germany Boosts Judaism," 2003.

18. Elena Burlina, "Vitamin "K" für Kultur," Hagalil.com (January 19, 2004); *http://www .berlin-judentum.de*.

19. May, personal conversation, 2003.

20. Rafael Seligmann, "Jude, Preuße, deutscher Patriot," *Berliner Morgenpost* (January 7, 2004); *http://morgenpost.berlin1.de*.

21. Albert Meyer, as cited in ibid.

22. Judith Kessler, "Resüme und Ausblick—Wenig Anlass zu Optimismus: Ein hoffnungsloser Fall?" Hagalil.com (May 8, 2002); *http://www.berlin-judentum.de*. I am grateful to Judith Kessler for her insights into Russian Jewish immigration.

23. Judith Kessler, "Umfrage 2002. Mitgliederbefragung der Jüdischen Gemeinde zu Berlin," Berlin, December 2002.

24. LD, personal conversation with the author, Berlin 2003.

25. Ibid.

26. Ibid.

27. Ibid.

28. Franziska Becker, *Ankommen in Deutschland: Einwanderungspolitik als biographische Erfahrung im Migrationsprozess russischer Juden* (Berlin: Dietrich Reimer Verlag, 2001).

29. Ibid.

30. Cited in Toby Axelrod, "Germany to Triple Its Funding for Country's Jewish Community," Jewish Telegraphic Agency (November 14, 2002); http://www.jta.org.

31. "Anti-Semitism Has Become Worse," Paul Spiegel, head of Germany's Jewish Community, in interview with *Der Spiegel* (March 21, 2005); Spiegel Online.

32. "That's Right, Germany," *WUPJ Brochure*, 2004.

33. Philip Gessler, "Schily pusht Union liberaler Juden," *Die Tageszeitung* (July 12, 2003).

34. Paul Spiegel, personal conversation with the author, Düsseldorf, March 2004.

35. Toby Axelrod, "Disagreement All in the Family at German Jewish Youth Forum," Jewish Telegraphic Agency (February 10, 2003); http:/www.jta.org.

36. Jewish Students' discussion with the author, Synagogen Clubhouse, Joachimsthalerstrasse, Berlin, December 11, 2003.

37. Ibid.

38. Lucian Kim, "Jewish Renaissance in Berlin," *Christian Science Monitor Online*; *http://csmweb2.emcweb.com*.

Chapter 4. Representing Jews in Germany Today

1. Paul Rabinow, "Representations Are Social Facts: Modernity and Post-Modernity in Anthropology," in *Writing Culture: The Poetics and Politics of Ethnography*, ed. James Clifford and George Marcus (Berkeley and Los Angeles: University of California Press, 1986), 234–261.

2. Virginia Dominguez, "Questioning Jews," *American Ethnologist* 20 (1996): 618–624.

3. Oliver Lubrich, "The Other and the Ordinary: Demystifying and Demusealizing the Jew" (unpublished manuscript).

4. Norman Kleeblatt, *Too Jewish? Challenging Traditional Identities* (New York: Jewish Museum of New York, 1996), 6–7.

5. Y. Michal Bodemann, "Die Landstriche Deutschlands sind für viele Juden nicht länger nur Diaspora," *Das Parlament* (July 28–August 2/4, 2003), 10.

6. Gruber, *Virtually Jewish*, 203.

7. Ibid., 202.

8. Ibid., 208.

9. Ibid., 208

10. Thomas Gross, "Der auserwählte Folk," *Die Zeit* (June 24, 2003).

11. Jörg Magenau, "Gibt es eine deutsch-jüdische Literatur?" *Das Parlament* (July 28/August 4, 2003).

12. Rafael Seligmann, *Rubensteins Versteigerung* (Munich: Deutscher Taschenbuchverlag, 1991), 189.

13. Wladimir Kaminer, *Russendisko* (Munich: Goldmann Verlag, 2000), 2.

14. Henryk Broder, *Jewish Voices, German Words: Growing Up Jewish in Postwar Germany and Austria*, ed. Elena Lappin and trans. Krishna Winston (North Haven, Conn.: Catbird Press, 1994), 85, 101.

15. "Is Auschwitz the Yardstick for Anti-Semitism?" in *Speaking Out: Jewish Voices from United Germany*, ed. Susan Stern (Chicago: Edition Q, 1995), 189.

16. Ibid., 188–189.

17. Rafael Seligmann, "Interview mit Ignatz Bubis," *Der Stern* (July 1999): 57–59.

18. Seligmann, "Jude, Preusse," 2004.

19. Brumlik, *Kein Weg*, 105.

20. Ibid., 107.

21. Ibid., 107.

22. Michael Blumenthal, *Stories of an Exhibition: Two Millennia of German Jewish History* (Berlin: Jewish Museum Berlin, 2001), 14.

23. Ibid.

24. Ibid.

25. Ibid.

26. Jewish Museum Berlin, *Exhibition Catalogue* (Berlin: Jewish Museum Berlin, 2001), 4.

27. Ibid., 7.

28. Ibid.

29. Ibid.

30. Susannah Reid, "Jewish Museum Berlin—A Review." In Virtual Library Museen (VL Museums and Museum Professionals, 2001), 2; http://www.vl-museen.de.

31. Ibid., 3.

32. For commentary on Broder's exhibition, see his homepage, *http://www.henryk-broder.com*.

Chapter 5. Jews and Turks

1. "Weder Heimat noch Freunde," *Der Spiegel* (June 7, 1993): 16.

2. Klaus Bade, ed., *Deutsche im Ausland, Fremde in Deutschland: Migration in Geschichte und Gegenwart* (Munich: Verlag C. H. Beck, 1992).

3. Leslie Adelson, "Opposing Oppositions: Turkish-German Question in Contemporary German Studies," *German Studies Review* 17, 2 (1994): 305.

4. Ibid.

5. Ruth Mandel, "Turkish Headscarves and the 'Foreigner Problem': Constructing Difference through Emblems of Identity," *New German Critique* 46 (1989): 31.

6. John Efron, personal conversation with the author, Seattle, Washington, 1990.

7. Gökçe Yurdakul and Michal Bodemann, " 'We Are Not Immigrants, We Are a Minority': The German Jewish Trope as Master Narrative Discourse Model for German Turks" (unpublished manuscript, 2004).

8. Borneman and Peck, *Sojourners*, 1995.

9. In a lecture given at the Paul-Löbe-Haus, as quoted in Jeffrey M. Peck, "The 'Ins' and 'Outs' of the New Germany: Jews, Foreigners, Asylum Seekers," in *Reemerging Jewish Culture in Germany: Life and Literature since 1989*, ed. Sander L. Gilman and Karen Remmler (New York: New York University Press, 1994), 130.

10. Joschka Fischer, speech at the Conference on Global Anti-Semitism, sponsored by the Anti-Defamation League, New York, November 1, 2002.

11. "Jeder achte Deutsche ein Antisemit," *Der Spiegel* 46, 4 (January 20, 1992): 44.

12. "Europe's Memory Stirred," *Washington Times* (September 1, 1992).

13. Eugene Meyer, "Violence in Germany," *Washington Post* (December 14, 1992).

14. Ibid.

15. Ibid.

16. A. M. Rosenthal, "Our German Crisis," *New York Times* (November 24, 1992).

17. Alan Dershowitz, "Nazism in Germany Is No Surprise," Jewish Telegraphic Agency, n.d.

18. Ibid.

19. "How Bad Is It?" *Time Europe* (June 17, 2002).

20. Arrigo Levi, "Wir alle sind Deutsche," *Frankfurter Allgemeine Zeitung* (September 9, 1992).

21. Marc Fisher, "13,000 Germans Demonstrate against Right-Wing Violence," *Washington Post* (August 30, 1992).

22. Ibid.

23. Ibid.

24. Ibid.

25. Susan Sontag, "Fascinating Fascism," in *Under the Sign of Saturn* (New York: Farrar Straus Giroux, 1989), 73–105.

26. For a more detailed discussion of this topic, see Jeffrey M. Peck, "Refugees as Foreigners: The Problem of Becoming German and Finding Home," in *Mistrusting Refugees*, ed. Daniel E. Valentine and John Knudsen (Berkeley: University of California Press, 1995), 102–125.

27. "Jeder achte Deutsche," *Der Spiegel*, 41.

28. "Die Rechte bombt—die Linke dividiert sich," *Die Tageszeitung* (September 30, 1992).

29. Ibid.

30. Rita Süssmuth, cited in ibid.

31. Wolfgang Kowalsky, *Rechtsaussen . . . die verfehlten Strategien des deutschen Denkens* (Berlin: Ullstein Verlag, 1992).

32. Elise Brayton, "Almost German: The Representation of Racial Difference and Belonging in Contemporary Germany" (Ph.D. diss., Georgetown University, 2000).

33. Birgit Rommelsbacher, "Rassismus Ost und West schaukeln sich hoch," *Die Tageszeitung* (February 11, 1992).

34. Rafael Seligmann, "Die Juden leben," *Der Spiegel* (November 16, 1992): 75.

35. Peck, "East Germany," 447–472.

36. Konrad Jarausch, "The Failure of East German Antifascism: Some Ironies of History as Politics," *German Studies Review* 14, 1 (1991): 96.

37. Nora Räthzel, "Germany: One Race, One Nation?" *Race and Class* 32, 3 (1991): 45.

38. Berndt Ostendorf, "The Politics of Difference: Theories and Practice in a Comparative U.S. and German Perspective," in *Multiculturalism in Transit: A German-American Exchange*, ed. Klaus Milich and Jeffrey M. Peck (New York: Bergham Books, 1998), 47.

39. "Jeder achte Deutsche," *Der Spiegel*, 41.

40. Although the opportunity to become German citizens became easier with the immigration law of January 1, 2000, fewer Turks have taken advantage of this opportunity, according to Leslie Adelson, because it meant giving up their Turkish nationality and the right to own or inheriting property in Turkey. See further discussion in Leslie A. Adelson, "Introduction," *Atlas of a Tropical Germany: Essays on Politics and Culture, 1990–1998* by Zafer Şenocak (Lincoln: University of Nebraska Press, 2002), xix. The Germany-info website reports that in 2000, 82,800 Turks or 44 percent became citizens out of 2,053,560 Turks in Germany.

41. Valentine and Knudsen, *Mistrusting Refugees*, 2.

42. "Weder Heimat," *Der Spiegel*, 21.

43. Andrea Klimt, "Returning 'Home': Portuguese Migrant Notions of Temporariness, Permanence, and Commitment," *New German Critique* 46 (1989): 70.

44. "Gefährlich fremd: Das Scheitern der multi-kulturellen Gesellschaft," *Der Spiegel* (April 1997).

45. Yurdakul and Bodemann, "We Are Not Immigrants," 2004.

46. Adelson, "Introduction," xiv.

47. Ibid.

48. Yurdakul and Bodemann, "We Are Not Immigrants," 2004, 3.

49. Ibid.

50. Ibid.

51. Ibid.

52. Interview with Malte Krause cited in Jonathan Laurence, "(Re)constructing Community in Berlin: Of Jews, Turks, and German Responsibility" (Paper presented at the Science Center Berlin for Social Research, Berlin, Germany, October 1999), 8.

53. Ibid., 9.

54. Ibid.

55. Şenocak, *Atlas of a Tropical Germany*.

56. Ibid., 53–57.

57. Adelson, in *Atlas*, xxx.

58. Ibid. Adelson's translation is more literal: "a history of touch."

59. Ibid.

60. Şenocak, *Atlas*, 6.

61. Ibid., 56–57.

62. On January 1, 2000, a new citizenship law was passed, which was less liberal than many had hoped, but did make substantive changes possible. For the first time children of foreign parents born in Germany acquire German citizenship at birth. The prerequisite of the parents has been legal residence in Germany for eight years and possession of a residence authorization or unlimited residence for three years. See Auswärtiges Amt website: Welcome to Germany, Law on Nationality (www.auswaertigesamt.de/www/en/willkommen) Staatsangehoerigkeitsrecht/index_html) (Federal Foreign Office, Facts about Germany: Nationality).

63. Michael Wolffsohn, "Allein auf weiter Flur. Nach der Bundestagswahl: Juden fühlen sich von keiner Partei vertreten," *Jüdische Allgemeine Wochenzeitung* (September 25, 2002).

64. Craig Smith, "Racism Grows against Jews and Muslims," *International Herald Tribune* (December 12, 2002), 5.

65. Şenocak, *Atlas*, 93.

Chapter 6. Creating a Continental Identity

1. Sergio DellaPergola, "An Overview of the Demographic Trends of European Jews," in *Jewish Identities in the New Europe*, ed. Jonathan Webber (London: Littman Library of Jewish Civilization, 1994), 61.

2. S. Ilan Troen, ed., *Jewish Centers and Peripheries: Europe between America and Israel Fifty Years After World War II* (New Brunswick, N.J.: Transaction Publishers, 1999), 4.

3. Troen, *Jewish Centers*, 4.

4. Bernard Wasserstein, *Vanishing Diaspora: The Jews in Europe Since 1945* (Cambridge, Mass: Harvard University Press, 1996).

5. Jonathan Webber, ed., *Jewish Identities in the New Europe* (London: Littman Library of Jewish Civilization, 1994). See especially his "Introduction," pp. 1–32.

6. Gruber, *Virtually Jewish*, 11.

7. Diana Pinto, "The Jewish Challenge in the New Europe," in *Challenging Ethnic Citizenship: German and Israeli Perspectives on Immigration*, ed. Daniel Levy and Yfaat Weiss (New York: Bergham Books, 2002) and in "Diaspora Manifest," in *Golem* 3 (2002): 94.

8. Andreas von Bülow, *Die CIA und der 11. September* (Munich: Piper, 2003).

9. Elaine Sciolino, "Europeans and Americans Seek Answer to Anti-Semitism," *New York Times* (February 20, 2004): 11, section A.

10. Robert Wielaard, "EU Vows to Fight Anti-Semitism, Urges Tolerance of Israel," Associated Press (February 20, 2004).

11. Sciolino, "Europeans and Americans," 11.

12. Ibid.

13. Jörg Lau, "Warum diese Angst? Ein neues Misstrauen prägt die deutsch-judischen Debatten der vergangenen Wochen," *Die Zeit* (July 8, 2004): 34.

14. Wielaard, "EU vows."

15. Werner Bergman and Juliane Wetsel, "Manifestations of Anti-Semitism in the European Union," Speech, Vienna, Austria, March 2003. Synthesis Report on Behalf of European Monitoring Centre on Racism and Xenophobia.

16. European Council of Jewish Communities (ECJC), "Strategic Plan"; *http://www.ecjc.org.*

17. Ibid.

18. Ibid.

19. Ruth E. Gruber, "5761: The Jewish World. European Jews Made Strides This Year Redefining Their Identity," *Jewish Telegraphic Agency*, January 6, 2003, *http://www.jewsweek.com.*

20. Toby Axelrod, "Family Ties? At Berlin Conference, Women Say Jewish Family Life Is Key to Rebuilding European Jewish Communities," Jewish Telegraphic Agency, January 13, 2003, *http://www.jewsweek.com.*

21. Toby Axelrod, "European Jews Unite for Israel," Jewish Telegraphic Agency (June 7, 2002); *http://www.jewishaz.com.*

22. ECJC website, "Two Hundred Leaders from across Europe, Israel, and the US Planned Future of European Jewry," July 2–5, 1995; http://www.ecjc.org.

23. Eric Johnson, "New Chapter in Jewish History Emerges in Europe," *Deutsche Presse-Agentur* (November 7, 2002).

24. Ruth E. Gruber, "Jewish Leaders Focus on Scourges That Confront Jews in Post-Oslo Era," Jewish Telegraphic Agency, November 5, 2002, *http://www.jta.org.*

25. Ibid.

26. Ibid.

27. "Wir sind viel weiter als die EU," *Jüdische Allgemeine Wochenzeitung* (February 18, 2003); *http://www.juedische-allgemeine.de.*

28. Eric J. Greenberg, "On Campus in Europe: Anti-Semitism: Jewish Student Leader Recounts Chilling Incidents below Media's Radar," *The Jewish Week* (April 6, 2004); *http://www.thejewishweek.com/news/newscontent.php3?artid=6174.*

29. Ibid.

30. Ruth E. Gruber, "E.U. Expansion Is Challenge and Chance for European Jews," *Jewish Telegraphic Agency* (December 17, 2003); *http://www.jta.org/html.*

31. Ibid.

32. Salomon Korn, as cited in "Zentralrat warnt vor wachsendem Antisemitismus. Vizepräsident Korn, Gefahr steigt durch EU-Erweiterung," *Berliner Zeitung* (April 27, 2004).

33. Gruber, "Jewish Leaders."

34. Johnson, "New Chapter."

35. Smith, "Racism Grows."

36. Wasserstein, *Vanishing Diaspora*, 290.

37. Ibid., 289.

38. Ibid., 289.

39. Gruber, *Virtually Jewish*, 27.

40. Webber, *Jewish Identites*, 85.

41. Ibid., 85.

42. Gruber, *Virtually Jewish*, 238.

43. Webber in ibid., 238–239.

44. Pinto, "The Jewish Challenges in the New Europe," 251.

45. Jan Gross, *Neighbors: The Destruction of the Jewish Community in Jewabne, Poland* (Princeton, N.J.: Princeton University Press, 2001).

46. Pinto, "Jewish Challenges," 243.

47. Nicola Galliner, ed., *Jewish Film Festival Berlin* (Berlin: Bebra, 2004).

48. Pinto, "Jewish Challenges," 239–252.

49. Möllemann statement as cited in *Die Tageszeitung* (May 23, 2002).

50. Frank Schirrmacher, "Tod eines Kritikers: Offener Brief von Frank Schirrmacher," *Frankfurter Allgemeine Zeitung* (May 29, 2002).

51. Marcel Gäding, "Festakt nach 'Juden Raus'—Rufen beendet," *Berliner Zeitung* (November 21, 2002).

52. Reported in *Time Europe*, "How Bad Is It?" (June 17, 2002).

53. Ibid.

54. Salomon Korn, "Ende der Schonzeit," *Frankfurter Allgemeine Zeitung* (May 6, 2002).

55. Marlies Emmerich, "Antisemitismus unter neuer Maske," *Berliner Zeitung* (June 6, 2002).

56. Michael Brenner, "Der neue alte Antisemitismusstreit," December 21, 1998; *http://www.hagalil.com/archiv/98/12/brenner.htm*.

57. Wolfgang Benz, "Antisemitismus ohne Antisemiten." *Tribüne: Zeitschrift zum Verständnis des Judentums*, 163 (2002): 85–92.

58. Henryk M. Broder, "Ein moderner Antisemit," *Der Spiegel* (May 27, 2002): 26.

59. Joschka Fischer, "Deutschland, Deine Juden," Frankfurter *Allgemeine Zeitung* (May 11, 2002); http://www.germanemb.org.il

60. Joschka Fischer, speech at the Conference on Global Antisemitism of the Anti-Defamation League, New York, November 1, 2002.

61. See OSCE website for all pertinent information and documents; http://www.osce.org.

62. Yehuda Bauer, speech at OSCE Conference.

63. Reformierte Nachrichten, "Israel: 27. Januar wird «Tag des Kampfes gegen Antisemitismus»," January 23, 2004; *http://www.ref.ch/rna/meldungen/7885.html*.

64. Newsletter of the Embassy of the State of Israel, "Der 27. Januar 2004: Israels Tag für den Kampf gegen Antisemitismus," January 23, 2004; *http://www.botschaft@israel.de*.

65. Ibid.

66. Ibid.

67. *Gesher—Forum for Diaspora Culture, Galut 2000: Towards a European Jewish Identity*, ed. Sandra H. Lustig and Jan Leveson; *www.galut2000@gesher-berlin.org*.

68. Fischer, speech to OSCE, April 28, 2004; *http://www.osce.org*.

69. Jörg Lau, "Warum diese Angst?" Feuilleton Judentum, *Die Zeit*; www.zeit.de/2004/29/Wolfssohn?=Kugelmann.

70. Fischer, speech to OSCE, April 28, 2004.

71. Ruth E. Gruber, "U.S. Jews Tell European Jews: You're Responsible for Your Future," *Jewish World Review* (February 21, 2000); *http://www.jewishworldreview.com/0201/your.future.asp*.

Chapter 7. The United States and Israel

1. Roger Cohen, "Israel's Ties with Germany Elude U.S. Jews," *New York Times* (March 4, 2001).

2. Lily Gardner-Feldman, "German Morality and Israel," in *The Federal Republic at Forty*, ed. Peter H. Merkl (New York: New York University Press, 1989).

3. Lily Gardner-Feldman, personal conversation with the author, Washington, D.C., 2004.

4. John McCloy, American High Commissioner to Germany 1949–1952. McCloy is also cited as the Roosevelt administration official who made the decision not to bomb Auschwitz. Consequently, he is condemned by some critics as "an oppressor" of the Jews.

5. Information from German Embassy website in Israel, *http://www.germanemb.org.il.*

6. Lily Gardner-Feldman, "Germany's Special Relationship with Israel Continues Despite Appearances to the Contrary," AICGS website, *http://www.aicgs.org.*

7. Shlomo Shafir, *Ambiguous Relations: The American Jewish Community and Germany since 1945* (Detroit: Wayne State University Press, 1999).

8. Ibid., 341.

9. Ibid., 344.

10. Ibid., 345.

11. George H.W. Bush, "Remarks to the Citizens in Mainz," at Rheingoldhalle, Mainz, Germany, May 31, 1989.

12. Kyle James, "Marketplace," Minnesota Public Radio, May 22, 2002.

13. George W. Bush, speech to the German Bundestag, May 22, 2002.

14. Ibid.

15. Ibid.

16. Ibid.

17. Ibid.

18. Tom Segev, *The Seventh Million: The Israelis and the Holocaust* (New York: Hill & Wang, 1994).

19. Ezer Weizman, "Das ist mein wunder Punkt," *Der Spiegel* (January 22, 1996): 6.

20. Bubis expressed this sentiment in many public statements. For a broader discussion, see Moritz Neumann, "Szenen eines Familienstreits," *Jüdische Allgemeine Wochenzeitung* (January 25, 1996).

21. Ignatz Bubis with Edith Kohn, *Ich bin ein deutscher Staatsbürger jüdischen Glaubens* (Cologne: Kiepenheuer & Witsch, 1993).

22. Weizman in *Der Spiegel* (January 22, 1996): 6.

23. "Das ist mein wunder Punkt. Interview mit jüdischen Studenten über ihre Entscheidung in Deutschland zu leben," *Der Spiegel* (January 22, 1996): 33.

24. Ibid.

25. Alice Brauner, "Die Jungen Juden von Berlin. Sie sind die Kinder der Holocaust-Generation. Ganz oft sind sie wütend über den deutschen Wunsch nach Vergessen. Und doch bleiben sie hier, weil sie in Berlin zu Hause sind," *Tip* (December 14, 1995).

26. Ibid.

27. Bodemann in personal conversation with the author, Berlin, 2004.

28. Brauner, "Die Jungen Juden."

29. "Katzav und Rau eröffnen Wuppertaler Synagoge," *Die Welt* (December 9, 2002).

30. Ibid.

31. Michel Friedman cited in Toby Axelrod, "Germany to Triple Its Funding for Country's Jewish Community," *JTA* (November 14, 2002).

32. Gerhard Schröder, speech at OSCE conference, April 29, 2004.

33. Ibid.

34. Richard Chaim Schneider, "Gute Gründe zur Vasallentreue," *Die Tageszeitung* (June 4, 2002).

35. "Interview mit Nathan Sharansky," *Jüdische Allgemeine Wochenzeitung* (July 17, 2003).

36. Judith Hart, "Ein Bild aus erster Hand. Solidaritäts-und Informationsreise des Zentralrats nach Israel: Spiegel übergab 250.000-Dollar-Spende für bedürftige Kinder," *Jüdische Allgemeine Wochenzeitung* (July 31, 2003).

37. Paul Spiegel, "Mit vorsichtiger Hoffnung. Das Präsidium des Zentralrats besucht Israel," *Jüdische Allgemeine Wochenzeitung* (July 17, 2003).

38. Ibid.

39. Ibid.

40. Lily Gardner Feldman, "The Jewish Role in German American Relations," in *The German American Encounter: Conflict and Cooperation between Two Cultures, 1800–2000,* ed. Frank Trommler and Elliott Shore (New York: Berghahn, 2001), 180.

41. Ibid.

42. Eugene Dubow, "Foreword," Dedication of the Berlin Office of the American Jewish Committee, February 1998.

43. Toby Axelrod, "Germany Committed to U.S., Israel, Leaders Tell Visiting Group," Jewish Telegraphic Agency, March 25, 2003.

44. Harold Tanner, president of AJC on occasion of the fifth anniversary of the Berlin office, 2003.

45. Pamphlet of the American Academy in Berlin; see *www.americanacademy.de.*

46. Susan Neiman, *Slow Fire: Jewish Notes from Berlin* (New York: Schocken Books, 1992).

47. Josh Spinner, personal conversation with the author, Berlin, December 2004.

48. Ibid.

49. Chabad, website, *http://www.chabad.org.*

50. Yehuda Teichtal, personal conversation with the author, Berlin, December 2004.

51. Ibid.

52. German Embassy website on Israel. See website of Coordination Centre for German-Israeli Youth Exchange, *www.conact-org.de.*

53. American Jewish Committee, memo, n.d.

Chapter 8. Toward a New German Jewish Diaspora in an Age of Globalization

1. Howard Wettstein, ed., *Diasporas and Exiles: Varieties of Jewish Identity* (Berkeley: University of California Press, 2002), 1–2.

2. Ibid., 1.

3. Ibid., 2.

4. Ibid.

5. Sander Gilman, *Jewish Frontiers: Essays on Bodies, Histories, and Identities* (New York: Palgrave, 2003).

6. Arjun Appadurai, *Modernity at Large,* 4.

7. Erich Gruen, *Diasporas,* 18.

8. Jonathan Boyarin and Daniel Boyarin, *Powers of Diaspora: Two Essays on the Relevance of Jewish Culture* (Minneapolis: University of Minnesota, 2002), 5.

9. Ibid., 721.

10. Jonathan Boyarin, *Thinking in Jewish* (Chicago: University of Chicago Press, 1996), 126.

11. Troen, *Jewish Centers,* 411.

12. Sufott in Troen, *Jewish Centers and Peripheries,* 402.

13. Larry Tye, *Home Lands: Portraits of the New Jewish Diaspora* (New York: Henry Holt, 2001), 12.

14. Mark Kurlansky, *A Chosen Few: The Resurrection of European Jewry* (Boulder, Colo.: Perseus Publishing, 1995).

15. Yossi Shain, "American Jews and the Construction of Israel's Jewish Identity," *Diaspora, A Journal of Transnational Studies* 9 (2000): 170.

16. Ibid., 180.

17. Igal Avidan, "Israelis Look to Germany for Refuge," *Jerusalem Report* (September 9, 2002).

18. Cited in ibid.

19. Greer Fay Cashman, "FSU Immigration to Germany More Than to Israel," *Jerusalem Post* (July 17, 2003).

20. Jerold S. Auerbach, *Are We One? Jewish Identity in the United States and Israel* (New Brunswick, N.J.: Rutgers University Press, 2001).

21. Deborah Dash Moore and S. Ilan Troen, eds., *Divergent Jewish Cultures: Israel and America* (New Haven, Conn.: Yale University Press, 2001),

22. Steven T. Rosenthal, *Irreconcilable Differences: The Waning of the American Jewish Love Affair with Israel* (Waltham, Mass.: Brandeis University Press, 2001).

23. Cited in Toby Axelrod, "Facing Reality of Jews in Germany, Zionist Arm Takes Indirect Approach," *JTA* (July 30, 2003).

24. Itty Abraham, "International Trends," *India Seminar* (August 19, 2003).

25. Pnina Werbner, "The Materiality of Diaspora—Between Aesthetic and 'Real' Politics," *Diaspora. A Journal of Transnational Studies* 9 (2000): 5.

26. Doomernik, *Going West*.

27. Ascheron in David Morley, *Home Territories: Media, Mobility, and Identity* (London: Routledge, 2000), 261.

28. Y. Michal Bodemann, *In den Wogen der Erinnerung: Jüdische Existenz in Deutschland* (Munich: Deutscher Taschenbuch Verlag, 2002), 194.

29. Ibid., 195.

30. Mike Featherstone, "Cosmopolis: An Introduction," *Theory, Culture and Society* 19 (2002): 1.

31. Werbner, *Diaspora*, 6.

32. Y. Michal Bodemann, "Global Diaspora? European Jewry? Brushing the Postmodern Debate against the Grain," *Golem* 3 (2002): 94.

33. Ibid.

34. Nathan Sznaider and Daniel Levy, "How Much Diaspora Is Bearable?" *Golem* 3 (2002): 28.

35. Bodemann, "Global Diaspora," 94.

36. Werbner, *Diaspora*, 6.

37. Yossi Shain, "Jewish Kinship at a Crossroads: Lessons for Homelands and Diasporas," *Political Science Quarterly* 117 (2002): 286–287.

38. Leon Wieseltier, "Lieberman," *The New Republic* (August 21, 2000): 6.

39. Shain, "Jewish Kinship," 289.

40. Ibid., 291.

41. Daniel Goldhagen, "The Globalization of Antisemitism," *Forward* (May 2, 2003).

42. Simon Schama, "Old Demons, New Debates: Anti-Semitism in the West" (Conference lecture at the Center for Jewish History, New York, 2003).

43. Ibid.

44. Mark Poster, *What's the Matter with the Internet?* (Minneapolis: University of Minnesota Press, 2001), 167. For a more detailed and academic analysis of the notion of a CyberJew, see Poster's "Virtual Ethnicity: Tribal Identity in an Age of Global Communication," in *Cybersociety 2.0: Revisiting Computer-mediated Communication and Community*, ed. Steven G. Jones (Thousand Oaks, Calif.: Sage Publishing, 1998) 184–211.

45. Harry Chauss, "Virtually Jewish, Virtually Connected: Searching for Jewish Identity Online" (Master's thesis, Georgetown University, 2001), 52.

46. Ibid., 61.

47. Ibid., 67–68.

48. Jola Merten, "Sieben Minuten zum Kennenlernen," *Jüdische Allgemeine Wochenzeitung* (September 25, 2003).

49. Thomas von der Osten-Sacken, "A German Jewish Internet Portal Combating Anti-Semitism," Hagalil.com, 2003; *http://hagalil.com*.

50. Poster, *What's the Matter*, 167.

51. Ibid., x.

52. Barbara Kirshenblatt-Gimblett, "The Electronic Vernacular," in *Connected: Engagements with Media*, ed. George Marcus (Chicago: University of Chicago Press, 1996), 32.

53. Ibid., 34.

54. Ibid., 22.

55. Ibid., 23.

56. Poster, *What's the Matter*, 103.

57. Shain, "Jewish Crossroads," 308.

58. Ibid., 304.

59. " 'Viele Zimmer unterm Dach,' Orthodoxe und liberale Juden streiten um Geld, Mitgliederzahlen und die Verwendung staatlicher Zuschüsse. Das Monopol des Zentralrats bröckelt," *Der Spiegel* (May 3, 2004). The title of this article is particularly telling in the way the article foregrounds the many problems in the Community, "Orthodox and Liberal Jews fighting about money, membership, and the application of state financial support. The monopoly of the Central Council is crumbling."

60. I want to thank Professor Karen Remmler for her discussion of the ethics of memory that took place at a conference entitled "Inter/Disciplinary Approaches to Memory: Trans/Formation of the Past in Contemporary German Literature and Culture" organized by Professor Frederike Eigler at Georgetown University on May 8–9, 2004. The presentations of other participants, such as Professors Katharina Gerstenberger, Leslie Adelson, Eric Langenbacher, and Eigler were very helpful for my thinking on the subject of memory.

61. Jeffrey M. Peck, ed., "The Jewish Voice in Transatlantic Relations," *AICGS German-American Issues* 1 (2004): 7.

62. Eric Langenbacher, "Memory Regimes in Contemporary Germany" (Ph.D. diss., Georgetown University, 2002).

63. Peck, "Jewish Voice," 10.

64. "Leben ohne Handlauf. Schimanski und die deutsch-jüdische Geschichte: Ein grosses Abenteuer und ein dreifacher Krimi," *Frankfurter Allgemeine Zeitung* (January 1, 2004).

65. Ibid.

66. Ibid.

67. Jody K. Biehl, "Jewish Comedy Kosher as Pork Chops," *Spiegel Online* (January 25, 2005); *http://service.spiegel.de/cache/international/91518,00.html*.

Bibliography

Adelson, Leslie. "Opposing Oppositions: Turkish-German Question in Contemporary German Studies." *German Studies Review* 17, 2 (1994): 305.

————. *The Turkish Turn in Contemporary German Literature: Toward a New Critical Grammar of Migration*. New York: Palgrave Macmillan, 2005.

Appadurai, Arjun. *Modernity at Large: Cultural Dimensions of Globalization*. Minneapolis: University of Minnesota Press, 1996.

Auerbach, Jerold S. *Are We One? Jewish Identity in the United States and Israel*. New Brunswick, N. J.: Rutgers University Press, 2001.

Bade, Klaus J., ed. *Deutsche im Ausland—Fremde in Deutschland: Migration in Geschichte und Gegenwart*. Munich: C. H. Beck, 1992.

————, ed. *Die multikulturelle Herausforderung: Menschen über Grenzen—Grenzen über Menschen*. Munich: C. H. Beck, 1996.

Berghahn, Klaus, ed. *The German-Jewish Dialogue Reconsidered: A Symposium in Honor of George Mosse*. New York: Peter Lang, 1996.

Becker, Franziska. *Ankommen in Deutschland: Einwanderungspolitik als biographische Erfahrung im Migrationsprozeß russischer Juden*. Berlin: Dietrich Reimler, 2001.

Benz, Wolfgang. *Integration ist machbar: Ausländer in Deutschland*. Munich: C. H. Beck, 1993.

————, ed. *Antisemitismus in Deutschland: Zur Aktualität eines Vorurteils*. Munich: Deutscher Taschenbuch Verlag, 1995.

————. *Rechtsextremismus in der Bundesrepublik: Voraussetzungen, Zusammenhänge, Wirkungen*. Frankfurt am Main: Fischer Taschenbuch, 1990.

Berenbaum, Michael. "The Americanization of the Holocaust." In *Bitburg and Beyond. Encounters in American, German, and Jewish History*, edited by Ilya Levkov. New York: SPI Books, 1987.

Biller, Maxim. *Land der Väter und Verräter*. Cologne: Kiepenheuer and Witsch, 1994.

————. *Die Tempojahre*. Munich: Deutscher Taschenbuch Verlag, 2003.

Blumenthal, Michael. *Stories of an Exhibition: Two Millennia of German Jewish History*. Berlin: Jewish Museum Berlin, 2001.

Bodemann, Y. Michal. *Gedächtnisstheater: Die jüdische Gemeinschaft und ihre deutsche Erfindung*. Hamburg: Rotbuch, 1996.

————. "Global Diaspora? European Jewry? Brushing the Postmodern Debate against the Grain." *Golem* 3 (2002): 86–95.

————. *In den Wogen der Erinnerung. Jüdische Existenz in Deutschland*. Munich: Deutscher Taschenbuch Verlag, 2002.

————. "Die Landstriche Deutschlands sind für viele Juden nicht länger nur Diaspora." *Das Parlament* (July 28/August 4, 2003): 10.

————, ed. *Jews, Germans, Memory: Reconstructions of Jewish Life in Germany*. Ann Arbor: University of Michigan Press, 1999.

Böhme, Gernot, Rabindra Nath Chakraborty, and Frank Weiler. *Migration und Ausländerfeindlichkeit*. Darmstadt: Wissenschaftliche Buchgesellschaft, 1994.

Borneman, John, and Jeffrey M. Peck. *Sojourners: The Return of German Jews and the Question of Identity*. Lincoln: University of Nebraska Press, 1995.

Boyarin, Jonathan. *Storm from Paradise: The Politics of Jewish Memory*. Minneapolis: University of Minnesota Press, 1992.

———. *Thinking in Jewish*. Chicago: University of Chicago Press, 1996.

Boyarin, Jonathan, and Daniel Boyarin, eds. *Jews and Other Differences: The New Jewish Cultural Studies*. Minneapolis: University of Minnesota Press, 1997.

———. *Powers of Diaspora: Two Essays on the Relevance of Jewish Culture*. Minneapolis: University of Minnesota Press, 2002.

Brayton, Elise. "Almost German: The Representation of Racial Difference and Belonging in Contemporary Germany." Ph.D. dissertation. Washington, D.C.: Georgetown University, 2000.

Brenner, Michael. *After the Holocaust: Rebuilding Jewish Lives in Postwar Germany*. Princeton, N.J.: Princeton University Press, 1997.

Broder, Henryk. *Erbarmen mit den Deutschen*. Hamburg: Hoffmann and Campe, 1993.

———. *Kein Krieg, nirgends: Die Deutschen und der Terror*, with Reinhard Mohr. Berlin: Berlin Verlag, 2002.

———. "Ein moderner Antisemit." *Der Spiegel* 22 (2002).

Brumlik, Micha. *Kein Weg als Deutscher und Jude: Eine bundesrepublikanische Erfahrung*. Munich: Luchterhand Verlag, 1996.

———, ed. *Zuhause, keine Heimat? Junge Juden und ihre Zunkunft in Deutschland*. Gerlingen: Bleicher Verlag, 1998.

Brumlik, Micha, Doron Kiesel, Cilly Kugelmann, and Julius H. Schoeps, eds. *Jüdisches Leben in Deutschland seit 1945*. Frankfurt am Main.: Athenäum, 1988.

Bubis, Ignatz. *Ich bin ein deutscher Staatsbürger jüdischen Glaubens*, with Edith Kohn. Cologne: Kiepenheuer & Witsch, 1993.

———. *Juden in Deutschland*, edited by Wilhelm von Sternberg. Berlin: Aufbau Taschenbuch, 1996.

Bubis, Ignatz, and Wolfgang Schäuble. *Deutschland wohin?*, edited by Frank Schirrmacher. Freiburg im Breisgau: Herder Freiburg, 1996.

Chauss, Harry. "Virtually Jewish, Virtually Connected: Searching for Jewish Identity Online." Master's thesis, Georgetown University, 2001.

Chow, Rey. *Writing Diaspora: Tactics of Intervention in Contemporary Cultural Studies*. Bloomington: Indiana University Press, 1993.

Cohn-Bendit, Daniel, and Thomas Schmid. *Heimat Babylon: Das Wagnis der multikulterellen Demokratie*. Hamburg: Hoffman und Campe, 1992.

Cohen, Roger. "Israel's Ties with Germany Elude U.S. Jews." *New York Times*, March 4, 2001.

———. "Uneasy Peace." *New York Times*, August 6, 2000.

Daniel, E. Valentine, and Jeffrey M. Peck, eds. *Culture/Contexture: Explorations in Anthropology and Literary Studies*. Berkeley and Los Angeles: University of California Press, 1996.

DellaPergola, Sergio. "An Overview of the Demographic Trends of European Jews." In *Jewish Identities in the New Europe*, edited by Jonathan Webber. London: Littman Library of Jewish Civilization, 1994.

Der Spiegel. "Das is mein wunder Punkt" (January 22, 1996).

———. "Gefährlich fremd: Das Scheitern der multi-kulturellen Gesellschaft" (April 1997).

———. "Jeder achte Deutsche ein Antisemit" 46:4 (January 20, 1992): 41–66.

———. "Lied'l fum goldenen Land" 50, 40 (1995):135.

———. "Schlag ins Wasser? Deutsche Muslime distanzieren sich von Jürgen Möllemann" (June 10, 2002).

———. " 'Viele Zimmer unterm Dach,' Orthodoxe und liberale Juden streiten um Geld, Mitgliederzahlen und die Verwendung staatlicher Zuschüsse. Das Monopol des Zentralrats bröckelt" (2004).

———. "Weder Heimat noch Freunde" (June 7, 1993): 16.

Diner, Dan. *Gedächtniszeiten: Über Jüdische und andere Geschichten*. Munich: C. H. Beck, 2003.

Dische, Irene. *Pious Secrets [Lies]*. New York: Viking, 1991.

Dischereit, Esther. *Joëmis Tisch: Eine jüdische Geschichte*. Frankfurt am Main: Suhrkamp Verlag, 1988.

———. *Übungen, jüdisch zu sein*. Frankfurt am Main: Suhrkamp Verlag, 1998.

Domansky, Elisabeth. "Kristallnacht, the Holocaust, and German Unity: The Meaning of November 9 as an Anniversary in Germany." *History and Memory* 4, 1 (spring 1992): 60–94.

Dominguez, Virginia. "Questioning Jews." *American Ethnologist* 20 (1996): 618–624.

Doomernik, Jeroen. *Going West: Soviet Jewish Immigrants in Berlin since 1990*. Brookfield, Vt: Avebury, 1997.

ECJC website. "Two Hundred Leaders from across Europe, Israel, and the US Plan Future of European Jewry." July 2–5, 2004; *http://www.ecjc@ort.org*.

Eisen, Arnold M. *Galut: Modern Jewish Reflection of Homelessness and Homecoming*. Bloomington: Indiana University Press, 1986.

European Council of Jewish Communities. "Two Hundred Leaders from across Europe, Israel, and the US Plan Future of European Jewry." July 2–5, 1995; *http://www.ecjc.org*.

Featherstone, Mike. "Cosmopolis: An Introduction." *Theory, Culture and Society* 19 (February–April, 2002): 1–16.

Feldman, Linda E., and Diana Orendi, eds. *Evolving Jewish Identities in German Culture: Borders and Crossings*. Westport, Conn.: Praeger Publishers, 2000.

Felman, Shoshana, and Dore Laub. *Testimony: Crises of Witnessing in Literature, Psychoanalysis, and History*. New York: Routledge, 1991.

Finkelstein, Norman G. *The Holocaust Industry: Reflections on the Exploitation of Jewish Suffering*. New York: Verso, 2000.

Finkielkraut, Alain. *The Imaginary Jew*. Translated by Kevin O'Niell and David Suchoff. Lincoln: University of Nebraska Press, 1996.

Fleischmann, Lea. *Dies ist nicht mein Land: Eine Jüdin verlässt die Bundesrepublik*. Munich: Wilhelm Heyne Verlag, 1987.

Friedlander, Saul, ed. *Probing the Limits of Representation: Nazism and the 'Final Solution'*. Cambridge, Mass.: Harvard University Press, 1992.

Galliner, Nicola, ed. *Jewish Film Festival Berlin*. Berlin: Bebra, 2004.

Gardner-Feldman, Lily. "German Morality and Israel." In *The Federal Republic at Forty*, edited by Peter H. Merkl. New York: New York University Press, 1989.

———. "The Jewish Role in German American Relations." In *The German-American Encounter: Conflict and Cooperation between Two Cultures 1800–2000*, edited by Frank Trommler and Elliott Shore. New York: Berghahn Books, 2001.

Gay, Ruth. *The Jews of Germany. A Historical Portrait*. With an introduction by Peter Gay. New Haven, Conn.: Yale University Press, 1992.

Gilman, Sander L. *Jewish Frontiers: Essays on Bodies, Histories, and Identities*. New York: Palgrave Macmillan, 2003.

———. *The Jew's Body*. New York: Routledge, 1991.

———. *Jews in Today's German Culture*. Bloomington: Indiana University Press, 1995.

———. *Smart Jews: The Construction of the Image of Jewish Superior Intelligence*. Lincoln: University of Nebraska Press, 1996.

Gilman, Sander L., and Karen Remmler, eds. *Reemerging Jewish Culture in Germany: Life and Literature since 1989*. New York: New York University Press, 1994.

Gilman, Sander L., and Jack Zipes, eds. *Yale Companion to Jewish Writing and Thought in German Culture, 1096–1996*. New Haven, Conn.: Yale University Press, 1997.

Goldberg, David Theo, and Michael Krausz, eds. *Jewish Identity*. Philadelphia: Temple University Press, 1993.

Goldhagen, Daniel Jonah. *Hitler's Willing Executioners: Ordinary Germans and the Holocaust*. New York: Alfred A. Knopf, 1996.

Gross, Jan. *Neighbors: The Destruction of the Jewish Community in Jewabne, Poland*. Princeton, N.J.: Princeton University Press, 2001.

Gruber, Ruth Ellen. *Virtually Jewish: Reinventing Jewish Culture in Europe*. Berkeley and Los Angeles: University of California Press, 2002.

Harris, David A. "Jews and Germany: Remembering the Past, Planning for the Future." Address given at University of the German Armed Forces, Hamburg, January 29, 2001.

Hartmann, Geoffrey H., ed. *Bitburg in Moral and Political Perspective*. Bloomington: Indiana University Press, 1986.

———. *Holocaust Remembrance: The Shapes of Memory*. Cambridge, Mass.: Blackwell, 1994.

———. *The Longest Shadow: In the Aftermath of the Holocaust*. Bloomington: Indiana University Press, 1996.

Heid, Ludger, and Julius H. Schoeps, eds. *Juden in Deutschland: Von der Aufklärung bis zur Gegenwart*. Munich: Piper Verlag, 1994.

Herf, Jeffrey. *Divided Memory: The Nazi Past in the Two Germanys*. Cambridge, Mass.: Harvard University Press, 1997.

Honigmann, Barbara. *Alles, alles Liebe!* Munich: Carl Hanser, 2000.

———. *Damals, dann und danach*. Munich: Carl Hanser, 1999.

———. *Eine Liebe aus Nichts*. Berlin: Rowolt, 1991.

———. *Soharas Reise*. Berlin: Rowolt, 1996.

Horrocks, David, and Eva Kolinsky, eds. *Turkish Culture in German Society Today*. Providence, R.I.: Berghahn Books, 1996.

Hubel, Helmut, ed. *Die trilateralen Beziehungen zwischen Deutschland, Israel und den USA*. Thüringen: Landeszentrale für politische Bildung, 2001.

Jarausch, Konrad. "The Failure of East German Antifascism: Some Ironies of History as Politics." *German Studies Review* 14:1 (1991): 85–96.

Jarausch, Konrad H., ed. *After Unity: Reconfiguring German Identities*, vol. 2, Modern German Studies. Providence, R.I.: Berghahn Books, 1997.

Jewish Community Publication. "Beware Lest the Nightmare Recur." Published by the Jewish Community of East Germany, 1988.

Jewish Museum Berlin. *Discovering the Jewish Museum Berlin*. Berlin: Stiftung Jüdisches Museum Berlin, 2001.

———. *Stories of an Exhibition. Two Millennia of German Jewish History*. Berlin: Stiftung Jüdisches Museum Berlin, 2001.

Junker, Detlef, ed. *Die USA und Deutschland im Zeitalter des Kalten Krieges: Ein Handbuch*, vol. 1, *1945–1968*. Munich: Deutsche Verlags-Anstalt, 2001.

———. *Die USA und Deutschland im Zeitalter des Kalten Krieges: Ein Handbuch*, vol. 2, *1968–1990*. Munich: Deutsche Verlags-Anstalt, 2001.

Kaminer, Wladimir. *Russendisko*. Munich: Goldmann Verlag, 2000.

Kaufman, Jonathan. *A Hole in the Heart of the World: Being Jewish in Eastern Europe*. New York: Viking, 1997.

Kirshenblatt-Gimblett, Barbara. "The Electronic Vernacular." In *Connected: Engagements with Media*, edited by George Marcus. Chicago: University of Chicago Press, 1996.

Kleeblatt, Norman L., ed. *Too Jewish? Challenging Traditional Identities.* New York: The Jewish Museum; New Brunswick, N.J.: Rutgers University Press, 1996.

Klimt, Andrea. " 'Returning Home': Portuguese Migrant Notions of Temporariness, Permanence, and Commitment." *New German Critique* 46 (winter 1989): 47–70.

Knowlton, James, and Truett Cates, trans. *Forever in the Shadow of Hitler? Original Documents of the Historikerstreit.* Atlantic Highlands, N.J.: Humanities Press, 1993.

Korn, Salomon. *Geteilte Erinnerung: Beiträge zur "deutsch-jüdischen" Gegenwart.* Berlin: Philo Verlagsgesellschaft, 1999.

Kowalsky, Wolfgang. *Rechtsaussen . . . und die verfehlten Strategien des deutschen Denkens.* Berlin: Ullstein Verlag, 1992.

Kurlansky, Mark. *A Chosen Few: The Resurrection of European Jewry.* New York: Addison Wesley, 1995.

Kurt, Kemal. *Was ist die Mehrzahl vor Heimat? Bilder eines türkisch-deutschen Doppellebens.* Hamburg: Rowolt Verlag, 1995.

LaCapra, Dominick. *History and Memory after Auschwitz.* Ithaca, N.Y.: Cornell University Press, 1998.

———. *Representing the Holocaust: History, Theory, Trauma.* Ithaca, N.Y.: Cornell University Press, 1994.

Land, Berel. *Writing and the Holocaust.* New York: Holmes & Meyer, 1988.

Langenbacher, Eric. "Memory Regimes in Contemporary Germany." Ph.D. dissertation, Georgetown University, 2002.

Langer, Lawrence L. *Admitting the Holocaust.* New York: Oxford University Press, 1995.

———. *Holocaust Testimonies: The Ruins of Memories.* New Haven, Conn.: Yale University Press, 1991.

Lanzmann, Claude. *Shoah: The Complete Text of the Acclaimed Holocaust Film.* New York: Da Capo Press, 1995.

Lappin, Elena, ed. *Jewish Voices, German Words: Growing Up Jewish in Postwar Germany and Austria.* Translated by Krishna Winston. North Haven, Conn.: Catbird Press, 1994.

Laurence, Jonathan. "(Re)constructing Community in Berlin: Of Jews, Turks, and German Responsibility." Paper presented at the Science Center Berlin for Social Research, Berlin, Germany, October 1999; *German Politics & Society* 19 (Summer 2001).

Leggewie, Claus, and Zafer Şenocak, eds. *Deutsche Türken—Türk Almanlar: Das Ende der Geduld—Sabrin sonu.* Hamburg: Rowolt Verlag, 1993.

Linenthal, Edward T. *Preserving Memory: The Struggle to Create America's Holocaust Museum.* New York: Viking, 1995.

Lorenz, Dagmar C. G., ed. *Contemporary Jewish Writing in Austria: An Anthology.* Lincoln: University of Nebraska Press, 1999.

Lubrich, Oliver. "The Other and the Ordinary: Demystifying and Demusealizing the Jew." Unpublished manuscript.

Magenau, Jörg. "Gibt es eine deutsch-jüdische Literatur?" *Das Parlament* (July 28/August 4, 2003): 2.

Maier, Charles. *The Unmasterable Past: History, Holocaust, and German National Identity.* Cambridge, U.K.: Cambridge University Press, 1988.

Mandel, Ruth. "Turkish Headscarves and the 'Foreigner Problem': Constructing Difference through Emblems of Identity." *New German Critique* 46 (1989): 31.

Markovits, Andrei S., and Beth Simone Noveck. "West Germany." In *The World Reacts to the Holocaust,* edited by David S. Wyman. Baltimore: The Johns Hopkins University Press, 1996.

Mattenklott, Gert. *Über Juden in Deutschland.* Frankfurt am Main: Jüdischer Verlag, 1992.

Menasse, Robert. *Das Land ohne Eigenschaften*. Weinheim: Suhrkamp Taschenbuch, 1995.

Moore, Deborah Dash, and S. Ilan Troen, eds. *Divergent Jewish Cultures: Israel and America*. New Haven, Conn.: Yale University Press, 2001.

Morley, David. *Home Territories: Media, Mobility, and Identity*. London: Routledge, 2000.

Morris, Leslie, and Jack Zipes, eds. *Unlikely History: The Changing German-Jewish Symbiosis*. New York: Palgrave/St. Martin's Press, 2002.

Mosse, George L. *Germans and Jews: The Right, the Left, and the Search for a 'Third Force' in Pre-Nazi Germany*. New York: Universal Library, 1970.

Münz, Rainer, and Myron Wiener, eds. *Migrants, Refugees, and Foreign Policy: U.S. and German Policies toward Countries of Origin*, vol. 2. Providence, R.I.: Bergham Books, 1997.

Neiman, Susan. *Slow Fire: Jewish Notes from Berlin*. New York: Schocken Books, 1992.

"New Jews in a New Germany." *European Judaism. A Journal for the New Europe* 33 (2000): 4–50.

Nirumand, Bahman, ed. *Angst vor den Deutschen: Terror gegen Ausländer und der Zerfall des Rechtsstaates*. Hamburg: Rowolt, 1992.

———. *Leben mit den Deutschen*. Hamburg: Rowolt, 1991.

Nolden, Thomas. *Junge jüdische Literatur: Konzentrisches Schreiben in der Gegenwart*. Würzburg, Ger.: Königshausen & Neumann, 1995.

Novick, Peter. *The Holocaust in American Life*. New York: Mariner Books, 1999.

Organization for Security and Cooperation in Europe. Website, *http://www.osce.org*.

Ostendorf, Berndt. "The Politics of Difference: Theories and Practice in a Comparative U.S. and German Perspective." In *Multiculturalism in Transit: A German-American Exchange*, edited by Klaus Milich and Jeffrey M. Peck. New York: Bergham Books, 1998.

Ostow, Robin. *Jews in Contemporary East Germany: The Children of Moses in the Land of Marx*. New York: St. Martin's Press, 1989.

———. "The Post-Soviet Immigrants and the *Jüdische Allgemeine* in the New Millennium: Post-Communism in German's Jewish Communities." *East European Jewish Affairs* 33 (2003): 54–70.

Peck, Jeffrey M. "East Germany." In *The World Reacts to the Holocaust*, edited by David S. Wyman. Baltimore: The Johns Hopkins University Press, 1996.

———. "The 'Ins' and 'Outs' of the New Germany: Jews, Foreigners, Asylum Seekers." In *Reemerging Jewish Culture in Germany: Life and Literature since 1989*, edited by Sander L. Gilman and Karen Remmler. New York: New York University Press, 1994.

———. "Refugees as Foreigners: The Problem of Becoming German and Finding Home." In *Mistrusting Refugees*, edited by Daniel E. Valentine and John Knudsen. Berkeley and Los Angeles: University of California Press, 1995.

———, ed. "The Jewish Voice in Transatlantic Relations." *AICGS German-American Issues* 1 (2004).

Pinto, Diana. "Diaspora Manifest." *Golem* 3 (2002): 4–13.

———. "The Jewish Challenge in the New Europe." In *Challenging Ethnic Citizenship: German and Israeli Perspectives on Immigration*, edited by Daniel Levy and Yfaat Weiss. New York: Bergham Books, 2002.

Poster, Mark. *What's the Matter with the Internet?* Minneapolis: University of Minnesota Press, 2001.

———. "Virtual Ethnicity: Tribal Identity in an Age of Global Communication." In *Cybersociety 2.0: Revisiting Computer-mediated Communication and Community*, edited by Steven G. Jones. Thousand Oaks, Calif.: Sage Publications, 1998.

Rabinbach, Anson. "From Explosion to Erosion: Holocaust Memorialization in America since Bitburg. Passing into History: Nazism and the Holocaust Beyond Memory. In

Honor of Saul Friedlander on His Sixty-fifth Birthday." *History and Memory* 9, 1–2 (fall 1997).

Rabinbach, Anson, and Jack Zipes, eds. *German Jews since the Holocaust and the Changing Situation in West Germany.* New York: Holmes & Meier, 1986.

Rabinow, Paul. "Representations Are Social Facts: Modernity and Post-Modernity in Anthropology." In *Writing Culture: The Poetics and Politics of Ethnography*, edited by James Clifford and George Marcus. Berkeley and Los Angeles: University of California Press, 1986.

Rapaport, Lynn. *Jews in Germany after the Holocaust: Memory, Identity, and Jewish-German Relations.* New York: Cambridge University Press, 1997.

Räthzel, Nora. "Germany: One Race, One Nation?" *Race and Class: A Journal for Black and Third World Liberation* 32, 3 (January–March 1991): 31–48.

Rebiger, Bill. *Das Jüdische Berlin: Kultur, Religion und Alltag gestern und heute.* Berlin: Jaron Verlag, 2000.

Remmler, Karen. "Reclaiming Space. Jewish Women in Germany Today." In *Writing New Identities: Gender, Nation, and Immigration in Contemporary Europe*, edited by Gisela Brinker-Gabler and Sidonie Smith. Minneapolis: University of Minnesota Press, 1997.

Rommelsbacher, Brigit. "Rassismus Ost und West schaukeln sich hoch." *Die Tageszeitung*, February 11, 1992.

Rosenthal, Stephen T. *Irreconcilable Differences: The Waning of the American Jewish Love Affair with Israel.* Waltham, Mass.: Brandeis University Press, 2001.

Roth, Andrew, and Michael Frajman. *The Goldapple Guide to Jewish Berlin.* Berlin: Goldapple Publishing, 1998.

Runge, Irene. *>>Ich bin keine Russin<<: Jüdische Zuwanderung zwischen 1989 und 1994.* Berlin: Dietz Verlag, 1995.

Sachar, Howard M., ed. *The Unlikely Partnership: Germany and Israel.* Washington, D.C.: Friedrich-Ebert-Stifting / Friedrich-Naumann-Stiftung / George Washington University, 1997.

Schmalz-Jacobsen, Cornelia, and Georg Hansen, eds. *Kleines Lexikon der ethnischen Minderheiten in Deutschland.* Munich: Deutscher Taschenbuch Verlag, 1997.

Schneider, Richard Chaim. *Fetisch Holocaust: Die Judenvernichtung—verdrängt und vermarktet.* Munich: Kindler Verlag, 1997.

———. *Zwischen Welten: Ein jüdisches Leben im heutigen Deutschland.* Munich: Kindler Verlag, 1994.

Schoeps, Julius H., Willi Jaspar, and Bernhard Vogt, eds. *Russiche Juden in Deutschland: Integration und Selbstbehauptung in einem fremden Land.* Weinheim: Beltz Athenäum, 1996.

Segev, Tom. *The Seventh Million: The Israelis and the Holocaust.* New York: Hill & Wang, 1994.

Selengut, Charles, ed. *Jewish Identity in the Postmodern Age: Scholarly and Personal Reflections.* St. Paul, Minn.: Paragon House, 1999.

Seligmann, Rafael. "Interview mit Ignatz Bubis." *Der Stern* (July 1999).

———. *Die Jiddische Mamme.* Munich: Deutscher Taschenbuch Verlag, 1996.

———. "Die Juden leben," *Der Spiegel* 46, 4 (1992): 41.

———. *Mit Beschränkter Hoffnung: Juden, Deutsche, Israelis.* Hamburg: Hoffman und Campe, 1991.

———. *Der Musterjude.* Hildesheim: Claassen Verlag, 1997.

———. *Rubensteins Versteigerung.* Munich: Deutscher Taschenbuch Verlag, 1991.

———. *Schalom meine Liebe.* Munich: Deutscher Taschenbuch Verlag, 1998.

Şenocak, Zafer. *Atlas of a Tropical Germany: Essays on Politics and Culture, 1990–1998.* Translated and edited by Leslie A. Adelson. Lincoln: University of Nebraska Press, 2001.

———. *Gefährliche Verwandtschaft*. Munich: Babel Verlag, 1998.

Shafir, Shlomo. *Ambiguous Relations: The American Jewish Community and Germany Since 1945*. Detroit: Wayne State University Press, 1999.

Shain, Yossi. "American Jews and the Construction of Israel's Jewish Identity." *Diaspora, A Journal of Transnational Studies* 9 (fall 2000): 163–201.

———. "Jewish Kinship at a Crossroads: Lessons for Homelands and Diasporas." *Political Science Quarterly* 117 (2002).

Sichrovsky, Peter. *Strangers in their Own Land: Young Jews in Germany and Austria Today*. Translated by Jean Steinberg. New York: Penguin Books, 1987.

Singer, David and Lawrence Grossman, eds. *American Jewish Yearbook 1992*. New York: American Jewish Committee, 1992.

———. *American Jewish Yearbook 2000*. New York: American Jewish Committee, 2000.

———. *American Jewish Yearbook 2003*. New York: The American Jewish Yearbook Committee, 2003.

Singer, David, and Ruth R. Seldin, eds. *American Jewish Yearbook 1999*. New York: American Jewish Committee, 1999.

Spiegel, Paul. *Was ist kosher? Jüdischer Glaube — Jüdisches Leben*. Berlin: Ullstein Verlag, 2003.

Steinweis, Alan E. "The Legacy of the Holocaust in Germany and the United States." In *The United States and Germany in the Era of the Cold War, 1945–1990*, vol. 1: *1945–1968*, edited by Detlef Junker. Cambridge, U.K.: Cambridge University Press, 2004.

Stern, Frank. *Dann bin ich um den Schlaf gebracht: Ein Jahrtausend jüdisch-deutsche Kulturgeschichte*. Berlin: Aufbau-Verlag, 2002.

Stern, Frank, and Maria Gierlinger, eds. *Die deutsch-jüdische Erfahrung: Beiträge zum kulturellen Dialog*. Berlin: Aufbau Verlag, 2003.

Sznaider, Nathan, and Daniel Levy. "How Much Diaspora Is Bearable?" *Golem* 3 (2002): 21–29.

Traverso, Enzo. *The Jews and Germany: From the 'Judeo-German Symbiosis' to the Memory of Auschwitz*. Translated by Daniel Weissbort. Lincoln: University of Nebraska Press, 1995.

Troen, S. Ilan, ed. *Jewish Centers and Peripheries: Europe between America and Israel Fifty Years after World War II*. New Brunswick, N.J.: Transaction Publishers, 1999.

Trommler, Frank, and Elliott Shore, eds. *The German-American Encounter: Conflict and Cooperation between Two Cultures, 1800–2000*. New York: Berghahn Books, 2001.

Tye, Larry. *Home Lands: Portraits of the New Jewish Diaspora*. New York: Henry Holt, 2001.

Valentine, Daniel E., and John Knudsen, eds. *Mistrusting Refugees*. Berkeley and Los Angeles: University of California Press, 1995.

von Bülow, Andreas. *Die CIA und der 11. September*. Munich: Piper Verlag, 2003.

von der Osten-Sacken, Thomas. "A German Jewish Internet Portal Combating Anti-Semitism," Hagalil.com, 2003; *http://hagalil.com*.

Wasserstein, Bernard. *Vanishing Diaspora: The Jews in Europe since 1945*. Cambridge, Mass.: Harvard University Press, 1996.

Webber, Jonathan. *Jewish Identities in the New Europe*. Washington, D.C.: Littman Library of Jewish Civilization, 1994.

Werbner, Pnina. "The Materiality of Diaspora—Between Aesthetic and 'Real' Politics." *Diaspora. A Journal of Transnational Studies* 9, 1 (2000): 5–20.

Wettstein, Howard, ed. *Diasporas and Exiles: Varieties of Jewish Identity*. Berkeley and Los Angeles: University of California Press, 2002.

Weiss, Iris. "Jewish Disneyland—die Aneignung und Enteignung des Jüdischen." *Golem* (March 6, 2002): 43–48.

Wolffsohn, Michael. *Ewige Schuld? 40 Jahre Deutsch-Jüdische-Israelische Beziehungen*. Munich: Piper, 1988.

————. *Meine Juden—Eure Juden*. Munich: Piper Verlag, 1997.

Wroblewsky, Vincent von, ed. *Zwischen Thora und Trabant: Juden in der DDR*. Berlin: Aufbau Taschenbuch, 1993.

Wyman, David S., ed. *The World Reacts to the Holocaust*. Baltimore: The Johns Hopkins University Press, 1996.

Young, James E. *The Texture of Memory: Holocaust Memorials and Meaning*. New Haven, Conn.: Yale University Press, 1993.

————. *Writing and Rewriting the Holocaust: Narrative and the Consequences of Interpretation*. Bloomington: Indiana University Press, 1988.

Yurdakul, Gökçe, and Y. Michal Bodemann. " 'We Are Not Immigrants, We Are a Minority': The German Jewish Trope as Master Narrative for German Turks." Unpublished manuscript.

Zelizer, Barbie. *Remembering to Forget: Holocaust Memory through the Camera's Eye*. Chicago: University of Chicago Press, 1998.

Index

About the Author

Jeffrey M. Peck is a professor in the Communication, Culture, and Technology Program at Georgetown University and a senior fellow at the American Institute for Contemporary German Studies in Washington, D.C. After occupying positions at the University of Washington and Georgetown University, he was director of the Canadian Centre for German and European Studies at York University (Toronto) and the University of Montreal. His publications include *Sojourners: The Return of German Jews and the Question of Identity* (with John Borneman, 1995) and *Culture/Contexture: Explorations in Anthropology and Literary Studies* (with E. Valentine Daniel, 1996).

305.892
Pec

Peck, Jeffrey M.

Being Jewish in the
new Germany
68757